Trekking in the Indian Himalaya

To my "fellow-traveller",
Xmas 1987 — how does
this look ?!
love,
Susan

S0-BDQ-664

Trekking in the Indian Himalaya
First Edition

Published by
Lonely Planet Publications
PO Box 88, South Yarra, Victoria, 3141, Australia
PO Box 2001A, Berkeley, California, USA 94702

Printed by
Colorcraft, Hong Kong

Photographs & line drawings
Garry Weare, Manmohan Singh Bawa & N N Badoni

First published
April 1986

National Library of Australia Cataloguing in Publication Data

Weare, Garry.
  Trekking in the Indian Himalaya

  1st ed.
  Includes index.
  ISBN 0 908086 61 X.

  1. India, Northern – Description and Travel – 1981 – Guide-books. 2. Himalaya Mountains – Description
and travel – Guide-books. 3. Hiking – Himalaya Mountains – Guide-books. I. Title.

915.4'0452

© Copyright Garry Weare, 1986

All rights reserved. No part of this publication may be reproduced, stored in a retrieval system or
transmitted in any form by any means, electronic, mechanical, photocopying, recording or otherwise,
except brief extracts for the purpose of review, without the written permission of the publisher and
copyright owner.

Garry Weare

Each trekking season over the last 10 years Garry Weare has covered over 1600 km researching and leading trips and consulting for TV documentaries in the Indian Himalaya. He has also established a west Himalayan trek agency, owned and run by local guides from Kashmir, Ladakh and Manali. He is currently researching a book on the history of Kashmir exploration.

This Edition

Trek contributions and advice also came from numerous other sources. In Kashmir and Ladakh the principle route descriptions were compiled by the author with advice from Meraj Din of Mountain Journeys (Kashmir), Wangchuk Shamshu and Rigzin Jowa of Indus Expeditions (Leh) and Iqbal Sharma Mountain Journeys (Manali). For the detailed trek reports out of Manali thanks must go to Terry Ryan (Adelaide) and to Manmohan Singh Bawa for treks across the Dhaula Dhar. In Uttar Pradesh, Lewie Gonsalves (Melbourne), Sarah Lauchlan (Sydney) and Captain Swadesh Kumar (Delhi) contributed the general trek advice, while Manmohan Singh Bawa provided the descriptions in the Badrinath region and N N Badoni on the Kedarnath regions. For the maps Jane Besley (Sydney) spent many hours working from Garry's rough outlines to produce the finished maps.

The author would like to thank Marina Haywood (Sydney), without whom the book would not have got started, and Anne Matthews (Kathmandu) who completed the manuscript. Thanks also to Rosemary Worthington (Sydney), Fiona Bell (Melbourne), Simon Baldestone (Melbourne) and David Frith (Sydney), trek companions of many km; and to the Badyari Houseboat family, whose houseboats are without equal on Nagin Lake.

Thanks also to Goronwy Price and Christine Gee of Australian Himalayan Expeditions who made my time in Kashmir possible and to Michael Langley and Lindy Cameron at Lonely Planet who edited the material. Finally thanks to all the trekkers who have trekked with me in Kashmir.

And the Next

This first edition of *Trekking in the Indian Himalaya* only scratches the surface of trekking possibilities in India. With future editions we intend to not only improve the current material but also add treks and trekking regions. Any suggestions, corrections or additions will be gratefully received either at Lonely Planet Publications or directly to the author, Garry Weare, Australian Himalayan Expeditions, 377 Sussex St, Sydney 2000, Australia. The best letters will be rewarded with a copy of the next edition.

Contents

Introduction

Trekking in India is still in its infancy compared with the volume of traffic that currently visits the Nepal Himalaya. In Nepal the attraction has been to trek to the Everest Base Camp or go around the Annapurna Massif. In India, however, attention has been concentrated on exploring the rich cultural and geographical features found in the passes and valleys of the Himalaya rather than trekking to the base of a particular mountain.

For people considering a first time trek to the Himalaya, India provides some superb opportunities. The trek routes vary to suit anyone prepared to give things a go. Trekking is not just a pastime for eccentrics and bushwalkers – trekking is simply a means of travelling and appreciating the mountains and the people in the most natural way – on foot. There is no technical climbing, only walking, sometimes strenuous, sometimes easy – but walking nonetheless. Sound preparation, both physically and mentally, is still vital. It would be a sorry individual who went to the Himalaya unprepared.

This guide has been classified into the regions of Kashmir, Jammu and Ladakh and the states of Himachal Pradesh and Uttar Pradesh, each with an overall assessment of their trekking possibilities.

The trekking regions are introduced by their geographical and historical features, a run-down of the treks covered, the season in which the trails can be followed and any hazards and difficulties that should be borne in mind. There is information on how to get to the various trek-off points, accommodation before setting off, and an assessment of the necessary or possible trekking arrangements including the cost and availability of supplies, porters and horsemen.

Finally there is a stage by stage description of each trek.

The treks outlined cover many of the popular routes in India. The structure of the trekking sections start with treks in Jammu & Kashmir and continue on to those in Himachal Pradesh. For example the trek out of Kishtwar (in Jammu) finishes at Chamba, a trek through Zanskar finishes in Lahaul, The Himachal Pradesh trek section is therefore restricted to treks mainly in or south of the Pir Panjal range. This in no way endorses the idea that this is the only way in which extended treks can be followed. Treks from Kulu, Chamba and Lahaul can extend right the way across Kashmir or Ladakh; it is only for convenience that many itineraries start in the state of Jammu & Kashmir.

There are numerous possibilities of combining treks in these regions of the Himalaya, and it's hoped that by linking some of the treks outlined you can fully exploit your experiences on the trail. For instance a trek from Pahalgam to Sonamarg in Kashmir can be completed in six to eight stages and from there it is possible to return to Pahalgam by an alternative pass, continue beyond Sonamarg through the north Kashmir range, or go by bus to Ladakh and start another trek out of the Indus Valley. It is up to you to combine treks to satisfy your time, interest or pocket.

Facts about the Region

CULTURE & HISTORY

From near the Nun-Kun mountains and from no other spot in Asia, we go westwards through countries entirely Mohammedan, eastward among none but Buddhists, and southwards over lands where the Hindu religion prevails to the extremity of the Indian peninsula.

Frederic Drew,
The Northern Barrier of India 1877.

Within the Indian Himalaya are the boundaries of Asia's three main cultures. The borderlands of Kashmir mark the eastern-most boundary of the Islamic culture, Ladakh is predominantly Buddhist, while the foothills of Himachal Pradesh and Uttar Pradesh contain some of the central sites in Hindu heritage.

For the Hindu, the Himalaya have been a constant source of religious inspiration. Pilgrimages are regularly conducted to the caves and shrines in the innermost mountain sanctuaries. Places such as the source of the Ganges, the Amarnath Cave and Vaishno Devi are intimately connected with the Hindu understanding of the Himalaya as the abode of the gods.

Although Buddhism was introduced comparatively early to the Himalaya by the emperor Ashoka, it took many centuries for the teachings of Buddha to gain a substantial foothold. One of the most decisive periods was when the sage Padmasambhava introduced Tantric Buddhism to the Himalaya. Its tenets were popularised in Tibet, and by the 10th century the kings of Ladakh had been fully converted.

In the 11th century Mahmud of Ghanzi overpowered the Hindu rulers of Kabul and established Islamic rule across north-west India. Kashmir's conversion to Islam was undertaken peacefully and its sultanate developed independently from the Turkish forces in the plains. In the 13th century Baltistan was converted to Islam and the Islamic armies from Baltistan and Kashmir attacked the Buddhist hierarchies of Ladakh. The Ladakhi culture however remained intact and part of the Tibetan world.

The Himachal, Garwhal and Kumaon kingdoms likewise guarded their autonomy from the Delhi sultanate. The three cultural worlds of Buddhist Ladakh, Mohammedan Kashmir and the Hindu foothills had evolved.

The founding of the Moghul empire realigned cultural boundaries. After consolidating his power over north India, the Moghul emperor Akbar was able to take Kashmir. The Moghuls were also able to extend their influence over the independent Himalaya kingdoms and demand at least some tribute to their courts.

To the north of the Himalaya, Ladakh had carved out a sizeable empire for itself. Yet after its war with Lhasa, its boundaries were reduced to the confines of the Indus Valley. The war would have reduced Ladakh boundaries even further had it not been for the intervention of the Moghuls. The Emperor Aurangzeb called for Leh to make a nominal tribute to Delhi – a mosque at the end of the Leh bazaar.

Following the decline of the Moghuls, a complex political situation developed. Kashmir was invaded by Kabul in the mid 18th century, Jammu secured a position of autonomy over its foothills, Kangra extended its influence across the Ravi and Kulu valleys to the Sutlej, and the Gurkhas of Nepal expanded their borders right across the Kumaon to the Simla hill states. To complete the picture, the Sikhs were establishing their empire over the Punjab while the British East India Company had set their sights far beyond the trading post of Calcutta.

Control over the Himalaya was to become the goal of Kangra, the Sikhs and the Gurkhas. The Gurkhas needed the assistance of the Sikhs, but the Sikhs had their own plans to expand beyond Lahore. The Gurkhas therefore lead a unified front with the deposed hill rajahs against the Kangra armies. The Kangra forces were driven back to Kangra and called on the Sikhs for assistance. The Sikhs complied, the Gurkhas withdrew to the Sutlej and the Sikhs assumed authority over the Himachal kingdoms. The Sikhs then lost little time in taking Kashmir and proceeded to establish their power over the Indian Himalaya.

The British were wary of the Sikh influence and were equally aware that a combined Gurkha-Sikh empire stretching from Sikkim to Kashmir would be a formidable force to deal with. The British were determined to forge a neutral zone between the Sikhs and the Gurkhas which they achieved after the Gurkha wars of 1815. The Gurkhas retreated to their present Nepalese boundaries, leaving the districts of Garwhal, Nainital, Kumaon and Dehra Dun under British control.

By the 1830s the Sikhs, with the assistance of the Dogras of Jammu, had taken Kishtwar, Ladakh and Baltistan. An historic manoeuvre followed. The British gained control of the Punjab following the Sikh wars in the mid-1840s, while the Dogras remained neutral. The political evolution of north-west India was nearly complete.

Regional Histories
Jammu

Following the Treaty of Amritsar, the Sikh Durbar agreed to cede 'the hilly and mountainous country' between the Beas and the Indus rivers on 9 March 1846. On 16 March a separate treaty was entered into between the British and Gulab Singh, the Dogra leader from Jammu. It transferred to him the country between the Ravi and the Indus. By granting rule to the Dogras, the British had, in effect, found a means of exercising control over the northern barrier of India. The Maharajah's state was vast, encompassing Jammu,

Baltistan, Ladakh and Kashmir, boundaries it maintained until the Indian partition of 1947.

Kashmir

In 1947 Hari Singh, the Maharajah of Kashmir was forced to choose between joining India or Pakistan. On paper the choice was clear: Kashmir was dominantly Muslim, and Pakistan the natural cultural alternative. However, Hari Singh remained indecisive. As a Hindu, he had little feeling for Pakistan; as a Maharajah he had even less inclination to lose his kingdom to India. His wish was for an independent Maharajah's kingdom – an utterly impossible dream. Pakistan seized upon the urgency of the situation and 'organised' a coup by sending in Pathan tribesmen to capture Srinagar. Hari Singh called to India for assistance and paid the political price: a full scale war that lasted until January 1949 and the loss of a substantial part of Kashmir to Indian control.

The line of control in Kashmir has been a constant matter of dispute between India and Pakistan, and further conflict arose in 1965 and 1971. The result is the state of Jammu & Kashmir, where Jammu is dominantly Hindu, Kashmir Muslim and Ladakh Buddhist – a state born more out of political accident than cultural design.

Himachal Pradesh

The evolution of Himachal Pradesh has been less politically sensitive. In 1947 the Himachal districts were divided into two zones – one around Chamba and the other including Mandi, Bilaspur and the nearby Simla hill states – but not including Simla. The rest of the mountain region was classified as part of the Punjab hill states – from Kangra through to Kulu and up to the Himalaya watershed north of Lahaul, with the administrative centre of the Punjab at Simla. In 1966 the Punjab was re-organised and the huge Himalayan region united. The states of Kangra, Kulu and

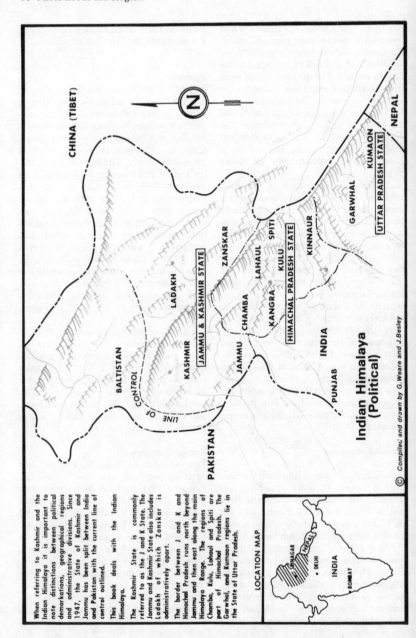

When referring to Kashmir and the Indian Himalaya it is important to note distinctions between political demarcations, geographical regions and administrative divisions. Since 1947, the State of Kashmir and Jammu has been split between India and Pakistan with the current line of control outlined.

This book deals with the Indian Himalaya.

The Kashmir State is commonly referred to as the J and K State. The Jammu and Kashmir State also includes Ladakh of which Zanskar is administratively apart.

The border between J and K and Himachal Pradesh runs north beyond Jammu and then east along the main Himalaya Range. The regions of Chamba, Kulu, Lahoul and Spiti are part of Himachal Pradesh. The Garwhal, and Kumoon regions lie in the State of Uttar Pradesh.

Indian Himalaya (Political)

© Compiled and drawn by G. Weare and J. Besley

CHINA (TIBET)

NEPAL

KUMAON

GARWHAL

UTTAR PRADESH STATE

ZANSKAR

JAMMU & KASHMIR STATE

LADAKH

LAHAUL

SPITI

KINNAUR

CHAMBA

KANGRA

KULU

HIMACHAL PRADESH STATE

JAMMU

BALTISTAN

KASHMIR

LINE OF CONTROL

INDIA

PUNJAB

PAKISTAN

LOCATION MAP

SRINAGAR

NEPAL

DELHI

INDIA

BOMBAY

Lahaul merged with the Simla hill states, Chamba, Mandi and Bilaspur to form Himachal Pradesh. The capital of Himachal was Simla, and in 1971 Himachal Pradesh was given full statehood status in the Indian Union, an essentially Hindu state devoid of the complex cultural anomalies of Jammu & Kashmir.

Uttar Pradesh

Since 1947 the Himalayan districts of Uttar Pradesh have been part of a state that essentially comprises the upper reaches of the Ganges from the confluence of the Ganges and Yamuna on the plains at Allahabad, to the peaks of the main Himalaya.

GEOGRAPHY

The Himalaya do not present themselves as one unbroken chain, but rather as a gigantic layer cake, as anyone taking a mountain flight to Kashmir or Ladakh will testify.

For the ancient Hindu geographer, Mt Kailash was the centre of the universe with the Indus, the Brahmaputra and the Sutlej rivers all flowing from its ridges. For the 19th century geographer, the task of tracing the river systems and defining the innumerable snow-capped mountain ranges from the plains to the Tibetan plateau, was a more formidable task.

The main Himalaya, the principle mountain range, divides the Indian sub-continent from the Tibetan plateau. From Nanga Parbat in the west it stretches for over 2000 km, to the mountains bordering Sikkim and Bhutan in the east, all with an average elevation of over 5500-6000 metres. In the west Himalaya it is the range that divides Kashmir and Himachal from Ladakh. In Uttar Pradesh it is the dividing line between India and Tibet, while in the Nepal Himalaya the main ridge line often coincides with the political boundary between Nepal and Tibet.

In Kashmir the ranges give way to subsidiary ridges such as the north Kashmir range beyond Sonamarg and the Kolahoi and Amarnath ranges, while in Himachal Pradesh the snowy boundaries broaden to encompass the mountains of Lahaul, Spiti and Kinnaur. In Uttar Pradesh and the Garwhal, the range is clearly defined and includes Nanda Devi which, at 7817 metres, is the highest mountain in the Indian Himalaya.

The west Himalaya range is breached only once, where the Sutlej cuts through the mountains en route to the plains. It maintains a path it has followed prior to the formation of the Himalaya.

To the south of the main Himalaya is the Pir Panjal, a range with an average elevation of some 5000 metres. In the north-east it begins at Gulmarg and follows the southern rim of the Kashmir Valley to the Banihal Pass. Here the Pir Panjal meets the north Pir Panjal ridge, a barrier that separates the Kashmir Valley from the Warvan Valley. From Banihal the Pir Panjal sweeps south-east to Kishtwar, where there is some discrepancy between topographical reference and geological formation. Topographically, the Pir Panjal is defined as that range between the Chandra Valley and the Ravi Valley. However, the geological continuation of the Pir Panjal is marked as the ridge between the Ravi and the Beas valleys, generally known as the Dhaula Dhar. For the purpose of geographic reference the Pir Panjal has therefore been classified as a double range both to the north and south of the Ravi Valley; the northern Pir Panjal, extending from Kishtwar to Kulu, divides the Chenab and Ravi valleys; the southern Pir Panjal (Dhaula Dhar) provides the division between the Ravi and the Beas. This range continues north of Dharamsala, through Dalhousie, to Bhadawah. There it meets the Murree Range, a ridge line that divides the Chenab Valley below Kishtwar and the Tawi Valley twisting south to Jammu. It is the range crossed at Panitop on the Jammu-Srinagar highway.

The Pir Panjal, like the Indian Himalaya, is breached only once – at Kishtwar, where the combined waters of the Marwa-

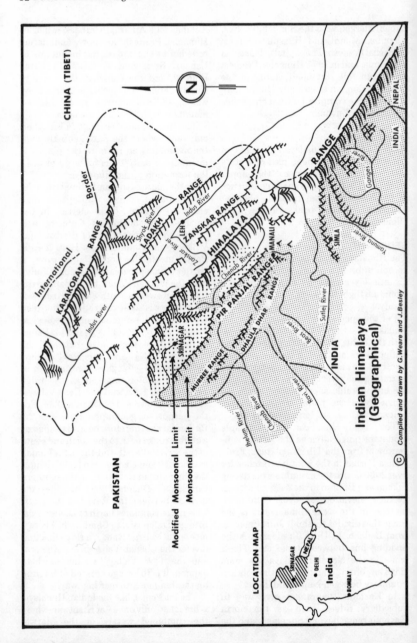

Indian Himalaya (Geographical)

© Compiled and drawn by G.Weare and J.Besley

Warvan River join the Chenab River and gorge through this range en route to the Indus.

South of the Pir Panjal are the Siwalik hills, which have an average elevation of 1500-2000 metres. Geologically they are separate from the Himalaya and refer to the first range of hills you meet en route from the plains. They include the Jammu hills and Vaishnu Devi, and extend to the Kangra hills and further to the range south of Mandi and across the foothills around Dehra Dun.

To the north of the Himalaya lie the Zanskar and Ladakh ranges, commonly referred to as the Trans Himalaya Zone, which mark the geological transition area between the Indian subcontinent and the Tibetan plateau. The Zanskar range lies to the south of the Indus Valley and the Ladakh range is to the north. Both have an average elevation of 5000 metres.

The Zanskar range forms the backbone of southern Ladakh, stretching from the ridges beyond Lamayuru in the west across to the Zanskar region where it is divided from the main Himalaya by the Doda and Tsarap rivers producing the Zanskar Valley. The Zanskar range is breached only where the Doda and Tsarap rivers converge and flow north to the Indus River. It follows a course carved out before the formation of the Trans Himalaya.

To the north of the Zanskar range is the Ladakh range bordered to the north by the Saser Kangri and to the north-east by the eastern ridges of the Karakorum.

Passes & Trails

Throughout the Himalaya a complex network of trails and passes has evolved, criss-crossing the ranges and linking the principle valleys from Kashmir to Kulu and on to the Garwhal.

In the main Himalaya the principle passes are the Zoji La at the head of the Sindh Valley, the Boktol Pass at the head of the Marwa-Warvan Valley, the Chilung Pass and the Umasi La to the immediate

west and east of Kishtwar, and the Shingo La and Baralacha La to the head of the Chandra/Bhaga valleys. To the side of the Sutlej Valley is the Shipki La, while the Mana La at the head of the Alaknanda Valley is the principle pass linking the Garwhal with the Tibetan plateau.

Of the passes in the west Himalaya, the Zoji La and the Baralacha La are only open to vehicles for up to six months of the year as heavy snow makes them unsuitable for vehicles during the winter months. The other glaciated passes however, remain trekking objectives from mid-June until mid-October.

In the Pir Panjal, the main passes are the Pir Panjal Pass due west of Srinagar; the Banihal Pass, which marks the headwaters of the Jhelum River due south of Srinagar; and the Sythen Pass linking Kashmir with Kishtwar. In Himachal the main passes are the Sach Pass linking the Ravi and Chenab valleys, and the Rhotang Pass linking the Beas and upper Chandra valleys in Kulu and Lahaul.

Roads are being constructed over all these passes; the Banihal is now tunnelled and work is being carried out on the Pir Panjal and the Sach passes. The roads over the Sythen and Rhotang passes are open during the summer months. For trekking, there are many alternatives to explore the range, notably the Kugti, Kalicho and Chobia passes between the Ravi Valley and Lahaul, while the Hampta and Sama Unga passes link the Kulu Valley with Lahaul. In the Dhaula Dhar there are many opportunities to cross the range and trek to the Ravi Valley.

The Siwalik hills are lower and broader and have not presented great obstacles to highway construction, the hill roads crossing freely to link the northern Indian plains with Kangra, the Kulu Valley, Simla and Dehra Dun.

On the Zanskar range the Fatu La, on the Leh/Srinagar highway, is considered the easterly most pass, while the Singi La, the Charcha La and the Rubarung La are the principle trekking passes into the Zanskar Valley. For the hardy Ladakhi the principle route in winter between the Zanskar Valley and the outside world is down the ice-bound Zanskar River gorges.

In the Garwhal, roads are being constructed to the main places of pilgrimage in the heart of the Himalaya. These include Yamunotri, Gangotri at the head of the Bhagirathi Valley, Kedarnath at the head of the Mandakini Valley, and Badrinath at the head of the Alaknanda Valley. While treks are followed from the roadhead to the river sources, alternative routes can be taken across the ridges which separate the headwaters of the Ganges.

Rivers

The Indus River and its tributaries provide the principle drainage system in the Indian Himalaya. From its source below the slopes of Mt Kailash, it flows along the northern boundaries of the Himalaya, before turning south en route to the Arabian Sea. On its path to the plains it is fed by the Jhelum, the Chenab, the Ravi, and finally the Sutlej which, with the Indus, comprise the five main rivers of north-west India.

Eastwards from the Sutlej the rivers drain into the Ganges basin: first the Tons flows into the Yamuna, which in turns drains into the Ganges at Allahabad, before sweeping across north-east India to the Bay of Bengal. The third main river system traversing the subcontinent is the Brahmaputra. It too has its source close to the headwaters of the Sutlej and the Indus but flows east along the Tibetan plateau before it loops around the Himalaya and into the Bay of Bengal.

CLIMATE

Climatically, the Indian Himalaya can be divided into three regions. The first is the ridges and valleys to the south of the Pir Panjal range and the monsoonal hill states from Jammu to Kumaon; the second, including the region south of the Himalaya but beyond the Pir Panjal, encompasses the Kashmir Valley and the valleys of Lahaul and Spiti, a modified monsoon climate; the third region, that of Ladakh

	New Delhi*			Srinagar**			Leh***		
	max	min	rain	max	min	rain	max	min	rain
January	21.1	6.7	22.9	5.0	-2.2	73.7	-1.1	-13.3	10.2
February	23.9	9.4	17.7	7.2	-1.1	71.1	0.6	-12.2	7.6
March	30.6	14.4	12.7	13.9	3.3	91.4	7.2	-6.1	7.6
April	36.1	20.0	7.7	18.9	7.2	93.9	13.3	-1.1	5.0
May	40.6	26.1	12.7	24.4	11.1	60.9	16.1	0.6	5.0
June	38.9	28.3	73.7	29.4	14.4	35.6	20.0	6.7	5.0
July	35.6	27.2	180.3	31.1	18.3	58.4	25.0	10.0	12.9
August	33.9	26.1	172.7	30.6	17.8	60.9	23.9	10.0	15.2
September	33.9	23.9	116.8	27.8	12.2	38.1	21.1	5.6	7.6
October	33.9	18.3	10.2	22.2	5.0	30.5	15.0	-0.6	2.5
November	28.9	11.1	2.5	15.6	-0.6	10.2	8.3	-6.7	2.5
December	22.8	7.8	10.2	10.7	-2.2	33.0	2.2	-10.6	5.0
annual rainfall			640.2			657.7			83.8

*1866-1943 **1899-1942 ***1881-1942

and its environs, is beyond the Himalaya, where climatic conditions result in a high altitude desert.

TREKKING SEASONS

The corresponding seasons to trek these regions are as follows: the monsoonal hill states of Kangra, Kulu, Simla and Kumaon in June, and from September till mid-October. In Kashmir the season extends from late May until October. The same period applies to Lahaul/Spiti although it is difficult to gain access to these regions until mid-June. In Ladakh the trekking season also extends from May until October.

Spring in the valleys of Kashmir and Kulu begins in mid-March and extends through until the end of May. At this time Kashmir experiences its heaviest rainfall with storms breaking over the Pir Panjal. In the valleys heavy rain can fall for two to three days; in the mountains it is snow, which in late spring plays havoc with early trek schedules. Late snow on the passes reduces extended walks at least until early June, and can persists until well into July. Late snows can also interrupt pre-monsoonal treks in Kulu and road access over the Rhotang Pass to Lahaul. It normally means that extended trekking itineraries are limited before the monsoonal rains affect Kulu in late June.

While the Kulu Valley experiences rain, the Kashmir Valley becomes hazy and humid in July and August. During summer temperatures often reach 35°C by midday. In Kashmir the mountain trails are generally clear, while in the Kulu region it is worthwhile going over the Rhotang Pass and beyond the Pir Panjal into Lahaul. Treks here are possible anytime between mid-June and October.

Autumn is the most settled period. The months of September and October are typically clear with a minimum of rain. Treks can be made throughout the Pir Panjal and the Himalaya from Kashmir, Kangra, Kulu and Kumaon. Night time temperatures begin to drop by mid-October and the early snows settle on the passes. However, this does not preclude valley treks and many of the main Indian valleys can be clear even up to December.

The winter months from December until March are marked some years by a heavy snowfall in early December. In other years the snows don't fall heavily in the Indian Himalaya, and particularly in Kashmir, until late January. Skiing schedules can be reliably undertaken from late January until April.

Ladakh is isolated from the brunt of the Indian climate. Humidity is always low and rainfall no more than a few cm a year. Until a few years ago, Ladakh was cut off completely for six months of the year from the time the snows fell on the passes in October until they melted again the following June. Rarely would the mail runner risk the avalanche-prone Zoji La in the middle of winter. Nowadays the commercial flights to Leh allow visitors in throughout the year, although the region is not all that comfortable in winter. For many Ladakhis the flight is an opportunity to get down to the plains, so in-bound flights often have only a few civilian passengers.

Ladakh experiences some of the coldest temperatures anywhere in the world, and it doesn't warm up until spring in late April/early May. In June, July and August, daytime temperatures frequently rise to the high 20°Cs and the snow on the passes melts. Occasional heavy rain can

be experienced in July and August, and care needs to be taken on river crossings. By September, conditions are perfect and normally continue until late October – even though night time temperatures may fall below freezing. By November, the early winter snows fall on the passes closest to the Himalaya. In winter the Ladakhis still travel, enduring the intense cold to follow the snow bridges in the depths of the valleys. For the well-prepared trekker, there are possibilities of exploring the Indus and Zanskar valleys in the winter months.

NATURAL HISTORY/ECOLOGY

Over the last decade there has been an increasing awareness of the delicate ecological balances in the Himalaya. Some regions that have been over-grazed or denuded of timber have been designated as national parks or sanctuaries, while there are plans to impose restrictions on many other alpine valleys in the west Himalaya.

Until 1947 the balance of wildlife in the hills was closely regulated. Sport was a prime attraction of the area and close control was kept over hunting regulations.

Since 1947 however, enforcement of the rules has lapsed and many of the protected species, including the snow leopard and the Kashmir stag, have been drastically reduced in number. It is only over the last few years that concerted action has been taken against poachers and fur traders.

In his book *The Wildlife of India*, the noted naturalist E P Gee, refers to the diminishing number of Hangul deer in the Dachigam Sanctuary in Srinagar. In 1947 the population was estimated at between 1000 and 2000; by 1954 it had dropped to 300; by 1964 to less than 200; and by 1970 to less than 150. Strong measures backed by the Jammu & Kashmir Wildlife Directorate and the World Wildlife Association have been responsible for checking this decline and the numbers today have increased to more than 500.

Recently the Uttar Pradesh government introduced restrictions on movement through the Valley of the Flowers (the Bhyundar Valley) and the Nanda Devi Sanctuary. Both local shepherds and climbers had caused a gradual erosion of the flora and fauna, so with traffic restricted for the next five years these regions will have time to regenerate.

In the high Himalayan valleys of Kashmir and Himachal Pradesh proposals have been made to regulate the shepherd migrations to the huge valleys that border the Great Himalaya. The regions northeast of the Marwa/Warvan valleys and north-west of the Chenab up to the main Himalayan watershed have been designated. This ambitious scheme would effectively control the movement of the Bakharval and Gaddi with their huge flocks of sheep and goats that have damaged the alpine hillsides. Alternative grazing areas will have to be found and the numbers strictly controlled before the plans will achieve any degree of success.

In the meantime, the Dachigam National Park is an example of successful regeneration by restricting movement through a region. The rich variety of wildflowers has been rejuvenated and, as a natural progression, the wildlife has returned and multiplied. This area had previously been over-grazed by the buffalo of the local Gujar. The park extends from the shores of Dal Lake to the 4000-metre high ridges beyond Tarsar Lake.

A day trek can be made in the lower sanctuary beyond Harwar, just 20 km from Srinagar. Alternatively, a week or more could be profitably spent trekking to the upper sanctuary, either from Harwar, Tral (near Avantipur), or from the ridges of Tarsar Lake. If accompanied by an experienced shikari, the experience is likely to be highly rewarding, and the chances of sighting the Hangul deer and other rare wildlife species are quite high.

Permits are necessary to visit the sanctuary; they cost Rs 20 per person per day and can be obtained from the Wildlife Directorate in Srinagar.

While demands on the mountainside are made by both the conservationists and the shepherds, trekkers have also made their mark over the last 20 years. While the trekker's awareness of the mountain ecology is likely to be greater than that of his counterpart who visits mountain regions by bus or jeep, there is still a need for regulation. In the most popular trek areas, of the Kulu Valley and the Sindh/Lidder valleys, the trails and campsites are beginning to deteriorate. Garbage is seldom burned, rain ditches are seldom filled in, and trees are often felled indiscriminately. In the west Himalaya the severe winters have, until now, been the one saving grace. The heavy snowfalls make the mountain regions wilderness areas for over half of the year, and gives the flora time to regenerate. Also there is a plentiful supply of deadwood so the forest erosion is not as acute as in other Himalayan districts, such as the Khumbu region of Nepal. Yet demands by both graziers and trekkers will soon exceed the environmental balance.

Two programmes should be initiated without delay before the damage is too great: one, the respective tourist departments should help fund a permanent staff to clear campsites, and in some cases, restrict camping at more popular sites; and second, an immediate programme of environmental education should be

launched for both foreign and local trekking companies to ensure that both trekkers and staff are aware of the delicate ecology of the mountains.

Flora

The west Himalaya can be broadly classified into three main vegetation/forest zones – each one varying with altitude. The highest is the alpine zone – the open grazing areas and flowered meadows above the treeline. The elevation of the alpine zone varies from 3500 to 4500 metres, though plant life is actually sustained up to the margins of the permanent snowline at about 5000 metres.

Immediately below this region is a transitional zone – or sub-alpine region, where birch groves, juniper and dwarf rhododendron grow at elevations between 3400 and 3800 metres.

The temperate forest zones comprise the lowest region. Generally the conifers are found on the higher levels, to 3500 metres, while the deciduous trees come at elevations lower than 3000 metres. Below 3000 metres many tree varieties – the pines, firs, spruces, holly, oaks, ash and alder are interspersed. Each tree grows in its own specific elevation band, eg the blue pine, the deodar and the white oak grow between 1500 and 2500 metres, while the silver fir and the brown oak are found between 2500 and 3500 metres. Bordering the forest regions are the farming settlements with orchards and walnut groves. Cornfields are at the higher altitudes, to 3000 metres, while rice paddies are cultivated below 2000 metres.

When trekking, these various vegetation levels are a very useful indication of altitude, especially if trekking for the first time. They are also reliable indications of the wildlife in the area.

While the forest and vegetation categories are useful indications of elevation south of the main Himalaya range, to the north of the Himalaya in Ladakh, Zanskar, and to some extent Lahaul, there are other relevant factors.

First, altitude. While the highest village in Kashmir is no more than 3000 metres, there are few villages in Ladakh below 3000 metres, so the forest regions of the latter are limited to the willow, poplar and sage bush. The lack of rainfall is the second variable. The vegetation is drier and the alpine zone is characterised by plant species that have little resemblance to those of Kashmir or Himachal Pradesh.

Bearing this in mind, the alpine regions of Kashmir, Himachal and Uttar Pradesh provide the best scope for appreciating the wildflower species, many of which are similar to the mountain flora of Europe and the USA. Here, Pollunin and Stainton's book *Flowers of the Himalaya* must be consulted for identifying the hundreds of varieties of wildflowers in the mountain districts.

The flowering season is dependent on the spring snow melt and can vary considerably from year to year. In the regions over 3500 metres, the alpine meadows become clear of snow sometime between mid-June and late July, depending on the harshness of the winter.

By summer, mid-July to late August, the alpine meadows of Kashmir, Himachal and Uttar Pradesh are at their best. In Kashmir occasional storms break over the Pir Panjal, while the Himachal Pradesh and Garwhal regions are subject to monsoon. However, compensations abound for the well-prepared trekker.

In Kashmir, the region beyond Sonamarg – to Vishensar, Krishensar and Gangobal – is always a popular locality for wildflowers, while the trekking trails into the main Himalaya pass through alpine meadows that support a wide variety of flora. For those based in Srinagar, a short trek to the upper Dachigam Sanctuary is recommended, and the valley above the Gujar village of Satlanjan, en route to the Kolahoi Glacier, is well worth visiting.

In Himachal Pradesh the alpine plateaus above the Kulu Valley, in particular the treks to Chandratal and Beas Kund, and the meadows over the Ravi Valley, en route to the Sach or the Kugti passes, are also renowned for wildflowers. In Uttar Pradesh the alpine meadows between Yamunotri and Har-ki-Dun are recommended, and anyone who has read Frank Smythe's *The Valley of Flowers* is sure to be attracted to the Bhyundar Valley in the heart of Garwhal.

In Ladakh, the wetter regions to the immediate west of the Himalaya, such as the Pensi La and the grazing grounds en route to the higher passes, support many wildflowers. As you move further away from the Himalaya, the alpine zones have less flowering species.

Fauna

The migration of wildlife in the Indian Himalaya, while dependent on the seasons and the respective vegetation zones, has also been considerably influenced by the migration of shepherds and villagers to the mountain regions. As a general rule, the more remote the area, the greater the chance of seeing animals in their natural state. The only outstanding exception to this is the wildlife found in the Dachigam National Park.

In the west Himalaya wildlife such as the black and brown bear, the red fox and stone marten, and members of the cat family, including the wildcat and the snow leopard, inhabit the upper forest regions during the winter months. In spring, as soon as the snows at 3000-3500 metres begin to melt, the animals migrate higher to the birch trees and open meadows. The animals are less wary of human encroachment during this period, and this is an ideal time to trek out of the valleys of Pahalgam, Sonamarg or Manali on skis and snowshoes.

The period between the snows melting and the arrival of the shepherds to establish their high camps, is the perfect time to explore the more remote valleys in the high conifer, sub-alpine zones. In May and early June it is common to see both black and brown bears with their cubs, foraging for food above the Lidder Valley and in the Kulu region. The wild sheep and goat herds, including the urial and the markhor, inhabit the denser birch and conifer forests, a habitat they share with the Kashmir stag and the musk deer. The bharal and the ibex seek higher altitudes, particularly in Ladakh, where they head for the most remote plateaus for summer grazing. Here the rare snow leopard, the wolf and the brown bear also roam during the summer months in search of prey – either wild goats or the domestic variety tended by the shepherds. The alpine and sub-alpine zones are also the habitat of the marmot – the most common animal in these regions, who whistle from the security of their burrows as soon as they sense danger. The common langur are

often seen in the Himalaya and their upward migration through the valleys to the conifer zones is seldom quiet. Family groups of these arboreal monkeys will occasionally wander close to camp sites.

In early autumn the bears are attracted to the valleys and villages by the ripening cornfields. Many tales are told of the destruction they cause and the measures that have had to be adopted to control them. The black bear is the main culprit and is not on the list of protected wildlife. The rarer brown bear is protected but tends to stick to the higher terrain anyway, until the first winter snows.

Most animals make their own way down in late autumn after the shepherds and buffalo wallahs have departed down-valley. In Ladakh the rarer wild goat and sheep species descend to the security of the more remote valleys and their migration can be appreciated between mid and late October. Their descent is followed by the packs of wolves and the lone snow leopard. After the first winter snows the wolf tracks are easy to follow and their migration has been well documented in both the Zanskar and Markha valleys. The snow leopard, the most elusive of the cat species, will also descend to the highest villages of Kashmir and Himachal Pradesh, particularly in the isolated valleys adjoining the main Himalaya.

Facts for the Trekker

VISAS

Since June 1984 all nationalities, including Commonwealth citizens, are required to have a visa for India. Visas are issued at Indian Embassies and are valid for 90 days and can be extended for a further 90 days. Visas must be obtained no more than six months before your arrival in India. Indian visas are usually triple entry so you can go to Nepal or Sri Lanka and return on the same visa.

Within India visas can be extended at the Foreigners' Registration Office in Delhi or Srinagar, or any office of the Superintendent of Police in the District Headquarters, eg Leh, Manali etc. Usually the application is straightforward and no particular hassles are encountered. It is not advisable to leave India and get a new 90-day visa – the embassy in Kathmandu, for instance, is wary of re-applications and may restrict a new one to two or three weeks.

If you stay in India more than 90 days be sure to hold on to your exchange certificates as you will need a tax clearance before leaving the country. An exemption form must first be completed in the area you registered, ie if you registered in Srinagar you must get a clearance from the local tax office in Srinagar and then get the relevant certificate endorsed at your port of exit in Delhi. There are no worries there but allow a day to complete formalities.

Restricted areas

You do not require special permits for visiting Kashmir, Ladakh or Himachal Pradesh. However, it is necessary to remember that all Himalayan border regions are politically sensitive. The area of Ladakh from one mile north of the Srinagar-Leh road is a restricted zone (completely barred to foreigners). The same restrictions apply to the area one mile east of the Leh-Manali road, although it is almost impossible to get permission to travel on this military road. At the time of writing, the regions of Rupshu and Nubra in Ladakh were still closed to foreigners, as is the region of Spiti to the east of Lahaul. In the Garwhal, similar restrictions apply as you get closer to the Chinese/ Indian border, and as a double check it is advisable to go to the Police Headquarters in Mussoorie before proceeding. It should also be noted that certain other trekking areas such as the Nanda Devi Sanctuary are at present closed to trekkers, while for similar ecological reasons there are restrictions on entry to the Valley of the Flowers.

It is necessary to carry your passport with you at all times. It is your only bona fide means of identification and will need to be shown at strategically placed checkpoints in Ladakh, Zanskar and Lahaul. No trekking permits are necessary for walking in the Indian Himalaya – although a system may be instituted in the next few years.

INSURANCE

Whether going it alone or through a trekking agency, it is imperative to take out some cover against loss of baggage, sickness or injury. Most policies also cover the reimbursement of cancellation fees and other non-recoverable expenses if you are forced to cancel your bookings or your air ticket because of accident or illness to yourself or a family member. If you are going to a more remote location then an evacuation cover must be considered. Evacuation by helicopter can be very expensive – up to $5000 or more, and one will generally not be sent unless the authorised officers have some guarantee of payment. Most agencies who run treks to the Himalaya can arrange policies to cover emergency evacuation. Do not rely on your consulate or embassy to help.

Most insurance companies will cover a trekking holiday at little or no extra cost to a normal holiday in India. But a substantially higher premium is involved if you're mountaineering, skiing or rafting.

If you purchase insurance and have a loss, you must submit proof of this in order to make a claim. If you have a medical problem you must save all your bills and get a physician's certificate stating that you were sick. If you lose something covered by insurance you must file a police report and get a copy to send to the insurance company, no matter how remote the location. Insurance companies will generally not consider claims without this documentation. Read your policy carefully and be sure you understand all its conditions.

MONEY

US$1	=	Rs 12.0
A$1	=	Rs 8.0
£1	=	Rs 16.2
C$1	=	Rs 7.5
NZ$1	=	Rs 6.2
DM 1	=	Rs 4.0

The rupee (Rs) is divided into 100 paise (p). There are coins of 1, 2, 3, 5, 10, 20, 25 and 50 paise and notes of Rs 1, 2, 5, 10, 20, 50, 100 and 500. At one time the rupee was divided into 16 annas and you may still occasionally hear prices quoted in annas in bazaars and markets – four annas is 25p.

The major travellers' cheques are all easily exchanged in India although US dollars and pounds sterling are the most recognised foreign currencies. In out-of-the-way centres you may find these are the only currencies readily accepted. Exchange rates tend to vary from bank to bank. Anything to do with paperwork in India is inevitably time consuming so you may find it easier to change a larger amount at one time (more than you would in other countries) – simply to minimise the time wasted in banks.

Deciding how much money to bring is a difficult consideration. If you are on a scheduled itinerary with most hotels, meals, sightseeing and/or trekking included then you will need little extra. A few hundred dollars will easily cover additional expenses like alcohol, laundry and airport taxes.

If however you're handling your own arrangements, you will naturally budget for the unexpected as well as the expected. A good idea is to double your original estimate. Itemise transport, food and accommodation. For trekking include guides, staff, horsemen, food and equipment. Remember that government rates for accommodation can usually be bargained down, while actual costs for horsemen and porters are generally higher than the government rates, especially when taking into account relocation costs of the horses and staff. Don't forget that cooking gear and additional food for staff, together with their clothing and equipment boosts the overall cost even further. A contingency fund should also be considered for those unforeseen delays and emergencies.

Try not to have money transferred to you in India, it is often painfully slow and laborious, particularly with the Indian banks. If you must have funds sent to India transfer them by cable or telex, not by mail, even if you have plenty of time on hand, and transfer them to a foreign owned bank. American Express have offices in Bombay, New Delhi and Calcutta but there are other banks operating throughout India which are still foreign owned and tend to be more efficient than the Indian-owned banks when it comes to foreign transactions. The Chartered Bank and Grindlays Bank (now owned by Australia's ANZ Bank) are two examples – Grindlays have an office in Srinagar on the Bund.

There are two particular points to be careful about with Indian money. First avoid dirty, grubby or torn notes – they can be unusable, particularly in out-of-the-way places. If you do get stuck with such a note try not to worry about it or cause any hassle if people refuse to accept it. You can generally get them changed at a bank (but not always!) or use them for some official purpose such as paying your airport departure tax.

The other money problem is big notes – changing a Rs 100 banknote is always difficult, in fact with India's perpetual small change deficiency changing anything is usually difficult. When changing foreign currency at a bank try to get as much of it in smaller denomination notes as possible. This problem applies particularly in Ladakh where, during the summer tourist season, there is sometimes a severe shortage of small denomination notes – bring as many one and two rupee notes as possible.

Away from the major centres changing travellers' cheques or foreign currency may be difficult, if not impossible. There are no facilities for changing foreign money in Zanskar, nor in Ladakh outside Leh or Kargil. Make sure that you have enough rupees with you.

It is illegal to import or export Indian currency although you can generally get Indian rupees in Bangkok or Singapore or in Europe at a useful discount – about the same as the blackmarket rate within the country. You are allowed to bring a bottle of whisky and a carton of cigarettes into India duty free and these are usually an excellent investment. In Kashmir and Ladakh good quality camping gear and down clothing will also find a ready market. 'Antique' dealers and carpet sellers are also often willing to take dollars under the counter as payment.

INFORMATION

The Government of India Tourist Office maintains a string of tourist branches overseas where you can get brochures, leaflets and some information about India. The tourist office leaflets have plenty of information and are worth getting hold of.

As well as the overseas offices in the following list there are also smaller 'promotion offices' in Osaka (Japan) and Dallas, Miami, San Francisco and Washington DC (USA).

Australia
    Carlton Centre, 55 Elizabeth St, Sydney, NSW 2000 (tel 02 232 1600)
    Elder House, 111 St George's Terrace, Perth, WA 6000 (tel 06 321 6932)
Canada
    Suite 1016, Royal Trust Tower (PO Box 342), Toronto Dominion Centre, Toronto 1, Ontario (tel 416 362 3188)
Japan
    Pearl Building, 9-18 Ginza, 7 Chome, Chuo ku, Tokyo (tel 571 5062/3)
Singapore
    Podium Block, 4th floor, Ming Court Hotel, Tanglin Rd, Singapore 10 (tel 235 5737)
Sweden
    Sveavagen 9-11 (Box 40016), 103-41 Stockholm 40 (tel 08 215081)
Thailand
    Singapore Airlines Building, 3rd floor, 62/5 Thaniya Rd, Bangkok
UK
    7 Cork St, London W1X QAB (tel 01 437 3677-8)
USA
    30 Rockefeller Plaza, 15 North Mezzanine, New York, NY 10020 (tel 212 586 4901)
    201 North Michigan Ave, Chicago, Illinois 60601 (tel 312 236 6899)
    3550 Wilshire Blvd, Suite 204, Los Angeles, California 90010 (tel 213 380 8855)

Government of India Tourist Offices within India that should be useful include:

Bombay
    123 M Karve Rd (tel 293144)
Calcutta
    4 Shakespeare Sarani (tel 441402)
Jammu
    Gulab Bhavan (tel 5121)
Madras
    35 Mount Rd (tel 86240)
New Delhi
    88 Janpath (tel 320005)
Srinagar
    Residency Rd

GENERAL INFORMATION

Mail

The Indian postal services and poste restante are generally excellent. Expected letters are almost always there and letters you send almost invariably get to the address you put on the envelope. American Express, in its major city locations, is an alternative to the poste restante system, but the latter is quite OK. Have letters addressed to you with your surname in capital letters and underlined. Many lost letters are simply misfiled under first names, so always check under both.

You can often buy stamps at good hotels, avoiding the interminable queuing in crowded post offices.

Telecommunications

Making a phone call from Kashmir to Delhi can involve hours of waiting; making an international call from Kashmir is practically impossible – unless you know somebody at the exchange. This also goes for Kulu, Simla and Dharamsala. If it's an emergency it's best to go to Delhi where the international phone service is satisfactory. In spite of the importance of tourism to the Himalaya, international communication facilities are very poor. Telexes are a hit and miss affair while telegrams are frequently garbled. The best way of achieving some success is to send two telegrams – the cost is not too high and there's some chance of the message getting through.

Time

India is 5½ hours ahead of GMT, 10½ hours ahead of New York, 13½ hours ahead of the west coast of the USA, 4½ hours behind Sydney, and 10 minutes behind Nepal.

Business Hours

Government and airline business hours are normally 10 am to 5 pm Monday to Friday and half day on Saturday. Take into account, though, the many holidays and festival dates, both local and national.

BOOKSHOPS & BOOKS

New Delhi, in the bookshops around Janpath and Connaught Circle, has the largest stock of books on the Indian Himalaya including the reprints listed below. Closer to the hills, the Kashmir Bookshop on Sharwani Rd, Srinagar has a comprehensive stock of volumes on Kashmir and Jammu while in Leh there is a useful selection on Ladakh. In Simla there are a few shops on The Mall.

General

Where Men & Mountains Meet by John Keay (John Murray, London 1977)
The Gilgit Game by John Keay (John Murray, London 1979)
Plain Tales from the Raj by Charles Allen (Futura Publications, London 1980)
Trespassers on the Roof of the World by Peter Hopkirk (Oxford University Press, Oxford 1983)
Himalayan Art by Madajeet Singh (Macmillan, New York 1968)
An Area of Darkness by V S Naipul (Penguin, London 1968)
A Portrait of India by Ved Mehta (Penguin, London 1968)
Journey to the Himalaya by Keith Adam (ABC, Sydney 1980)

Guidebooks

Guide to Kashmir, Ladakh and Skardu by Arthur Neve (Srinagar)
Holidaying & Trekking in Kashmir by NL Bakaya (Srinagar)
Kashmir, Ladakh & Zanskar by Rolf & Margret Schettler (Lonely Planet, Melbourne 1985)
Trekking in the Himalayas by Tomoya Iozawa (Yama-Kei, Tokyo)
Trekkers' Guide to the Himalaya & Karakoram by Hugh Swift (Sierra Club Books, San Francisco 1982 and Hodder & Stoughton, London 1982)
Trekking in the Nepal Himalaya by Stan Armington (Lonely Planet, Melbourne 1985)
The Himalayas, Playground of the Gods by Captain Mohan Kolhi (Vikas, Delhi 1983)

19th Century Accounts

Kashmir by Younghusband (reprint 1909)
Travels in Kashmir, Ladakh & Skardu by Vigne (reprint 1842)
Northern Barrier of India by Drew (1877)
West Himalaya & Tibet by Thompson (reprint 1852)
Himalayan Districts of Kulu, Lahaul & Spiti by A F P Harcourt (reprint 1871)

Contemporary Accounts

This is Kashmir by P Gervis (Universal Publications, Delhi 1974)
Kashmir by F Brunel (Runca & Co, Delhi 1979)
Cultural History of Ladakh vols I & II (Vikas, New Delhi 1977 & 1980)
Ladakh by Heinrich Harrer (Penguin, London 1980)
Kulu, End of the Habitable World by P Chetwold (John Murray, London 1972)

MAPS, DISTANCES & ALTITUDES

An average group will cover two to three km an hour along an average trail. Perhaps four km an hour along a jeep track but considerably less – say 1½ km an hour – on a demanding pass ascent. Bearing this in mind a five or six hour day will average 12 to 14 km – sufficient to appreciate the trek and achieve a decent walking stage.

Altimeters have the disadvantage that the trekker cannot unduly exaggerate his or her performance after he or she returns home. However, there is always some leeway. I have watched Leh rise and fall nearly 100 metres in a day – not from any strange hallucinations but simply by recording altimeter readings on a stormy day. Barometric pressures change considerably in mountain regions and I have not yet spent sufficient time with an altimeter to record every pass and valley in a variety of weather conditions. Altitude figures when given on passes or in villages are estimates and should be taken as such. Spot heights referring to mountains on the maps are more accurate and have been taken from the Indian ground survey.

Compass bearings in the Himalaya are only as good as the maps you are following. The trekking maps are basic ridge and river profiles, principally based on the Indian ground survey. The 1:250,000 trekking maps compiled by the Ground Survey of India with local information supplied by the Jammu & Kashmir Tourist Department have the advantage of being very clear. They are available through the Jammu & Kashmir Tourist Department in Delhi and Srinagar – two sheets, one for Kashmir and one for Ladakh, at approximately US$2 each. For Himachal Pradesh there are three similar sheets, one for Chamba-Kangra-Kishtwar, a second for Kulu-Lahaul-Spiti and a third for Kinnaur-Simla.

The US Army maps (U 502 series) 1:250,000 are the best commercially available countour maps. The originals, published in 1948, were in colour, but the series reprints are in black and white and somewhat difficult to follow. It is best to colour in the river and glacial systems and get a general profile of the region. The most relevant to Jammu and Kashmir are 43.6 Srinagar, 43.7 Kargil, 43.8 Leh, 43.11 Anantnag, 43.12 Padam. The most relevant to Himachal Pradesh and Uttar Pradesh are 43.16, 44.13, 43.4, 44.1 Himachal Pradesh and 44.6 Nanda Devi. These are generally available through Stanfords, 12-14 Long Acre, London, England, a leading map supplier who regularly print updates on what is available both in the U 502 series and also of new maps published in Europe.

WHERE TO TREK

Once you have decided to go to India, the first step is to decide where you want to trek, whether it is the right season for a particular area and whether that area is the most attractive in terms of walking conditions and culture. Check out the guidebooks and follow this through with background reading on the area; write off for travel brochures and information from the Indian Tourist Office; talk to people who have recently returned, compare their experiences with your own expectations and see how they measure up. Be as flexible as possible at this stage – there are many opportunities in the Indian Himalaya and some careful thinking at the outset will go a long way towards ensuring a successful trek.

The bottom line is, of course, what is available and what you can afford. Itemise the cost of organising a trek on your own: calculate how much you will need to spend on clothing, equipment, medical supplies, the cost of insurance, food and cooking gear, the additional cost of horsemen and perhaps a cook and a guide. Then compare and consider the alternatives and variables: the number of people who are interested and can share costs, their degree of commitment. Compare these with the costs of an organised travel company and decide which plan of action suits you.

For many, the financial alternatives are also dictated by time. Consider how long you are going to be away and the length of your trek. Never follow a too-ambitious itinerary if time is strictly limited by work or other travel commitments. You must structure your goals to meet the pace of India. You may experience delays waiting for flight connections or for guides or horsemen to assemble at the right spot on the right date. Plan an itinerary and then modify it. Remember that the stages outlined in this guide need to be scheduled also in terms of inclement weather, acclimatisation, sickness and other delays.

It is up to you to assess your outdoors experience. Trekking in India is more of a wilderness experience than trekking in Nepal. Attention must be paid to pass and river crossings, and sound common sense is not only essential, it can be a lifesaver. Remember to structure you trek on the weakest member of your party. A weekend bushwalk is one thing but a trek in the Himalaya for two weeks or more is quite another. A trek can be an exhilarating experience, but it can also be a frustrating one for those not fully aware of what it's really like to camp for weeks at a time. Friendships can become strained unless each member is fully aware of what they are letting themselves in for. After considering the cost, the time available, and your outdoors experience, it is worthwhile to re-examine the options open.

WHAT STYLE OF TREK
Adventure Travel Company

Over the last decade many of these travel companies have expanded their programmes from Nepal into the Indian Himalaya. The Indian tourist offices in Europe, the UK, the USA and Australia have a file of bona fide organisations. Points to keep in mind when considering any of these companies are: their experience in handling trips to India, the leaders employed, equipment used, the type of food provided, the medical kits, clothing lists, specialist interests and evacuation cover. Ultimately, any adventure travel company is only as good as its local ground agent.

Local Agent

You can organise your trek through a local agent. This can be done by writing to the state trek offices. They will provide the names and addresses of local agents. You can either contact these agents beforehand or on your arrival. Quotes should be taken from two or three companies; check out their degree of experience and what exactly you're paying for in terms of guides, cooks, horsemen, equipment and food. This takes time so weigh it against the option of doing-it-yourself.

Self-Organised

At a hill station or trek starting-point you can arrange your own equipment, food and staff. If you have sufficient time and patience organising things either directly or through a local man can, besides saving money, be a rewarding experience. You must, however, be aware of or ready to deal with a different culture and all its unique qualities. This especially applies to negotiating the employment of staff. Negotiations with horsemen may take days, and must include such hidden costs as an extra allowance if the trek is going to a remote area, some clothing and a mess tent. Generally they are reluctant to go on their own and an individual trekker, planning an extended trek, would be well advised to find someone to help share costs.

A cook is a valuable asset – he will save you the expense of buying pots and pans and can recommend what food to bring and what to leave behind. He can also bargain far harder in the bazaars, saving you endless amounts of otherwise wasted time. In return, he will expect some clothing allowance, normally local walking boots, plus a decent tip at the end of the trek.

Your choice of a guide is vital because depending on his experience and reliability he can make or break a trek. It is essential to check over his experience in the area you are going to, his attitude towards the other staff, and his general knowledge of the area. Once a daily rate has been fixed for him, he is your representative and should need little reminder that he is to act always in your interests in negotiations with the cook, horsemen or equipment suppliers.

As contractor, you are liable, strictly speaking, if something goes wrong, and it is good protection on your side to be well equipped – particularly with medicines in case of accident.

Backpacking

This can be easily undertaken on short treks where the payload is light and the stages easy. On a long trek your rucksack may weigh you down to the point where you see more of your feet than the mountains. In Nepal this method has been used widely to trek from one village hotel to the next. In India the system has no direct counterpart. The British forest rest-house or dak bungalow equivalent is a long way down the line and food supplies en route are generally unreliable. In Zanskar a teashop/travellers'-inn system has evolved, but the facilities are limited in comparison with what is provided in Nepal. It is one thing to carry your own gear for a few days but quite another to do it for two weeks or a month. Some trekkers compromise – a porter or a horsemen is generally necessary unless you're very fit and experienced in the wilderness.

Whatever option you choose, whether it be backpacking or with an adventure travel company or something in-between, the magic of the Himalaya should be experienced in conjunction with the local people. A local crew can enhance your experience in a way that is sometimes not appreciated by people wary of anything that hints of the 'Raj'. Besides providing employment, the local cook, guide or horsemen's sense of involvement and humour can remain with you for a long time after you return home. Experiences in the Himalaya are shared experiences and there is nothing finer than having these enhanced by a great crew.

State Tourist Offices

Jammu & Kashmir

Trekking Officer in Charge, Tourist Reception Centre, Srinagar, Kashmir, India

Himachal Pradesh

Trekking Officer in Charge, Tourist Office, Manali/Dharmoda/Simla, Himachal Pradesh, India

Uttar Pradesh

Trekking Officer in Charge, Tourist Office, Mussoorie, Uttar Pradesh, India

CLOTHING

Clothing considerations differ widely from trek to trek. A short hike up the Lidder Valley in the middle of August could be undertaken in shorts, T-shirt, a warm pullover, sandshoes and a sun hat; a traverse from Kashmir to Ladakh in June, however, would require a far more comprehensive checklist. One of the most important considerations is the method by which you trek – if you are using pack horses then weight is not such an important consideration as when you are carrying all your own gear. The checklist below must, therefore, be interpreted liberally. Experienced bushwalkers will already have their own preferences, while for those with less outdoors experience, some of the following hints may prove useful.

In all mountain areas you should be prepared for inclement weather. On the other hand, excessive clothing is an expensive burden and most clothing worn on a weekend bushwalk is suitable for the Himalaya. Remember that you are walking essentially in summer-time in the Indian Himalaya, and heat is just as much a consideration as cold. It should be borne in mind that for the majority of treks, you will not be above the snow line and it is not necessary to have heavy down gear or double boots suitable for an ascent on Everest. A sturdy pair of walking boots is always recommended, as is a good wind and waterproof jacket and a comfortable rucksack to carry excess clothing during the day. An invaluable extra is a sturdy walking stick – useful on muddy trails, river crossings and for warding off over-friendly shepherd dogs.

If you're travelling exclusively in India and are not prepared to carry huge quantities of trekking gear around all the time, you can practically equip yourself in India. A local tailor can make up a pair of shorts and comfortable long trousers in an afternoon. Raw wool pullovers, long johns, string vests, gloves, socks and balaclavas can be purchased in the bazaar, while local hunter boots are just adequate for a short valley trek. A good windproof/waterproof jacket and rucksack are therefore the only minimal requirements. The Tourist Office in Kashmir has a stock of boots and jackets for hire, but as yet there are none of the local trek-clothing shops similar to Kathmandu.

Clothing Checklist

Walking boots These are the most important item in any clothing list. Boots must give adequate ankle support and have a sole flexible enough to meet the walking conditions anticipated. A sole fitted with a three-quarter length shank is not necessary unless you intend to tackle extensive glacial and snow walks. Make sure your boots are well walked-in beforehand and don't forget to bring spare laces and dubbin or other waterproofing application. Keep the receipts for new boots as most are guaranteed, or should be. Too many these days seem to fall apart in less than a month on the trail – an unfortunate sign of contemporary workmanship. Canvas boots are available in the markets for those taking an easy ramble.

Anorak A nylon/cotton windproof/waterproof is essential. Check that the proofing is adequate before going on a trek.

Down vest Recommended for chilly evenings. A full down jacket is generally not needed on most treks unless you feel the cold.

Wool shirt/pullover A thick woollen shirt is worth its weight in gold. I have worn mine solidly for five seasons and it is still nearly as good as new. Alternatively, raw-wool pullovers can be purchased in Srinagar, Leh and Manali for about Rs 50.

Breeches A pair of woollen walking breeches is ideal, or ex-army woollen pants. Pile trousers provide a satisfactory alternative or even track suit bottoms if you're not going over 3500 metres. Jeans are totally unsuitable in wet conditions.

Over-trousers A strong nylon pair is indispensable in wet weather.

Shorts Ideal for most walking in this part of the Himalaya. Some Australians even wear their shorts in blizzards rather than change into breeches.

Shirts T-shirts are OK but include at least one shirt with a collar to protect the back of the neck from sunburn. Ex-army shirts with plenty of pockets are ideal.

Thermal underwear Both pants and top really make a difference on those chilly mornings or when you are uncertain of the adequacy of your sleeping bag.

Gloves & balaclava Both items can be purchased locally in Srinagar, Manali and Leh bazaars. A balaclava is particularly important as considerable body heat is lost through the head.

Woollen socks A sufficient supply of thick and thin pairs should be taken. Normally use cotton inner and woolen outer on the trail.

Sandshoes For campsites and 'blistery' days.

Bush hat Absolutely essential.

Tracksuit A bit of a luxury for campsite and early morning wear, but still worth bringing along.

Snow gaiters Recommended, especially during the early and late parts of the season when snow covers the passes.

Snow goggles/sunglasses Good quality snow or ski goggles are necessary to combat the side glare on snow. Even if you're not actually walking on snow, glare on the ridges in late spring makes goggles indispensable. For non-snow conditions, Polaroid sunglasses are adequate.

EQUIPMENT

Over the last few years a number of outlets in Delhi and Srinagar have begun to stock lightweight equipment for hire. In Delhi it is best to check with the Indian Tourist Office in Janpath for up to date lists of agencies and equipment stockists. In Srinagar Choomti Treks, on the Bund, and the Tourist Office stock a limited supply of tents, sleeping bags, stoves and rucksacks. However, serious trekkers making their own arrangements are advised to bring their own tent, sleeping bag and insulated mat as quality items are always in short supply. For those undertaking an organised trek, professional agencies usually provide these basic essentials, though it's advisable to double check with your agent before you leave for India to establish exactly what is provided.

The following information is divided into equipment for *all* trekkers, whether you're making the arrangements yourself or going on an organised trek; and equipment to bring as an independent trekker. As with the clothing list, some items are more essential than others.

Equipment Checklist

Hold-all A strong hold-all or ex-army sausage bag for carrying your gear on a pack pony; preferably one large enough to carry your sleeping bag and insulated mat as well.

Stuff bags For protecting clothes from the elements, as most hold-alls are not waterproof. Strong plastic bags are ideal.

Rucksack Internal frame rucksacks are ideal on longer walks. Ensure that the sack is big enough to carry your toilet gear, camera and also your waterproof jacket and sweater as the pack ponies may not be at hand during a sudden change of weather. It is not recommended to bring a large rucksack as a means of packing gear onto horses as the condition of the sack will deteriorate rapidly after a few weeks of being handled by over-zealous ponymen.

Water bottle An aluminium or ex-army make is recommended but plastic bottles can be purchased locally.

Swiss Army knife The pride of any shepherd's possessions and always useful for peeling fruit and opening tins; one with a small screwdriver is invaluable for carrying out repairs on cameras.

Torch (flashlight), candles Available in India. Don't forget spare batteries and bulbs.

Umbrella For rain and shielding yourself from the sun; also handy for making discreet calls of nature. Available locally.

First aid kit A basic kit should include band aids, gauze pads, cotton bandages, sterile dressing, adhesive tape, antiseptic and burn creams, a low reading thermometer, scissors and tweezers. (Suggested medicines are detailed in the section on Health and Fitness.)

Miscellaneous Toiletries, toilet paper, waterproof matches, sun cream, towel, laundry soap, sewing kit, safety pins, a length of cord and small plastic bags for toilet paper and holding litter before disposal.

Optional extras Altimeter, compass, binoculars.

Equipment for Independent Trekkers
Tent A double-walled tent is necessary on most treks except for a short ramble up the Lidder Valley as there are few of the overnight teashop/hotels common in Nepal.

Sleeping Bag A good quality sleeping bag is imperative. Fibrefill bags dry a lot faster than down, though a down bag is more compact and lighter for backpacking.

Foam Mat A closed-cell foam mat should provide adequate insulation from the

ground; a space blanket can double as a ground sheet when sleeping in huts, monasteries or village halls.

Rope Whatever trek you are undertaking, a 40-metre length of rope is highly recommended for ensuring safe river crossings in the early part of the season in Kashmir, Kulu and Garwhal, and during the mid-season in Ladakh and Zanskar.

Cooking utensils Cooking pots and pans, enamel mugs, plates and cutlery, in fact, all kitchen utensils can be purchased in India. Gas containers or refills are not available. Local kerosene stoves provide a cheap and efficient alternative, although most locals use wood for cooking the evening meals. Remember to take spare parts and an ample supply of stove pins.

Miscellaneous Plastic drums for carrying kerosene, mustard oil, etc can be purchased locally. Large canvas mess tents can be hired for the crew and ponymen or porters to sleep in throughout the trek.

High altitude treks For exploring glaciers or climbing minor peaks, you'll need to bring ice-axes, crampons, harnesses, carabiners and rope with you as they are not readily available in India.

PHOTOGRAPHY
Ideally you should bring with you two single lens reflex cameras – one for colour and one for black and white film. For lenses, you could bring a wide angle for village profiles and monastery interiors, a macro lens for wildflowers, a telephoto for dramatic mountain shots and people close-ups and a zoom for on-the-move photography. Also a flash unit, light meter and tripod should be carried, together with a polaroid camera so that every child in each village you pass through can have a memento of your visit. All this, of course, requires at least 10 rolls of colour film for each day to cover every aspect of your trek.

In practice, most of us have to settle for less and get by with an Instamatic or SLR camera with a standard 50 mm lens. If you have never used a camera before, then a trip to the Himalaya is an ideal time to start. If you have used a camera before I would advise a reliable SLR body with a standard and telephoto lens. A telephoto lens is ideal for non-intrusive people photography. You can get a full-frame photograph of a shy villager without them noticing you're taking their picture. If you can afford it, buy a zoom lens the same make as your SLR system. If you can't, one of the widely available zoom lenses adaptable to most SLR bases will provide a satisfactory alternative.

Bring a change of ultra-violet filters. Extra camera and flash batteries are vital, plus a blower brush and cleaning equipment. The temperatures in summer do not necessitate your camera being 'winterised'. If, however, you're going to ski in Kashmir, or trek in Ladakh in winter then this should be considered. Don't forget, waterproof containers are essential to protect your film and camera gear in prolonged rainy conditions.

Film is very expensive in India and all colour film should be brought with you. If possible, allow a roll a day. If not try to ration your film carefully for the whole trip or you are bound to run short. Some fast film – ASA 400 – is desirable, especially if using a zoom or telephoto lens in low light conditions. Slide film is cheaper than prints and your best slides can be reprocessed as prints. Don't send film back from India by post – it may never get there. Keep it cool and secure until your return. Colour film can be processed in Bombay and Delhi, but the quality is uneven.

If you are buying new equipment, check it out thoroughly beforehand and make sure you know how to use it. Keep a record of light conditions and compare the results when your photos are developed. If you haven't used your camera for a while, have it serviced before you leave.

Finally, consider that you will be carrying the majority of your photographic gear with you each day. Your camera gear will almost certainly be the heaviest component of your daysack. Don't weigh yourself down with too much excess gear. Taking photographs should complement the enjoyment of your trek and not be viewed as an end in itself.

HEALTH & FITNESS
Having a suitable temperament is the most important consideration for going on a walk in the Himalaya. If you have any doubts as to whether you can handle being 'away from it all' for a period of a few weeks, then it is advisable to restrict your initial outdoors experience to a shorter trek nearer to home. I have led many groups over the last decade and am convinced that if someone thinks they can successfully complete a trek, then they will do so. Encouragement is often necessary but most problems arising on the trail are in the head rather than the feet. Trekking is not an activity exclusive to youth – age is no barrier. In fact, people of more mature years often do better than the younger generations. It is essential to approach the Himalaya with a sound and tolerant attitude.

Medical Preparation
Before visiting India a thorough medical check-up is necessary. It is advisable for people with a history of chest, asthma, bronchial and heart problems not to go. A visit to the dentist is also recommended as there's not much that can be done about a toothache when you're in the mountains. Before arriving in India you should have vaccinations against typhoid and tetanus which are generally recommended and shots against hepatitis may also be advisable. For the effectiveness of cholera shots you should consult your doctor. For anyone spending time in India, especially during the monsoon, anti-malarial tablets are a must. Kashmir is a non-malarial area but Kulu and the Garwhal are malarial.

Fitness

Having made the decision to go to the Himalaya, get fit! Jogging, swimming, cycling – in fact any regular physical exercise is desirable. Begin your programme preferably three months before and try to exercise daily for at least half an hour. The fitter you are the more you get out of your trek. If you do nothing beforehand, you will probably finish the trek but feel completely exhausted for the first week to 10 days. Most people have never felt better than after two or three weeks continuous walking in the mountains. The mountains, the exercise and wholesome food are an ideal combination for rejuvenating the mind and the body.

Food

A healthy diet makes for a healthy trek. The wide range of fresh fruit and vegetables, dairy products, fresh baked breads and wholegrains, contribute towards a highly nutritious eating pattern. When trekking try not to depend on tinned or imported freeze dried foods. Selective shopping or a preference made out initially to the cook will stand you in good stead.

Besides the fruit and vegetables available in the local markets, fresh meat – namely mutton and chicken – eggs, pulses, fish, goat's cheese, ghee, flour and rice are generally available anywhere in the Himalaya. Butter and dried milk are available in tins. Nuts and raisins, honey, peanut butter, jams, tea, coffee, sugar, biscuits and chocolate can also be purchased locally. The cost of locally produced goods such as rice, flour, fruit, vegetables and pulses is low, while the cost of meat, tinned goods, butter, cheese, fish, and dried fruit is on a par with western prices.

It is important to have a balanced diet of carbohydrates, proteins and fats on the trek; it is equally important not to miss the delicacies of Indian cooking. Have delicious *pooris* and *paratha* with honey first thing for breakfast instead of white bread and biscuits. A succulent mutton curry, cooked with local vegetables and *dahl*, is more appetising than roast mutton and boiled vegetables. Sausage, beans and chips may be OK, but a simple chicken or vegetable *pillau* with chutneys and local curd for lunch tastes so much better. Exploit your time in India – try the local honey rather than weak blends of peanut butter; try Kashmiri *kawa* instead of coffee.

Eric Shipton, the British explorer who specialised in small, lightweight expeditions in the Himalaya, reduced his catering requirements essentially to just porridge. Food was calculated by simply multiplying the number of days to trek by the quantity of oatmeal porridge per day. Apparently he spent considerable time

Top: Kashmiri Villagers
Left & Right: *Yatra* trail to Amarnath Cave, Kashmir

Top: Trekkers and local shepherds in Lidder Valley in late spring, Kashmir
Left: Bakharval women in Warvan Valley, Kashmir
Right: Dal Lake in late autumn, Srinagar, Kashmir

debating whether salt was a luxury that could be dispensed with.

For us lesser mortals, it is easy to exist, quite happily for three or four weeks at a time on a substantial diet of porridge, pooris and honey in the morning, with day-time snacks of nuts, raisins and tea, and an evening meal of rice, dahl and vegetables. On such treks I have found little need for imported freeze dried food or for artificial tinned or packaged items.

Living off the land may be all very well in other parts of the Himalaya, particularly Nepal, where you can purchase food from village to village, or tea stall to tea stall. But this style of trekking has not yet developed in India, except on a few valley walks in Kashmir. You may be able to buy some rice or flour in the villages, together with an occasional chicken, while shepherds may sell off a sheep or perhaps some goat's cheese and curd. Biscuits, dried milk, sugar and tea are available in some of the larger villages but supplies are by no means reliable. It is essential, therefore, for you to be self sufficient during your time in the mountains and you must calculate food rations accordingly. Remember that your appetite, and that of the staff you employ, will be huge. A competent cook can help ascertain how much is needed for your trek and can be an invaluable link between you and the variety of food available.

Water

Iodine kills all common forms of water-carried diseases including amoebic cysts, salmonella and some hepatitis virus.

The inclusion of an iodinisation kit in your medical supplies will allow you to fill your water bottle from any stream, treat it, and 20 minutes later have safe, cold drinking water. This saves having to wait for boiled water at night and saves scarce firewood by eliminating the necessity of building a fire each evening to boil the water.

The amount of iodine to be added depends on the temperature and degree of pollution of the water. If the water is heavily contaminated or cold, either add more iodine solution or wait more than 20 minutes before drinking the water.

Medicines

Prior to your trek, you will need to prepare a medical kit. What medications you take with you will, to a large extent, depend on whether you are going on an organised trek. I have led three-week treks with a full group and never had occasion to open the medical kit, but it is essential to carry certain items.

If trekking alone I would take along a medication for headache, a general course of antibiotics, a solution to cure severe gastro problems, moleskins (for blisters), UV and blockout (sunburn) cream, lip seal, and heat rub for aching limbs. Also iodine for the porters and guides as they're perpetually cutting themselves, and eyedrops to provide relief from snow glare, though if you wear sunglasses this shouldn't be a problem.

If you have a medical background then medications for severe pain, local anaesthetics, scalpels, syringes, needles and sutures, will cover emergencies. An invaluable book to take with you is *Medicine for Mountaineering* edited by James Wilkerson and published by the Mountaineers, Washington, USA.

Sickness – prevention

On the trek there is an obvious link between common sense and good health. Don't drink the water from streams no matter how 'clear' the water may appear as most have been polluted by animals and humans. Drink only from springs when you are sure they are springs. Use water purifiers or an iodine solution, or boil it. Best of all, just drink tea. Wash vegetables and avoid fruit that cannot be peeled.

Personal hygiene is also essential. Wash your hands thoroughly before each meal, and also wash your body every few days to counter prickly heat or skin infection. There have been times when I thought washing was just a western hang up, after all, most Zanskaris very rarely wash. A few years ago I decided to experiment, and dispensed with my daily cold bath. Apart from hands and face, I didn't wash my hair or body for a month during a trek in Ladakh. The result, after a few encounters with monks and donkeys, was a splendid case of body lice.

Sickness – treatment

Gastroenteritis Gastro problems are the main concern for trekkers. However, when you are in the mountains you are self-sufficient and have control over your kitchen and food preparation. So, with a little care, you may be able to avoid stomach disorders completely. If you should get diarrhoea, don't worry or panic – it happens to nearly everyone. Let nature take its course and bowel movements will probably normalise with 24 hours and the diarrhoea should subside within a few days. Remember to keep up fluids, rest sufficiently on the trek and take a medication such as codeine for stomach cramps.

Dysentery Despite the problem of a positive diagnosis while in the mountains, if you should contract dysentery then a more specific medical treatment is necessary. High temperature, nausea and blood or mucus in the stools is indicative of dysentery. Patients should be kept at rest and fluids maintained until they feel strong enough to move. This can take anything from two to four days, or longer, and a corresponding course of antibiotics should be followed. If this treatment doesn't work effectively then it is advisable to return to Leh, Srinagar or another large town and have a blood and stool test to determine the correct treatment.

Altitude Sickness This is a specific problem of trekking in the Himalaya. It occurs when a trekker ascends too quickly beyond altitudes of 3000-3500 metres without adequate time for acclimatisation. If acclimatisation is not heeded, fluid may build up on the lungs or brain, causing death by either pulmonary or cerebral oedema. If ascending beyond 3500 metres, at least one week should be spent for every 1000 metres ascended. This does not rule out higher daytime climbs over passes in excess of this limit. The crucial factor is the camping height or the height at which most time is spent during the day.

No connection has yet been made between altitude sickness and age, degree of health or fitness or sex. It can affect anyone, even those who have previously gone to high altitudes without problems.

It is important to distinguish between acclimatisation problems and severe altitude sickness. Poor acclimatisation produces headaches, sleeplessness, irregular breathing, general nausea, loss of appetite, and swelling of glands and fingers. In this case the remedy is simply not to go too much higher for a day or two until the symptoms subside.

The symptoms of severe altitude sickness include one or more of the following: extreme breathlessness which continues when at rest, coughing up water or body fluid, blueness around the mouth, severe nausea, pounding headaches and sometimes drowsiness and derangement. Perhaps the most important single symptom is water retention. If you are experiencing some of the above symptoms and are passing significantly less water than normal, then there is cause for concern. In the case of altitude sickness a descent to lower altitudes is imperative. A descent of 1000 metres is normally enough to bring improvement, but try to descend as fast as possible to promote rapid recovery.

Hypothermia This is caused by a severe drop in the body's temperature. Literally, the body cannot sustain the heat necessary to perform its muscular functions. The changeable conditions in any mountain area make hypothermia a very real possibility. A prolonged wet and windy pass crossing with inadequate clothing, or a river crossing mishap without protection, may induce symptoms.

Symptoms normally associated with exhaustion and exposure are indicative of hypothermia. Apart from extremely low body temperature and shivering, the trekker is likely to appear mentally confused and have little muscular co-ordination – an inability to walk or use the hands. If immediate treatment is not undertaken, death can occur in a few hours. Recognition of the symptoms, and quick treatment, is vital. First, find emergency shelter without delay, remove and replace wet clothing and get the patient into a sleeping bag. If there is little sign of recovery, get a second person in the sleeping bag with the patient. Body warmth – any warmth – is vital. Hot liquid should be prepared, if possible, but no alcohol as this increases core heat loss. Evacuation should not be attempted. In most Himalayan wilderness areas the distance to be covered would be outside the capabilities of the patient and would probably exacerbate the situation.

Rabies Talked about and worried about, but particularly rare in the west Himalaya, rabies can be contracted either by being bitten by a rabid dog or by its saliva entering an open wound. It is only during the dog's final rabid days that you can actually contract the disease, and if you have any doubts, a return to civilisation – generally to Delhi – is necessary in order to have the required injections.

Before treatment can be administered, if you think you've been attacked by a rabid dog, you must determine whether it was in fact a diseased dog or one acting for other 'rational' canine reasons. Was it protecting the village you were entering? Was it a mother 'warning' you away from her pups? In the overwhelming number of cases, a reason can be attributed to the attack, and the chances are that the bite is not rabid. If, however, the dog seemed to attack without reason, more enquiries about whether the area is generally supporting rabies must be made. If in doubt, the dog must be watched for a week to 10 days in order to detect the symptoms of rabies. Should it be detected, the patient must undergo the injections without further delay and the authorities informed.

While the chances of getting rabies is negligible, dog attacks in the mountain regions are not so unlikely. To help avoid attacks, it is recommended not to enter a village or shepherd encampment without first letting the villagers see you. Any stray guard dogs can then be chained up and you will be welcomed in. This is particularly necessary at early morning and late evening when dogs are let out to ward off bears and wild animals. If you should be bitten, clean the wound immediately and thoroughly with soap, water and iodine to lessen the risk of infection.

White Man's Medicine
On the trail, villagers and shepherds will ask you for medications, usually for headaches, colds and bowel complaints. Many believe that every westerner is a doctor and therefore equipped with wonder drugs that can cure anything. If your guide is with you, ask him to explain that not every westerner is a doctor and that you do not possess a cure-all for every illness. It cannot be over emphasised that the practice of freely dispensing drugs for headaches and illnesses will cause more harm than good.

The Indian state governments have instituted a system of para-medics to help villagers who do not need to be referred to qualified physicians. The para-medics are normally based in isolated regions and need support. To freely dispense medications on the trail will seriously undermine the role and status of the para-medic who is trying to establish himself in the community, and is also endangering the villager's likelihood of recovery should he be suffering from a serious illness. In isolated emergency cases when no paramedic or doctor is available, trek doctors or nurses should be wary of prescribing drugs or administering first aid until a good interpreter is at hand. In any case, no medical aid should be given unless the ailment is clearly diagnosed.

Getting There

Getting to the Indian Himalaya essentially means going to New Delhi first. The following section details air fares to India. To get to Kashmir, Himachal or Uttar Pradesh see the various regional sections.

FROM THE UK

The official fare from London to Bombay or New Delhi is £522 economy one-way or £927 in 1st class. Return fares are double. There are two different round trip excursion fares available but only to UK residents. The 28/90 (28 day minimum, 90 day maximum stay) ticket is £662 and permits one stopover on the roundtrip. The 14/120 day excursion costs £570 but no stopovers are permitted.

If economy is important then you can do considerably better than that through London's many cheap ticket specialists or 'bucket shops'. Check the travel page ads in the *Times, Business Traveller*, the weekly what's on magazine *Time Out*, or in giveaway papers like the *Australasian Express* or *LAM*. Two reliable London bucket shops are Trailfinders at 46 Earls Court Rd, London W8 and STA Travel at 74 Old Brompton Rd, London SW7 or 117 Euston Rd, London NW1.

Typical fares being quoted range from around £200 one-way or £300 return. Fares depend very much on the carrier. The very cheapest fares are likely to be on something like Ariana Afghan Airlines or Iraqi Airways which (surprise, surprise) nobody wants to fly on these days. You'll also find very competitive fares to the subcontinent with Bangladesh Biman or with Air Lanka.

If you want to stop in India en route to Australia you're looking at about £500. You'll probably find fares via Karachi (Pakistan) or Colombo (Sri Lanka) are slightly cheaper than fares via India.

FROM THE USA

Air India has the lowest fare for round trip regularly scheduled flights – US$1323 from New York to Delhi. There's a minimum 14 day, maximum 120 day stay requirement. Out of San Francisco the same ticket is US$1413. Some travel agencies will discount these tickets about US$150. The US west coast has plenty of ticket discounters who offer cut price tickets to Asia – check the travel sections of the Sunday papers for their ads. In New York AM-Jet Travels (tel 212 697 5332) has daily charters from New York to Delhi for US$1150 roundtrip. Their address is 501 Fifth Ave, Room 2008, New York, NY 10017. CIEE, with offices all around the country, are also good for cheap fares.

FROM CANADA

The regular one-way economy fare from Toronto to New Delhi is C$1479. The round trip excursion fare from Toronto, with a 14 day minimum, 120 days maximum stay, is C$1800. One-way apex fares, with the usual advance booking and cancellation penalties, are C$1132 in the low season, C$1240 in the high. Round the world fares which take in India are available through Canada for around C$2000.

FROM AUSTRALIA

The regular one-way fare to Bombay or Delhi from the Australian east coast is A$1081 in economy, A$1513 in 1st class. Return fares are double. There are also 10/270 (10 day minimum stay, 270 day maximum stay) round trip excursion fares available. From the Australian east coast (Melbourne, Sydney, Adelaide, Brisbane) to Bombay or Delhi the fare is A$1451. From Darwin or Perth it's A$1233. Fares are slightly cheaper to Calcutta, slightly cheaper again to Madras, but the largest difference is only A$23. You are allowed one stopover in each direction – which usually means Singapore.

Alternatively there are advance purchase tickets available one-way or return. These must be booked and paid for 21 days in advance and after that time the usual cancellation penalties apply. There's a minimum five day and maximum one year stay requirement. One stopover is permitted on the one-way or the roundtrip tickets. The year is divided into two periods – basic March to September, peak October to February.

The one-way fare from the Australian east coast to Bombay or Delhi is A$725 basic or A$824 peak. From Darwin or Perth it's A$616 or A$701. Calcutta and Madras are somewhat cheaper. The round trip fare from the east coast to Bombay or Delhi is A$980 basic or A$1218 peak. From Darwin or Perth it's A$834 and A$1036. Again Calcutta and Madras are somewhat cheaper.

FROM NEW ZEALAND

Round trip excursion fares are also available from Auckland. To Bombay or Delhi it's NZ$2059, slightly cheaper to Calcutta or Madras.

ROUND THE WORLD FARES

Round the world (RTW) fares have become all the rage in the past few years. Basically they're of two types – airline tickets and agent tickets. An airline RTW ticket usually means two or more airlines have joined together to market a ticket which takes you right round the world on their combined routes. Within certain limitations of time and number of stopovers you can fly pretty well anywhere you choose using their combined routes so long as you keep moving in the same direction. Compared to the full fare tickets which permit you to go absolutely anywhere you choose on any IATA airline you choose so long as you do not exceed the 'maximum permitted mileage' these tickets are much less flexible. But they are also much cheaper.

Quite a few of these combined airline RTW tickets go through India. The Air India-Continental Airlines one allows you to make several stopovers within India. RTW tickets typically cost from around £1000 (US$1500) for northern hemisphere routes. If you want to include the southern hemisphere (ie Australia) then you're probably looking at about US$2000.

The other type of RTW ticket, the agent ticket, is simply a combination of cheap fares strung together by an enterprising agent. This will probably use a wider variety of airlines and may provide routes which the 'off the shelf' tickets cannot manage.

OVERLAND

The classic way of getting to India from Europe has always been overland and despite the hassles in Iran and Afghanistan you can still travel by land all the way from Europe. Check Lonely Planet's *West Asia on a Shoestring* for more details. Similarly from Australia you can travel country to country through South-East Asia to India – see *South-East Asia on a Shoestring* for the full story.

GETTING TO TREKKING REGIONS
By Air

Indian Airlines are the principle internal air carrier. You can fly to Srinagar from Delhi or via Jammu, and you can fly to Leh either directly from Delhi twice a week, or from Srinagar three times a week. If undertaking a trek in the Kulu-Manali region you can fly by Vayadoot Airlines to Bhuntar just below Kulu – there is a daily service in the peak season and two or three times a week at other times until November. There is no winter service. Vayadoot Airlines also fly to Dehru Dun three times a week.

The cost of a flight from Delhi to Srinagar is Rs 631 and from Srinagar to Leh is Rs 314. The direct flight from Delhi to Leh costs Rs 697. The flight from Delhi to Kulu is Rs 425, and Delhi to Dehru Dun is Rs 350.

A major problem with flying Indian Airlines is the booking system. Your first consideration is that an 'OK' ticket is only OK when your name appears on the flight manifest. If you have purchased your ticket in conjunction with an international ticket, it is vital to re-confirm as soon as you arrive in India. If you purchase a ticket in Delhi it must be paid for in an acceptable foreign currency, or in rupees on receipt of a foreign exchange encashment certificate. A 25% discount is applicable to foreigners under 30 years of age on Indian Airlines flights.

Buying a ticket is one thing – getting it confirmed is another. Often you will get a chance number. Don't despair! Still go to the airport, be polite – the Indian Airline staff, particularly in Delhi, are always obliging and the chances are a seat will become available at the last minute. Likewise in Srinagar – but not in Leh. There a heavy waiting list means just that and a change of plans is often necessary.

If you have been ticketed on an Indian Airlines flight in conjunction with an international ticket, then generally there is no cancellation fee. However, on tickets purchased in India, there is a 10% cancellation fee on tickets altered up to 48 hours before departure, a 25% fee between 25-48 hours, 50% between 12-24 hours, and a no-show or change in reservation below 12 hours resulting in a cancellation means no refund at all.

By Land

You can get to the trekking regions by rail, bus or a combination of the two. Beware of theft, particularly on the Jammu train from New Delhi station; there have been sad stories over the past few years of packs, passports etc disappearing just before the train pulls out from the station.

If you're taking the bus, the central bus depot at Kashmir Gate in Delhi is the place to go. Both private and government buses operate during the day. Many now have videos, air-conditioning and reclining

seats – your only problems from then on are Indian roads and Indian drivers.

Jammu & Kashmir To reach Kashmir by land, you can either go by train to Jammu and from there by road to Srinagar, or by bus directly from Delhi to Srinagar; both trips take about 24 hours. The train from Delhi to Jammu departs in the evening and arrives in Jammu the following morning. This allows sufficient time to catch the bus to Kashmir which arrives in Srinagar that evening.

Train tickets from Delhi to Jammu cost Rs 193 1st class, Rs 62 2nd class. The super deluxe bus from Jammu to Srinagar is Rs 100, deluxe buses are Rs 65, an 'A' class bus is Rs 42, a 'B' class is Rs 32; taxis cost Rs 675 one-way and can be hired on a per seat basis.

Himachal Pradesh To reach Chamba and Dharamsala it is best to get the Jammu train from Delhi and get off at Pathankot (three hours before Jammu); from Pathankot get the local bus to Dharamsala (three to four hours) or to Chamba (five to six hours) from the Himachal Pradesh bus stand.

By train from Delhi to Pathankot costs Rs 180 1st class, Rs 50 2nd class; the local bus to Dharamsala is Rs 15, and to Chamba is Rs 25. To reach Kulu-Manali there is a direct bus service which normally leaves Delhi in the evening and arrives in Manali 18-20 hours later. The super deluxe bus costs from Rs 100-150, depending on the season.

Uttar Pradesh To reach Mussoorie, Hardwar or Rishikesh, there is a regular bus service from Delhi and an overnight train from Delhi Station. Both these services cost about Rs 40-100.

If leaving Delhi by train there is a tourist quota that is open up to 48 hours before the train departure. To get a train reservation, first go to Baroda House, New Delhi (any scooter man knows it). From Baroda House, you get a chit and then go to the relevant railway station to purchase your ticket.

LEAVING INDIA

Although you can also get cheap tickets in Bombay and Calcutta, it is in Delhi where the real wheeling and dealing goes on. There are countless bucket shops around Connaught Place, but enquire with fellow travellers about their current trustworthiness. If you purchase any cheap ticket you have to pay the full official fare through a bank – the agent gets you a bank form stating what the official fare is, you pay the bank, the bank then pays the agent. You then receive a refund from the agent – but in rupees. So it is wise to either buy your ticket far enough in advance that you can use up those rupees or, have plenty of bank exchange certificates on hand in order to change the rupees back. This also applies to credit card purchases.

Typical fares from India would be Delhi-Australia for about Rs 6000; and Delhi to various European capitals for around Rs 4000 (a bit less from Bombay).

The cheapest flights to Europe are on carriers like Aeroflot, LOT, Kuwait Airlines, Syrian Arab Airways, or Iraqi Airways.

It is important to re-confirm your international booking as soon as you are sure of your return date. Reconfirmation in Delhi or Bombay is necessary. Apart from an Air India office in Srinagar, there are no other airline represented in the mountain regions. You could confirm with a phone call or telegram, but there is no guarantee that your message will not be garbled.

India now has one of the highest airport taxes in the world for international flights. For flights to neighbouring countries such as Pakistan, Sri Lanka, Bangladesh and Nepal, it is Rs 50, but to more distant countries it is a hefty Rs 100. India's neighbours are also getting into the act – it is Rs 100 in Nepal and Sri Lanka, although fortunately, that's a fair bit less than Indian Rs 100 – in both cases. Note that this airport tax applies to everybody, even to babies who do not occupy a seat.

Kashmir

The Maharajah's state essentially comprises four separate regions, Kashmir, Jammu, Ladakh and Baltistan. Since the creation of the 1949 ceasefire line, some mountain regions have been the subject of dispute between India and Pakistan so as a consequence many border regions have been closed to tourism. Ladakh was only opened to tourists in 1974, and regions such as the Zanskar from 1976. Even so, the closed areas remain strictly closed and only the ill advised would flaunt the current regulations.

The Kashmir Valley was, until quite recent geological times, a vast lake enclosed by the snow-capped peaks of the Pir Panjal range. The range was breached to the northern end of the valley and the lake was drained by the Jhelum River, which flows north-west out of Kashmir and into the Indus River.

The Vale of Kashmir is one of the most fertile valleys in the entire Himalaya, and for centuries has captured the imagination of traders, pilgrims and conquerors intent on escaping the heat and humidity of the Indian plains. Even as early as the 3rd century BC Kashmir was well and truly marked on the travellers' map.

Due to its isolation Kashmir developed an independent cultural and historical tradition and until the conquest of the region by the Moghul Emperor Akbar in 1585 it was ruled by local dynasties. Kashmir also remained an essentially Hindu state, until the arrival of Islam in the 14th century, despite the early introduction of Buddhism by the Emperor Ashoka. Buddhist belief was strong and widespread in the region and in fact around the time of the birth of Christ the third Buddhist Congress was held in Kashmir and monks from the region were sent on journeys to Tibet and China; journeys that would take years to complete.

By the 7th century, however, Buddhism had lost its influence and the Hindus once again flourished. The teachings of the Buddha had not undermined the worship of the Hindu gods, whose habitat was believed to be the great mountains themselves. The Amarnath Cave and the Shiva lingam drew pilgrims from all over northern India and sages would go in search of sanctuary high in the mountains. Mt Haramukh on the north-east perimeter of the valley has long been revered as the abode of Lord Shiva and Konsarnag, a lake on the southern rim of the Pir Panjal, was known as Vishnupad – the foot of Lord Vishnu.

A succession of Hindu dynasties followed during which time the rulers exercised tolerance towards the Buddhist communities. The high point of Hindu rule was in the 7th to 9th centuries under the Karokta and Utpala kingdoms, when the boundaries of Kashmir stretched much further than the valley itself. The temples at Martand, on the Anantnag-Pahalgam road, and at Avantipuru, 30 km north of Srinagar beside the Jhelum River, were founded in this period.

Following the introduction of Islam by Shah Hamadan who came from Persia in the 14th century, the Kashmiris gradually began to follow the teachings of Mohammed and a series of Muslim rulers began their long rule from the 1300s.

One of the most respected and best-known of these local rulers was Zain-ul-Abidin, who was known generally as *Badshah* – the great king. His popular rule contrasted greatly with that of his father, Sultan Sikander, who with the guidance of a fanatical prime minister, had persecuted the Hindus and virtually ended the historical religious tolerance of the valley. *Badshah's* tomb still stands by the Jhelum River in Srinagar.

Islam had spread right through Kashmir

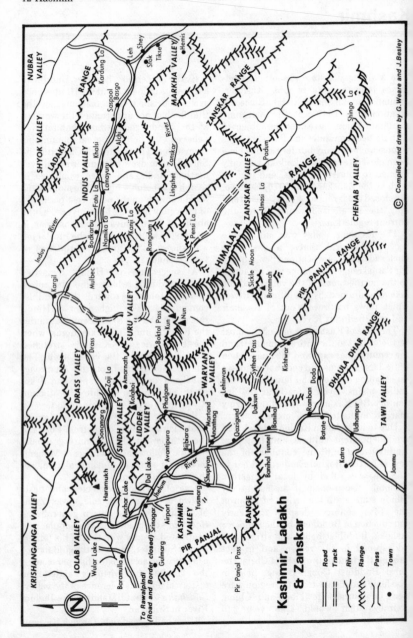

© Compiled and drawn by G. Weare and J. Besley

Kashmir, Ladakh & Zanskar

Road
Track
River
Range
Pass
Town

and Baltistan by the 15th century and from then the combined Balti/Kashmiri armies warred frequently with the Buddhist kings of Ladakh in order to gain control of the upper Indus Valley.

In 1585 the Emperor Akbar crossed the Pir Panjal pass and established Moghul rule over the valley. Following the conquest Kashmir entered its renaissance, and there was a period of stable political conditions and great cultural activity. The Moghuls chose Kashmir as their summer residence and built many beautiful gardens. Shah Jahan's summer court and palaces at Nishat and Jehangir's pleasure gardens at Shalimar must have been the most idyllic setting for any administration. No other rulers had so great an impact on Kashmir and their reign lasted nearly 200 years.

The decline of the Moghuls however, marked a period of unrest in Kashmir. From 1756 the valley was subject to harsh Afghan domination and the Sikh rule that followed, from 1819, was little better. But the Sikh administration covered such a vast area, from the Punjab to the Himalaya, that they were incapable of ruling effectively.

The treaty of Amritsar marked the end of the Sikh era in Kashmir and the introduction of the Dogra Maharajahs, rulers from Jammu. Under the Hindu Dogra dynasty, the state of Jammu & Kashmir arrived at more-or-less its present shape.

During the Raj period the British also left their mark. Kashmir's rulers would not permit the British to own land so they took to the water and adopted the superbly British solution of building houseboats – each one a little piece of England afloat on Dal Lake.

In 1947 with the independence of India from Britain and the partition of the country, Kashmir became a thorn in the side of India-Pakistan relations and has remained that way to this day.

As Kashmir was a 'Princely State', and therefore technically already independent,

the British could not simply grant it independence but had to persuade it to join one side or the other. The Maharajah, Hari Singh, wanted a totally independent Kashmir so his decision not to join either country or rather his indecision over which way to go, was fateful.

Kashmir was predominantly Muslim, with a Hindu Maharajah; geographically it was closer to Pakistan, economically it was tied to India. The Pakistanis realised that although the Maharajah had not elected to join with India, as a Hindu, Hari Singh certainly didn't intend to join Muslim Pakistan, so they organised an unofficial takeover bid. A ragtag Pathan army crossed the border from Pakistan, intent on getting to Srinagar and annexing Kashmir without provoking a real India-Pakistan conflict. Unfortunately for Pakistan the Pathans had been inspired in this endeavour by the promise of plunder and they spent so much time looting along the way that when Hari Singh turned to India for assistance the Pathans were still a long way from Srinagar. Indian troops were flown in, confronted the Pathans in Baramulla and a full scale war between India and Pakistan was soon underway, lasting until a UN cease fire came into effect on 1 January 1949.

In calling for assistance from India indecisive Maharajah paid the obvious price and made his decision – Kashmir joined the Indian union.

At first Kashmir was run as an autonomous region with its own government and president. Karan Singh, son of the Maharajah, was the first to hold this office. In 1957 Kashmir was formally made part of the Indian union despite protests from Pakistan. In 1965 India and Pakistan were again at war over the issue and the Pakistanis again nearly captured Srinagar. In 1971, during their conflict over Bangladesh, it was India who took the offensive and Pakistan was pushed back.

The India-Pakistan cease-fire line runs from Akhnoor northwards to near Keran on the Kishenganga – a rugged, dry,

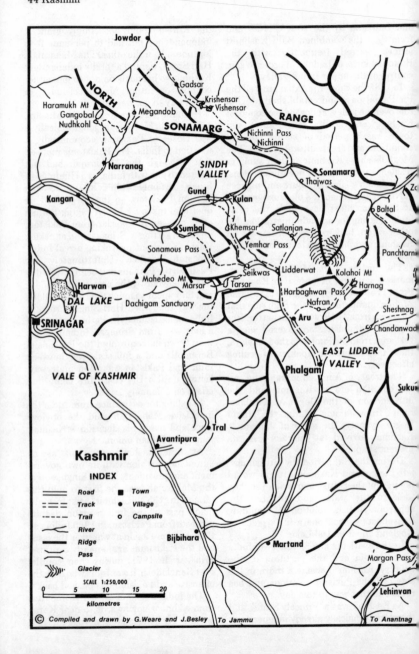

Kashmir

INDEX

═══	Road	■	Town
═ ═ ═	Track	●	Village
- - -	Trail	○	Campsite
∿	River		
▬	Ridge		
≍	Pass		
⑅	Glacier		

SCALE 1:250,000

0   5   10   15   20

kilometres

© Compiled and drawn by G.Weare and J.Besley

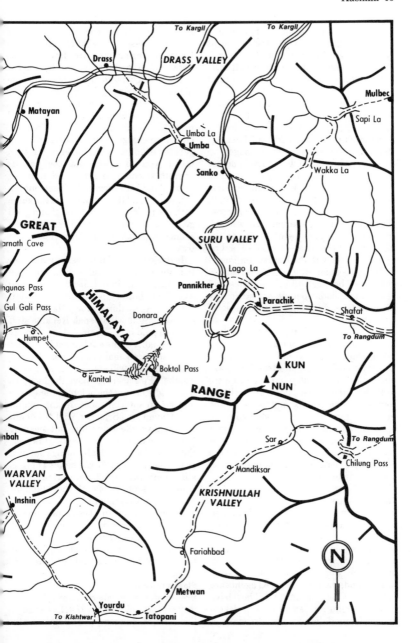

sparsely populated strip 25 km wide and 250 km long. From Keran the line turns east through Minimarg in the Gurais Valley and ends in the Karakoram Range. Gilgit, Hunza and Baltistan are north of the line under Pakistani control.

Earlier, in 1962, the Indians found themselves up against a different foe. The Ladakh region of the state was so neglected, because of the preoccupation with Pakistan, that the Chinese actually managed to construct a high altitude road right across the area they now hold, without India being aware of it. When the ensuing conflict eventually ground to a halt, another cease-fire line was drawn across the region. The Chinese control a desolate, bleak and cold plain nearly 5000-metres high and approximately east of a line joining Chusul with the Karakoram Pass.

Today Kashmir, which includes Ladakh, is divided between three countries and essentially-related people are artificially divided into different nationalities by enforced lines.

It is recommended to spend a few days in Srinagar, paddling the lakes or undertaking some day walks before driving to a hill station to embark on a trek. The treks out of the Lidder Valley and Pahalgam are probably the most popular trekking routes outside Nepal, and some of the most scenic alpine terrain can be appreciated throughout the summer months. For more strenuous treks over the main Himalaya, a section covering the Kashmir to Ladakh treks via the Warvan Valley is included.

Trekking Agents

In Kashmir there isn't the distinction between a travel agent and a trekking agent, as there is in Nepal. Until a couple of years ago, anyone could register himself as a travel agent and the registration procedures were extremely lax. Bearing this in mind, the reliable travel agents are normally 'All India' agents. They have offices in Delhi and can arrange air tickets and accommodation for you elsewhere in India. The reliable trek agencies, those that specialise in trekking rather than travel arrangements, are few and far between. Remember also that every houseboat owner and his son will call himself a trekking agent. Some are highly experienced, others are best avoided.

On arrival in Srinagar it is recommended to go to the Mountaineering & Trekking Officer in charge at the Tourist Office to get a list of approved trek agents. It is then up to you to check out the various operators, compare rates and find out what is and isn't included. Check out the equipment and the familiarity of the guide with the region. Bear in mind that a good guide or cook, recommended by a reputable agency, will make all the difference on the trek.

In dealing with a large agency make sure that the trek is not sub-contracted. You will start at an initial disadvantage and would do better to organise the staff yourself. Again don't expect the prices to be comparable with Nepal. Reliable staff are well paid in Kashmir.

The quality of the equipment is another vital factor, so make sure that sleeping bags and tents will stand up to inclement weather. Few agencies have the facilities to provide these at the height of the season and as an interim measure the tourist department in Srinagar and Choomti Trekkers on the Bund hire out sleeping bags, insulated mats and tents. However, the maxim 'when in doubt, bring your own gear' remains true in Kashmir. There is still a long way to go before Srinagar can boast trekking shops of the standard common in Kathmandu.

If uncertain of your plans, arrangements of a less inclusive nature can always be made at the various trekking-off points at Pahalgam, Sonamarg or Gulmarg. Details are covered in the relevant sections.

Places to Stay

Present day travellers coming to Kashmir may still stay at *Nedou's Hotel*, or even at the former Maharajah's Palace, now converted to a luxury hotel; but most stay on houseboats – an endearing legacy of the British Raj. To visit Kashmir and not stay on a houseboat would be rather like visiting Agra and not seeing the Taj Mahal.

Houseboats are comfortable floating homes, normally 30-50 metres long, consisting of a dining room, lounge, sundeck and two or three bedrooms with private facilities. Constructed of pine lined with cedar or sandalwood the boats are inevitably furnished in what could only be described as '1930s chintz', but the English drawing room atmosphere is superb.

When staying on a houseboat you rent a room on a full-board basis and share a lounge and dining room with other visitors. Houseboats are divided into various classes, ranging from deluxe to the local dunga style. Most boats are moored on the western edge of Dal Lake near the Boulevard, the main thoroughfare of Srinagar. For those intent on getting away from it all, Nagin Lake, seven km out of town, is a good alternative.

Houseboats provide an ideal opportunity for gaining an insight into the Kashmiri lifestyle. Each boat is owned by a family who will cook and maintain the boat for you. Friendships are often made and you can become an accepted part of the family in no time.

To find a houseboat to your taste and pocket, wander down to Dal Lake, hire a shikara and check out the 'To Let' signs. Remember that government rates are *maximum* rates, and can always be bargained down as many boats remain unoccupied, even during the peak summer season. (This, of course, doesn't give you licence to try and deprive someone of their livelihood). The current government rate per night for a deluxe boat is Rs 325 for a double room (full board), Rs 250 for 'A' class, Rs 190 for 'B' class, Rs 100 'C' class, and Rs 50 for dunga boats.

Getting There

Since partition in 1947 the Kashmir land borders between India and Pakistan have been closed. Apart from flying direct from Delhi to Srinagar, the only way to enter Kashmir is through the Banihal Pass. Until the late 1950s this route took three days, the first from Delhi to Pathankot by train, the second to Banihal and the third over the pass to Srinagar. The opening of the Banihal tunnel in 1958 has reduced the travelling time between Jammu and Srinagar to eight to 10 hours and has made Kashmir accessible to vehicles all year round.

It takes 24 hours by train and bus from Delhi to Srinagar. The trains from Delhi to Jammu leave from both the New and old Delhi stations in the evening and arrive in Jammu the following morning. The bus leaves Jammu after the trains arrive and reach Srinagar that evening. The train from Delhi to Jammu costs Rs 193 in 1st class or Rs 62 in 2nd. The super deluxe bus from Jammu to Srinagar is Rs 100, the deluxe is Rs 60, an A class is Rs 42, or a B class is Rs 32.

Getting Around

You can explore Srinagar by foot, bike or shikara. Walking is the only way to explore the back alleys of the old city and around Hari Parbat and Shankaracharya Hill. Sooner or later you will succumb to the delights of being paddled across the lakes by a shikara, Kashmir's answer to the gondola. For those shunning the easy way, small shikaras can be hired from your houseboat-man or from the small boys that hang out around Dal Lake. It's then up to you to master your strokes – it's not as easy at it looks – and paddle around to Nagin Lake or the Moghul Gardens. There are bicycles galore if you want to hire one and go further afield to places like Harwan, or the quieter rural villages beyond Srinagar.

From Srinagar there are three ways to travel to the hill stations before embarking on a trek. You can go by taxi which is convenient but quite expensive; by local tourist bus which is cheaper and permits some sightseeing en route; or you can take a local bus – as always very ethnic, very slow and very crowded. The drive to Gulmarg, Sonamarg, Pahalgam, Yusmarg and Arabal doesn't take too long: a couple of hours by car, three or four by bus. To give you an idea of the cost, a taxi to Pahalgam is at present Rs 250 one way, Rs 350 return. The tourist bus is Rs 20 one-way, Rs 30 return, and the local bus is what you expect for Rs 7 one-way.

PIR PANJAL HILL STATIONS
Gulmarg

Gulmarg, or the 'Meadow of Flowers', is 50 km east of Srinagar, at an altitude of 2900 metres. Until the early '70s the road ended at Tangmarg where riding ponies could be hired to complete the journey up through the pine forest; nowadays the road is sealed to Gulmarg and the drive from Srinagar takes 1½ hours.

Like Kashmir generally, Gulmarg is also said by those who knew it in the old days to be now spoiled. With the increasing numbers of visitors, with the numerous huts springing up year by year in every direction, with dinners and dances, it it said to have lost its former charms and it is believed that in a few years it will not be worth living in.

So wrote Francis Younghusband, leader of the British military expedition to Tibet, in his book *Kashmir*, in 1909.

A different perspective of the situation at the time was expressed by a now forgotten arbiter of public opinion.

Man cannot live forever on walks. His soul yearns for company. In Gulmarg ... there is a Residency, a hotel with a theatre and ballroom and more than a hundred huts built and owned by Europeans.

The sad, dilapidated bungalows are still there, while the original Nedou's Hotel, the church and the golf links remain as testimonies to a bygone era. Whatever the shortcomings of the British in India, the lack of foresight in planning in the nearly 40 years since Indian independence has taken its toll. Midway between the entrance road and the open meadows lies a muddy shanty town which does little to enhance the natural beauty of the area.

Accommodation in Gulmarg ranges from the luxury *Highland Park Hotel* to the simple government huts. There is certainly no shortage of places to stay but if you have any difficulties the Tourist Officer at the Golf Club can help out.

Day-walks from Gulmarg are the saving grace. An hour or so's climb to Kilarnmarg in the early morning provides a spectacular view of Nanga Parbat, while the climb to Mt Apharwat (4143 metres) takes 2½ to three hours. Before undertaking treks further afield it is necessary to consult the Tourist Officer as many of the ridges beyond Gulmarg are subject to military control.

En route to Gulmarg, a side trip can be made to the tomb of Baba Rishin, a noted Muslim saint and follower of Sheik Noor-ud-Din, who lived here in the Moghul period. A trek to the site can also be undertaken via the bridal path leading directly from Gulmarg.

Yusmarg

While Gulmarg has increasingly become the tourist destination in the Pir Panjal, Yusmarg has retained some of its character. Few incongruous developments spoil this hill station – which is simply an open meadow at 2700 metres with a few tourist bungalows to accommodate any overnight visitors. Day-walks from Yusmarg can be made either to the surrounding pine ridges and to Nilanag, or over the ridge to the Dudh Ganga Valley. Extended walks can be made to the base of Sunset Peak (5021 metres), taking a minimum of three days return, while the trek can be extended over the Pir Panjal Pass and return to Shupiyan. A further trek can be undertaken from Yusmarg to Toshmadidan and then to Gulmarg – a five-day return trek, or three days should be allowed for one way. Horses can be hired from Yusmarg in the season while local guides are available to complete these comparatively simple itineraries.

Now that the road is open even in January, Yusmarg is worth visiting at any time of the year. The villagers are able to make a living during the winter by supplying the townsfolk of Srinagar with charcoal for their *kangris*. The kangri is a small earthenware pot for burning charcoal, encased in a wicker basket and held against the body under the Kashmiri woollen cloak, the *ferun*. The kangri is Kashmir's unique way of keeping warm, and it would be a brave person indeed who separated a Kashmiri from his kangri.

En route to Yusmarg it's worthwhile visiting Chari-charif, the shrine of Sheik Noor-ud-Din, the patron saint of Kashmir. Approximately 600 years ago this renowned poet retreated to the wooded slopes beyond the village to study and meditate. During this time of solitude he devised a form of Islamic theology particularly suitable to the Kashmiris, and did much to popularise the religion throughout the Vale of Kashmir.

Arabal

The village of Arabal consists of a few houses and a small tourist complex. Apart from the waterfalls on the Visha River, which fall violently through the gorge, this place has little to offer. However, from Arabal it is possible to take an impressive trek to Konsarnag Lake, the legendary resting place of Lord Vishnu. From Arabal the trek can be completed in three days: the first stage through Kongwattan to the meadow of Mahinag; the second to the lake – involving a short steep climb to 3700 metres; and the third, to return to Arabal and Srinagar. The only problem is that horses are not generally available and you may have to budget for hiring local porters, arranged through the local Tourist Office.

During a climb to Konsarnag a short while ago I began to realise that there are some superb treks in the Pir Panjal. In comparison with the Lidder Valley, trekkers are few, while the surrounding peaks, the multitude of Gujar settlements and the unspoiled camping areas give the region great potential. Pass crossings often reach an altitude of about 4000 metres, which is not a great height, but if you're undertaking an extended walk in the region, be warned that the storms here are more severe than anywhere else in Kashmir. A number of Bakharval herdsmen died here on their way back to Jammu during an early autumn snowstorm a few years ago so good clothing and equipment are essential.

Sindh & Lidder Valleys

The alpine ridges between the Sindh and Lidder valleys are the most popular areas for trekking in Kashmir. The trails follow the inner rim of the Pir Panjal range to where it merges with the Amarnath, Sonamarg and Kolahoi ranges. The picture postcard scenery, not-too-demanding trails and comparative ease of arrangements made from Srinagar and the hill stations of Pahalgam and Sonamarg have helped to popularise this region.

The area beyond the village of Aru in the Lidder Valley is a wilderness region for more than six months of the year. During the short summer grazing season from June to mid-September, the Kashmiri shepherds, the Gujar buffalo herdsmen and the Bakharval goat herders drive their animals up the Lidder and Sindh valleys. This annual migration follows a grazing pattern whereby the three groups occupy different levels of grazing territory.

The 'locals' are the Kashmiri shepherds who rarely take their flocks of sheep into the high valleys, preferring to settle in the pastures a few km from the main hill stations of Pahalgam, Sonamarg or Gulmarg. The Kashmiri shepherd is easily distinguishable by his *ferun* – the woollen smock under which he carries his *kangri*.

The Gujar, with their herds of huge water buffalo, migrate higher up the valleys than the local shepherds. They earn part of their living by selling buffalo milk in the local villages and hill stations and usually have a small flock of sheep to supplement that income. Originally from Gujarat, they made their way to the Himalayan foothills many centuries ago and in the past crossed the Pir Panjal from the Jammu area each year to graze their herds in the high valleys. These days the Kashmir government has followed a policy of resettlement for the Gujar and many now spend the winter months in villages closer to their traditional grazing territory. For instance the Gujar who graze their animals at Satlanjan settlement live in the villages below Pahalgam during the winter, while the Gujars at Sonamous take their buffalo to the villages in the lower Sindh Valley. Easily identified by their Pathan features, their turbans and brightly woven blankets, the Gujar are an insular group, who rarely adopt local customs and remain socially separate from the Kashmiris.

The third group are the Bakharval – the goat herders who take their huge flocks to the higher more remote pastures during summer. Theirs is a lucrative business as the goats are shorn at the end of the season to make the famous Kashmiri shawls. The Bakharvals still lead a nomadic existence not only driving their herds through Kashmir and the main Himalayan valleys but also into the much higher grazing areas of Ladakh. As the winter approaches they begin the journey 'home', back across the Pir Panjal to the Jammu district of Raesi, a migration that takes almost two months to complete every year.

Essentially it is these three groups of shepherds who make it possible for us to trek in Kashmir. They assume the responsibility of reconstructing bridges after the snow bridges collapse and they also clear the trails of much of the scree brought down by the early spring avalanches.

Trekking Season

The trekking season, from mid-June to late October, although longer than the grazing season, is still very much dependent on the shepherds clearing the trails and re-making the bridges. It is possible however, to make a return trek from Pahalgam to the Kolahoi glacier from early May, although most of the upper valley will still be under snow. For pass crossings it is not advisable to plan an itinerary out of Pahalgam before mid-June and in some bad seasons the passes can be still deep under snow in mid-July. July and August are good months for trekking but although Kashmir lies beyond the full brunt of the monsoon there can be heavy periods of rainfall at this time, sometimes for up to three days. September and October are ideal, as night time temperatures are still above freezing and the days are generally very clear. The first snows on the ridges appear in late October although the hardy trekker can still tackle the pass crossings in early November, and the Lidder Valley treks can be undertaken as late as mid-December.

Each month, however, has its own delights: in June, the shepherds establish their camps for the season, and the first flowers are to be found at the margins of the snow melt. July is the month of mists and the first glimmer of summer; August is *the* month of wildflowers, while September sees the shepherds on the move again, and the birch trees gaining their autumn hues which last till mid-October.

Fishing If you have the tackle and the inclination, trout fishing is possible in the East and West Lidder Valleys, further away at Vishensar and Gangobal and also in the Bringi River over to the south of the Kashmir Valley towards Daksum. Permits are issued by the Fisheries Office at the Tourist Department in Srinagar – Rs 50 per rod per day. There is a maximum quota of six fish per day. A fishing inspector is at hand on all beats to check permits and offer advice. Remember, though, that 'Spinning is sinning' and fly fishing only is permissible.

Trail Sanitation

Unfortunately, the upsurge of trekking in these regions has exerted a toll, the all too familiar problem of litter and garbage marring the main camping areas. There is increasing concern that campsites such as Aru, Lidderwat and Gangobal will soon not be able to recover, even after the long winters. There is a dire need for some kind of trekking permit system to be instigated in these areas in order to pay to have the area 'de-garbaged' and 'controlled' until sufficient ecological awareness is developed among both Kashmiri and western trekkers. It is the latter, however, who must take responsibility for trail and campsite litter as it was this group who introduced the dreaded plastic bag, the tin-can, tissue paper and other near indestructible refuse. So, until litter consciousness comes to Kashmir it cannot be overemphasised that there is a real obligation to leave the campsites and trails in a state suitable for others to enjoy.

Getting Ready

From Pahalgam ponies are readily available, and local guides are generally reliable. Pony rates, usually Rs 40 per horse per day, are displayed on the tourist board in Pahalgam, and at the pony-wallah union's stand. Remember to budget for the ponyman's return journey.

All provisions can be purchased in Pahalgam and although basic supplies such as rice, potatoes, and dahl are available at Aru, Lidderwat and on the Amarnath trail, these supplies are not always reliable. Meat can be purchased from shepherds, however it is normally 'by the sheep' and can be expensive for a small party. Owing to the sensitivity of the Hindu people, meat and alcohol should not be taken on the Amarnath walk.

Camping equipment of the old style, such as dressing tables and bathtubs, can

be hired in Pahalgam. For tents, sleeping bags and other more practical items, it is best to enquire at the trekking lodges, where gear is sometimes available.

Although these treks are undoubtedly popular, this is no excuse for not being fully equipped. Rivers, especially in June and early July, must be crossed with extreme care. I heard of some very sad accidents that occurred because trekkers were ill-prepared for these mountains. I have also witnessed some near accidents where individual trekkers and trekking parties have crossed swift flowing torrents without rope or support.

Snow bridges are less of a hazard than is generally thought. Wide cracks appear well before the ice is going to collapse and these trails are long abandoned by the shepherds before they become dangerous.

Places to Stay

Accommodation in Pahalgam varies from the deluxe hotels adjacent to the main bazaar, to the popular alpine lodges two km beyond in the pine forests on the far side of the West Lidder Valley. Many individual trekkers manage to organise themselves into groups while staying at one of Pahalgam's delightful lodges.

Here, if no mention is made of Mohammad Yasin and the *Aksa Lodge* then my many happy days sipping tea on the verandah will be strictly limited in the future. They have double rooms from Rs

50 a day, with blankets, hot water and some classical music recorded from the author's tape collection. *Windrush Lodge*, below the Aksa, is under new management and the Windrush proprietors have a small hotel further along the Lidder. Doubles again from Rs 50, good food and a comfortable atmosphere. Both lodges also offer cheaper dormitory style accommodation.

Treks

Three routes are outlined in this section:
1. From Pahalgam to Kulan and Sonamarg via the West Lidder Valley and the Yemhar Pass.
2. From Pahalgam to Harnag and Sonamarg via the Harbaghwan Pass.
3. From Pahalgam to Sonamarg via the East Lidder Valley and the Mahgunas Pass.

Each of these treks has its own attraction. The route via the Yemhar Pass provides you with the opportunity to continue on to Tarsar Lake and the Kolahoi Glacier. The Harnag route is little trekked and there is the option of exploring the 'remoter' side of the Kolahoi massif. The Amarnath trail via the Mahgunas Pass is steeped in tradition and each August full moon the trail is followed by many thousands of devout Hindus making their annual *Yatra* (pilgrimage) to the Amarnath Cave.

The treks can be completed in six to 10 days. For those with less time to spare, a shorter trek to the Kolahoi Glacier and Tarsar Lake can be completed in four or five days.

A recommended extension to a trek between the Lidder and Sindh valleys is to continue beyond Sonamarg around the 'lake district' of Kashmir to Haramukh Peak. A trek from Pahalgam to Haramukh will take 15-20 days and commits you to crossing a number of passes beyond Sonamarg, the highest being Vishensar Pass at 4350 metres.

LIDDER TO SINDH VALLEY via Yemhar Pass

(Includes Pahalgam-Lidderwat-Kolahoi Trek)

Stage 1: Pahalgam-Aru

(Average walking time 3 hours)

Leaving Pahalgam, take the road along the west fork of the Lidder. The trail follows the road almost the whole way to Aru. En route there are spectacular views looking back down the valley to Pahalgam. Aru is the last permanently populated village and a number of lodges have been constructed, unfortunately, on the beautiful meadow. To get to the campsites it's recommended to leave the main trail and make a detour for a km or two above the open meadow. From the campsite, there are excellent walks following the ridge behind Aru to one of the many Gujar encampments. A challenging day-walk can also be made by climbing one of the obvious snow gullies to the north of Aru village.

Stage 2: Aru-Lidderwat

(Average walking time 3 hours)

From Aru, follow the main trail above the village and ascend the the rather muddy track through the pine forest for two or three km. The trail opens on to a veritable arcadian setting with Gujar shepherds tending their buffalo and local Kashmiri shepherds grazing their flocks of sheep on the undulating meadows. The trail follows the Lidder River until it's opposite Lidderwat where a sturdy bridge crosses the river.

There is a *Government Rest House* at Lidderwat, complete with a *chowkidar* (nightwatchman/cook) who can arrange fresh milk from the Gujars and supplies of vegetables from his home at Aru. Like Aru, the meadow at Lidderwat is rapidly being spoiled. Over recent seasons a number of wooden shanty huts have been constructed with government approval. There are good camping areas about two km further up the Lidder Valley.

Black bears are common in Lidderwat in April and early May. However, by June they have moved well up into the crags. I have been fortunate enough to see brown bears in the side valleys between Lidderwat and Satlanjan, both in early June and late autumn.

Stage 3: Lidderwat-Satlanjan

(Average walking time 2½ hours)

From Lidderwat, the trail follows the west bank of the Lidder. You do not have to re-cross the bridge. By early June the trail has become well defined, and there are likely to be Gujar settlements, complete with buffalo herds, scattered through the area. It should be mentioned that these seemingly docile creatures sometimes become uneasy with foreign scents. It is advisable to give them a wide berth whenever possible. Satlanjan is the largest Gujar village in the Lidder Valley and accommodates about a dozen extended families during the season. For those camping here a worthwhile option is to ascend the valley immediately above Satlanjan which leads to Sonasar and Handilsar.

Stage 4: Satlanjan-Kolahoi Glacier-Return to Lidderwat

(Average walking time 7 hours)

The trail from Satlanjan is initially well defined across the open meadows, then less so through boulders and scree. Kolahoi (5734 metres) looms above the upper valley. The peak tends to cloud over by mid-morning, so an early start is essential. It is not necessary to go to the glacier to view Kolahoi. You have a choice of either ascending the scree ridge opposite Kolahoi or fording the Lidder stream and climbing to Dodsar – a 1½ hour climb and well worth the effort.

For many trekkers the walk to Kolahoi can be completed from Lidderwat in one long tiring day. However, this is not recommended unless you are on a very tight schedule.

Stage 5: Lidderwat-Sekiwas

(Average walking time 3 hours)

From Lidderwat the trail follows the route behind the Rest House and ascends steeply for 400 metres. From the top of the ridge the track winds across open meadows and crosses two side nullahs before reaching the meadow at Sekiwas. From mid-June the area abounds with wild flowers – primulas, iris, marsh marigolds, gentians and buttercups. Climbing the rocky crags, you may also be fortunate enough to find an occasional Himalayan blue poppy.

Stage 6: Optional walk to Tarsar Lake

(Average walking time 5 hours return)

Great care is needed to cross the stream above Sekiwas, especially in June and July when the snow melt turns the nullah into a torrent. After the crossing, there is a steady climb to Tarsar Lake. The glacial lake is about two km long, one km wide and one of the most impressive in Kashmir. From Tarsar it is recommended to climb the ridge beyond the far end of the lake. From the pass you can descend into the upper Dachigam Sanctuary. From the ridge, you can also see Marsar, the lake which few locals will visit through fear of a legendary serpent. The stream from Marsar flows through the Dachigam Sanctuary into Dal Lake.

If you make Lidderwat your base, it is possible to visit Tarsar and return, making a long eight to 10 hour day. Take special care with river crossings when returning in the afternoon as the water level will rise with each day's snow melt.

Stage 7: Sekiwas-Yemhar Pass-Khemsar

(Average walking time 6 hours)

From Sekiwas the valley splits into three: the left gully leading to the Sonamous Pass (3960 metres), the centre gully to an unnamed pass (4200 metres), and the right gully to the Yemhar Pass (4350 metres).

The ascent to the Yemhar Pass should take about three hours, and is rewarded by some superb views from the top. The descent follows a rather exposed trail on the left side and packponies have to descend with care. There is an ideal camping area near the small glacial lake.

Stage 8: Camp-Sindh Valley-Kulan

(Average walking time 3-4 hours)
Below the camp, the trail to the Sindh splits; the main trail descends to Kulan, while the lower trail winds through birch and pine forests to the village of Gund. Both trails go through scattered Gujar settlements, generally more hospitable than their counterparts in the Lidder Valley. From Kulan or Gund you can either drive to Srinagar or catch the local bus to Sonamarg.

Trek Extension
LIDDER TO SINDH VALLEY via the Sonamous Pass

Until mid-June, and sometimes into July, the route to the Yemhar Pass from Sekiwas is subject to soft melting snow. It is advisable, therefore, during this period to cross the lower Sonamous Pass to the Sindh Valley by the following stages.

Stage 7: Sekiwas-Sonamous via Sonamous Pass

(Average walking time 5 hours)
Follow the left gully immediately above Sekiwas. The trail crosses the main stream after one hour, then there's a very gradual climb to the pass at 3960 metres. The first part of the descent is very slippery and steep, over boulders and snow fields – ponies may have to be unloaded. At Sonamous there is a Gujar encampment where fresh milk is available.

Stage 8: Sonamous-Sindh Valley at Sumbal

(Average walking time 4 hours)
Cross the side stream coming from the Sonamous Pass. The trail descends steeply through the forest and is by no means easy to follow so watch for the Gujar huts and don't descend to the main

river bed too quickly. After two to three km the trail becomes well defined and there is a steep descent to a side nullah. Beyond here the trails cuts over and back across the main river, by sturdy log bridges, before reaching the cornfields on the outskirts of Sumbal village. Here the ponies take a long route skirting the village fields, but you can head straight for the Sumbal bazaar on the main Sindh Valley road. From there you can catch a bus to Srinagar or Sonamarg that afternoon.

It would be possible, leaving Sekiwas in the very early morning, to reach Srinagar in one long day. In fact, for those backpacking, it is possible to ascend the middle gully from Sekiwas to the unnamed pass in three hours. Care has to be taken on the initial descent until the valley widens out to meet the trail from Sonamous. Packponies cannot be taken over this route.

LIDDER TO SINDH VALLEY via Harbaghwan Pass
Stage 1: Pahalgam-Aru

(Average walking time 3 hours)
Follow the Trek 1 description of the first stage to Aru.

Stage 2: Aru-Nafran

Climb through the Gujar encampments beyond Aru and follow the trail above the Nafran nullah. The trail frequently splits and you must be careful to remain in the main valley. By mid-June the Gujars have established a track which frequently fords the main nullah. The Gujar village at Arumin lies just below the Nafran meadow and provides an excellent campsite.

Stage 3: Nafran-Harnag

(Average walking time 4 hours)
The ascent to the Harbaghwan Pass (4200 metres) is quite steep. An extensive snow field has to be crossed early in the season before ascending the narrow gorge to the pass. Huge boulders often block the trail to the pass and packponies find this

section of the trail exceptionally difficult and sometimes impossible. There is a short descent from the pass to Harnag and it is advisable to camp towards the far end of the lake. Harnag is held sacred by the shepherds and each spring a lamb is sacrificed at the water's edge to ensure good weather throughout the grazing season.

The first time I visited Harnag the waters were completely frozen over and covered in snow. I didn't recognise the area as being a lake and traipsed over it for many hours before realising my mistake. From the camp, a day at least should be reserved to climb the ridges to view the main buttress of the Kolahoi massif.

Stage 4: Harnag-Baltal

(Average walking time 4 hours)

The shepherd-trail descends from Harnag on the right-hand bank. During the early season the trail relies heavily on the residual snow bridges. Later in the season it is necessary to ask the shepherds at Harnag for an alternative trail. Before reaching Baltal, the 'Harnag Valley' meets the track coming down from Amarnath. It is advisable to camp here by the small Gujar settlement rather than continue on to Baltal.

Stage 5: Baltal-Sonamarg

(Average walking time 4 hours)

Follow the track below the military encampments. You can either ascend to the road and hitch a ride to Sonamarg, or take the lower trail, following the Sindh River going via Sarbal. This avoids the main Kargil/Srinagar road until three km above Sonamarg.

The sprawling shanty village at Sonamarg has little to recommend it. Local buses go from here to Srinagar, the last leaving at 4 pm. Supplies can be replenished here if you're continuing on another trek or camping in the nearby Thajwas Glacier area, three km above Sonamarg.

LIDDER TO SINDH VALLEY via Mahgunas Pass & Amarnath

The trek to Amarnath Cave is the most important in the Kashmir Himalaya. Every year on the August Shavan full moon, about 20,000 Hindu pilgrims walk to the cave to view the ice statue which represents Lord Shiva, the god of destruction. For Hindus throughout India, a *Yatra* (pilgrimage) to the statue is necessary once a lifetime if they wish to enhance their chance of achieving immortality.

There are many legends regarding the existence of Amarnath, but little historical fact. It was probably discovered by local shepherds over 2000 years ago. The huge isolated cave, high in the Himalaya, is an ideal place for meditation. According to legend, Lord Shiva related his theory of immortality to his consort Parvati in a cave in the Kashmir Himalaya. Amarnath seemed to fit the description and sages made the pilgrimage to meditate in the cave and worship the ice statue.

For the *sadhu* (wandering holymen), the pilgrimage actually starts in Srinagar and takes a week to reach Pahalgam, resting at the Hindu temples at Bijbihara and Martand en route. At Pahalgam they rest at the Shankar temple, where the holy mace, or trident, symbolising the Hindu trinity of Vishnu, Shiva and Brahma, is shown to the pilgrims. The following morning the sadhus set off in the very early hours, with the main pilgrim column leaving at a more respectable time.

For some, walking with 20,000 pilgrims isn't exactly the ideal way to trek as moving with such a large mass of people rather undermines any notion of isolation. On top of which you have to contend with all the associated hygiene problems. One alternative is to visit the cave before the August full moon: the trail is open by late June/early July and remains open until October. However, most people who have walked to the cave with me during the *Yatra* have not regretted it – although most admit they would not want to repeat it. It's very much a once in a lifetime experience.

For those making their own arrangements, food can be purchased from the numerous tea stalls en route and limited tent accommodation is available at the 'camp cities' that form each night to accommodate the pilgrims. It is necessary to emphasise that drinking water from the streams should be avoided at all costs, and a strict eye must be kept on baggage. Ponymen are available for the trek. It is advisable to book your requirements in advance with the Tourist Office in Pahalgam. Prices are significantly higher during this period and a packpony for the five-day walk from Pahalgam to the cave and back is approximately 50% more than the normal season rates. It's also possible to be carried to the cave by a *dandy* – a wooden platform supported by five or six bearers who charge about $250 for the round trip!

During the *Yatra* the stages of the walk are carefully controlled by the authorities. The first stage is to Chandanwadi, the second to Sheshnag, the third over the Mahgunas Pass to Panchtarni and then a final stage to the cave. Most pilgrims visit the cave and return to Sheshnag that day, walking back to Pahalgam on the fifth day. There is an alternative approach via Sonamarg and Baltal; some pilgrims drive to Baltal and start very early the following morning for the cave. In this way they can get to Amarnath and back to Baltal in one very long day.

Stage 1: Pahalgam-Chandanwadi
(Average walking time 4 hours)
The trail leaves Pahalgam along the bitumen road, past the Shankar temple and into the East Lidder Valley. The trail is easy to follow, as it is open to vehicles as far as Chandanwadi. There are many obvious shortcuts on the route to a pleasant camping area just below Chandanwadi.

Stage 2: Chandanwadi-Sheshnag
(Average walking time 5-6 hours)
From Chandanwadi the trail winds steeply for 500 metres to Pisu Top. Here you gain good views back down the East Lidder to Pahalgam. There is a gradual climb to Wawajana, an ideal rest stop before the climb to Sheshnag. The glacial lake is set in remarkable surroundings, its waters reflecting the snow-capped peaks of Vishnu, Shiva and Brahma. Rumour among the pilgrims is that the lake is inhabited by a serpent of Loch Ness proportions – so it's *advised* that you don't camp by the water's edge.

Stage 3: Sheshnag-Panchtarni
(Average walking time 6 hours)
The trail follows the Sheshnag stream before the long steady ascent to Mahgunas Pass. Signs of encouragement appear along the way, like *Just a hop and you're on top*, to help the weary trekker/pilgrim. A sign at the top of the pass claims the altitude is 4580 metres. En route to the pass there are many vantage points to view the mountains back beyond Sheshnag and it's also possible to glimpse the Gulgali Pass, leading over to the upper Warvan Valley. The descent to Panchtarni involves crossing the main stream several times. There are more spacious campsites one km upstream from the main camping area.

Stage 4: Panchtarni-Amarnath-Baltal
(Average walking time 6 hours)
The *Yatra* trail crosses the Saint Sindh ridge before veering into the Amarnath Valley. The trail to the cave crosses a permanent snow bridge and follows the Amarvati stream to 150 metres below the cave entrance. Here a series of steps have been constructed to aid the pilgrims on their final climb to the cave at 3600 metres.

It's not hard to imagine why the pilgrims believe the cave to be sacred. It is 50 metres wide and high, and contains a natural ice lingam, the symbol of Lord

Shiva. Formed by the waters trickling through the limestone roof, the statue usually reaches its largest size during the full moon, particularly during the Shavan July-August moon. Occasionally the ice does not form at all, and this is considered extremely ominous for the pilgrims. If you're going up to the cave during the full moon or during the following morning be prepared for a considerable wait as only a limited number of pilgrims are allowed into the cave at any one time.

Most pilgrims return to Pahalgam from Amarnath. However to continue to Baltal it's necessary to return to the junction of the Panchtarni and Amarvati valleys. Here the trail splits. The trail from Amarnath to Baltal is subject to landslides and should not be undertaken during heavy rainfall periods. Transport is possible from Baltal during the pilgrimage period which will take you to Srinagar that night. Alternatively, you can camp at Baltal and descend to Sonamarg at a more leisurely pace the following day.

SONAMARG TO HARAMUKH via Vishensar, Krishensar & Gangobal

A trek in this region offers spectacular mountain scenery, beautifully flowered campsites and excellent fishing. It is an ideal extension for a trek between the Lidder and Sindh Valleys, and can be completed in one week between June and October. Trekkers must take *all* their provisions with them, including fuel as wood is not readily available. Packponies are available at Sonamarg at rates similar to Pahalgam. If you're going it alone, it is advisable to check your daily route with the shepherds as the trail frequently splits as it crosses the grazing routes.

A few days camping, before heading off, is recommended at Thajwas. There are some idyllic camping areas below the main glacier and there is also a *Government Rest House* in the vicinity. It takes four hours to reach Sonamarg from Srinagar by local bus.

Stage 1: Sonamarg-Nichinni
(Average walking time 5-6 hours)
Descend the Thajwas nullah to the main Sonamarg/Srinagar road. Cross the road bridge and follow the right-hand trail. The route ascends quite steeply along the Gujar trails. If this is your first day's trekking a few rest periods will certainly be the order of the day. After 800 metres the trail opens out on to the meadow at Shok Dharan, providing panoramic views back towards the Zoji La and Sonamarg. Shok Dharan offers a perfect camping site if you've come from Srinagar that day, or have plenty of time to spare. The trail then continues across the open meadow and along through birch forest before a short steady climb over the boulder fields to Nichinni.

Stage 2: Nichinni-Krishensar
(Average walking time 5 hours)
The ascent to Nichinni Bar is quite gradual. The pass, just below 4000 metres, is generally under snow until mid-July. However, the shepherds usually herd their flocks up the valley by mid-June and clear something of a trail. The initial route from Nichinni crosses the stream and follows the right-hand side of the nullah. The average trekking time to the pass is about 2½ hours.

From Nichinni Bar it is possible to climb the gully to the south. The climb should take about two hours over snow and scree, and is rewarded with an unimpeded view to the north-east of the Baltoro Glacier region and K2. No technical climbing is necessary, but an ice-axe comes in very handy for cutting steps.

The descent to Krishensar is through open meadows covered in wildflowers. The trail follows the valley downstream before veering over a minor ridge that separates the valley from Krishensar Lake. There is no wood at this campsite and it can get quite chilly when the wind blows off the lake. Trout fishing is possible here though by mid-autumn the fish don't exactly jump onto your line.

Stage 3: Krishensar-Gadsar
(Average walking time 5-6 hours)
The trail crosses the open marshland between Krishensar and Vishensar Lakes. From Vishensar there is a steep and rather slippery climb to the pass (4300 metres) from where there are views of Nanga Parbat, providing you get there before the morning clouds have settled. The descent to the small tarn at Gadsar is gradual and a good campsite beside the Gujar encampment can be found some two or three km downstream. Again there is no wood here.

Stage 4: Gadsar-Megandob
(Average walking time 4 hours)
Cross the Gadsar stream over the permanent snow bridge and follow the trail up along the Satsaran Ridge, a steep climb of about 1½ hours before the trail winds through open pastures. The valley at the head of the pastures marks the northern end of Megandob. The trail continues over boulders for some two or three km to a magnificent sheltered campsite. Wood is available about two or three km down the valley.

An alternative to the above walking stage is to divert down the Gadsar nullah for four or five km to the village of Jowdor. This is the only permanently populated village in the region and is completely cut off from Srinagar by snow for three months each year. The village produces potatoes, wheat, fodder crops and coarse-spun wool. It seems that many of the villagers may have originally migrated here from Gurais. It is interesting that the locals here have reported sighting both Kashmir stags and muskdeer in the crags above the village. In late autumn/early winter the herds apparently descend to the nullahs below Jowdor, making it imperative that these species be completely protected from hunters capable of reaching them at this altitude.

From Jowdor the trail climbs steeply to Megandob, meeting the Satsaran trail shortly before the northern end of the pass. Six hours should be allowed to complete this stage between Gadsar and Megandob via Jowdor.

Stage 5: Megandob-Gangobal
(Average walking time 4-5 hours)
From Megandob the trail descends for half a km before climbing the rather ill-defined goat track. The ascent takes up to two hours. From the pass there are impressive views across to Mt Haramukh (5755 metres) and the lakes of Gangobal and Nudhkohl. The initial descent to the lakes is quite steep and often muddy, so a stout stick is a prize possession. There are camping areas beside the lakes and excellent trout fishing. Ghulam Rasool Baig, the fishing inspector from Narranag, is particularly helpful, having spent many frustrating hours trying to teach trekkers how to fish.

There's a proposal to dam Gangobal Lake for hydro-electricity and the appalling structural remains of the first exploratory excavations have done much to scar the serene banks of the lake – it's better to camp at Nudhkohl.

From Gangobal you can undertake an optional climb to the ridge south of Haramukh where there are clear views across the Vale of Kashmir. The Bakharval follow this trail on their autumn migration back across the Pir Panjal.

It is not hard to understand why Haramukh was traditionally revered by the Hindus of Kashmir. Its impressive position can be appreciated from afar, even at Gulmarg, as it dominates the lower Kashmir valley. Not surprisingly, Haramukh and the sacred waters of Nudhkohl became a destination for Hindu pilgrims. Indeed, it is said that this *Yatra* pre-dated, and was generally held more important than the annual Amarnath pilgrimage.

Stage 6: Gangobal-Narranag
(Average walking time 4-5 hours)
From Nudhkohl, the trail descends across open meadows for four or five km; take

care not to follow any of the divergent shepherd trails. There is a steep descent through the forest to Narranag.

While descending, you'll appreciate why it is not recommended to follow this trek in the reverse direction; such a climb on the first day's walk would be quite dispiriting.

At Narranag there are Hindu temple ruins which date from the 9th century and a *Forest Rest House*. From Narranag you need to walk about five or six km along the road to Wangat, where you can get a bus to Kangan and from there to Srinagar.

The Warvan Valley

Trekking from Kashmir to Ladakh

The Warvan Valley – like the Chenab Valley in Himachal Pradesh – is an intermediary valley between the Pir Panjal ranges and the main Himalaya. It is essentially followed for some stages on the route from Kashmir to Ladakh. While walking the Warvan is an ideal trek in itself (see Jammu section) to most it provides a fascinating insight into a Kashmiri village lifestyle that is rapidly disappearing in the Vale of Kashmir. The Warvan is essentially free of roads and cut off by the winter snows from the rest of Kashmir for more than four months every year.

Getting Ready

Basic food supplies can be purchased from the larger villages in the Warvan Valley. These, however, cannot be relied upon and it is advisable to bring all supplies from Srinagar. Pack mule-trains frequently ply the route from Lehinvan and occasionally the muleteers will agree to load their mules when returning. Porters can also be hired en route in the Warvan, although village labour is in constant demand during the harvest period from late August until mid-September.

Treks

Three main treks are outlined in this section:

1. From Lehinvan (in the Kashmir Valley) over the Margan Pass, then up valley to the Kanital Valley and the Boktol Pass to Pannikher, in the Suru Valley, Ladakh.
2. From Pahalgam over the Gulgali Pass then down valley to the Kanital Valley and the Boktol Pass to Pannikher.
3. From Lehinvan over the Margan Pass then down valley to the Krishnullah Valley and the Chilung Pass to Rangdum and Ladakh.

Treks from Kashmir to Ladakh should not be attempted until mid-June. The season generally extends to late September/early October when snowfalls once again block the main Himalayan passes in Kashmir. If undertaking a trek solely in the Warvan Valley it is possible to cross the Margan Pass – the main pass above the village of Lehinvan – by early May, although horses generally cannot cross until early June. Trekking the lower Warvan to Jammu can be undertaken right up to December – refer to the section on Jammu. Vigne's *Travels in Jammu, Kashmir & Skardu*, written in the 1840s, also describes this area.

The most popular pass for trekking across the Himalaya, the Boktol Pass, is relatively low at 4420 metres. Even so, trekkers should be mindful of acclimatising fully and spending a few extra days in the Warvan villages or at the Bakharval encampments in the Kanital Valley.

River crossings do not constitute a major hazard on these treks although the snow bridge crossing above Sukunni village does need to be approached with caution by late spring. It is vital at these times to be guided by the Bakharval who are establishing their summer camps – likewise for the Krishnullah walks.

Forest Rest House accommodation is available in the Warvan. The wooden bungalows were originally designed for the forest officers on their tours of duty. Facilities are basic, with string or wooden beds, the occasional chair and an open verandah on which to pass the late afternoon. The *chowkidar* (caretaker) assigned to each rest house is normally very obliging, and it makes interesting reading to look through the register and discover what the Major and his wife thought of the place during the summer of '36.

Beyond the villages, the shepherd huts can be used at the margins of the season, but beyond that it is necessary to have a tent with you.

KASHMIR TO LADAKH via Lehinvan-Warvan Valley-Kanital Valley-Boktol Pass-Ladakh

This trek can generally be made in a week and provides an insight into the contrast between the settled village life of the upper Warvan and the semi-nomadic existence of the Bakharval herdsmen of the Himalaya. The trek can be extended for a few days by either camping by the villages and encampments or going higher and exploring some of the adjoining valleys in the main Himalaya. The trek reaches an altitude of 5000 metres so take care not to over-exert yourself.

Stage 1: Srinagar-Lehinvan-Camp

The drive from Srinagar to Lehinvan takes about four hours. There is a comfortable *Rest House* at Lehinvan, however it's advisable to put in a couple of hours walking during the first day by going up the valley and camping beyond the forest. Although there is a four-wheel-drive track in construction on the Kashmir side of the pass, it is not necessary to follow this as the shepherd trail is adequately graded.

Stage 2: Camp-Margan Pass-Inshin

(Average walking time 6 hours)
From the camp the trail ascends steeply to the pass. It is not the easiest introduction to walking in Kashmir, so take frequent breaks and make the most of the misty views back down to the Kashmir Valley. There is a cairn at the top of the ridge (3380 metres) which marks the beginning of the wide open pass. Midway across the pass there is a shelter hut and an adequate camping area. On clear days you are rewarded with views of the Himalaya. The trail down to Inshin is well defined and the descent takes about two hours. On reaching Inshin it's advisable to stay at the *Forest Rest House* rather than going on to the village. There is an Octroi Post here where Bakharval pay their toll for the summer grazing and ponymen pay a small amount for going on to the higher Himalaya.

Although the Margan Pass is normally open to the villagers by late April, late spring snow falls are still a hazard. Even today the Bakharval have not been able to master the tell-tale signs of these spring storms. In June the trail is littered with lambs that have perished, testimony to the unpredictable weather conditions experienced in the region.

Stage 3: Inshin-Sukunni

(Average walking time 7 hours)
The pack horse trail from Inshin ascends on the left-hand bank to the village of Gumbah, halfway to Sukunni. Cross the bridge over the river and continue on the opposite bank for six or seven km before re-crossing to Sukunni.

The Kashmir villages, though untidy in details, are very picturesque. The cottages are two-storied; in some parts they have mud walls, with a low sloping gable-roof of thatch or of rough shingle; in others, where wood is more plentiful, they are entirely of timber, made like a log-hut. They are sure to have some rooms warm and cosy, to live in in winter time; and a balcony sheltered by the overhanging eaves makes a good sitting-place in summer. The lower story of the cottages is used in winter for stabling the cattle; their heat sensibly warms the house, and partly counteracts the coldness of the season.

Drew, *Northern Barrier of India*, 1877.

That was 100 years ago. Today the description is still applicable to the 20 or 30 rather poorly constructed farmhouses that compose a typical village in the upper Warvan Valley. The essentially subsistence economy has not changed significantly either; corn is the principle crop grown, along with red barley for fodder. Simple water mills grind the corn, which is then stored in outhouses for the winter. Rice from government stores is brought by horse from Srinagar to supplement their supplies. During the long winter the villagers engage in coarse weaving, and some of the smocks and pullovers find their way into the markets in Srinagar.

Stage 4: Sukunni-Humpet

(Average walking time 6 hours)

From Sukunni ascend the trail along the left bank; do not re-cross the bridge immediately above the village. The trail ascends five or six km before forking. The higher trail leads to the Sain nullah and Permandal, while the lower trail follows the shepherd tracks across the river over a snow bridge early in the season or by a simple wooden bridge by July onwards. This lower trail continues along the main river bank for two or three km until it meets the Kanital nullah. Follow the Kanital trail upstream and a short steep ascent to the open plateau at Humpet. Beyond the Bakharval encampments there is a beautiful, if rather exposed, campsite. Birch wood is available for campfires.

A rest day can be spent at Humpet and groups can buy and barbecue sheep during the season. The Bakharval here are over-keen to check out new arrivals and are willing to offer goat's milk, curd and corn chappatis in exchange for the odd Swiss Army knife or two. Give the shepherds ample warning when visiting their encampments as the dogs are particularly fierce and will need to be chained. The valley opposite Humpet is open for exploration. You must, however, consult the shepherds for a suitable river crossing point to ensure that the day's snow melt will not cut off your safe return.

Stage 5: Humpet-Kanital

(Average walking time 3 hours)

Leaving Humpet, the trail follows the right-hand bank of the river, winding around to the campsite at Kanital. It is advisable to rest here for the day and get used to the altitude before ascending to the pass.

There is an ideal campsite beside the waterfall, two km before the glacial moraine. Wood is not available and the shepherds in the vicinity collect their supplies from below Humpet.

Stage 6: Kanital-Donara via Boktol Pass

(Average walking time 8-10 hours)

It's best to have a Bakharval guide through the moraine as the trail is difficult to follow. Walk towards the right-hand side of the glacier, avoiding obvious crevassed areas. Caution is needed after late snowfalls and rope should be carried. The ponymen may also need a hand. On a number of occasions I have helped rescue ponies whose forelegs have slipped into narrow crevasses.

The pass is approximately 5000 metres high and to the left of the main glacier. The final climb to the head of the col is often snow bound and quite tiring. From the pass a close inspection can be made of the unnamed 6000-metre peak which dominates the pass, while there are good views of the icefall leading across to the Nun massif.

The trail on the Ladakh side crosses the main valley before the terminal moraine. The first meadow campsite is three hours down from the pass and can be used in times of bad weather; otherwise continue for half an hour to where the glacial stream meets the main valley at Donara and camp there. There is a Bakharval encampment on the opposite bank.

Stage 7: Donara-Pannikher

(Average walking time 3 hours)

Cross the Cholong River and follow the trail downstream on the left-hand side. The women from Suru climb this valley each day in summer to collect juniper wood. There are also some shepherd encampments where the villagers from Pannikher graze their goats. Before you reach Pannikher the trail joins the jeep track. Follow it to the road bridge and cross over to the main village. There are impressive views of the Nun massif while the barren hills in the vicinity provide a sure indication that you are now on the lee side of the Himalayan watershed.

The best camping area is the shady grove beside the river and a nominal camping fee is charged. Trekkers are warned to pitch their tents with care as the small children from the village delight in opening up irrigation canals and swamping the unwary. Ponies can be hired in Pannikher as Kashmiri ponymen are seldom enthusiastic about continuing the trek into Ladakh.

From Pannikher you can either descend the Suru Valley to Kargil, a drive by local bus or truck of some five hours, or follow the track into Zanskar. Details of these routes are given in the Suru Valley section.

KASHMIR TO LADAKH via Pahalgam-Sheshnag-Gulgali Pass-Kanital Valley-Boktol Pass-Ladakh

The initial stages of this trek follow the Amarnath pilgrim trail from Pahalgam to Sheshnag before crossing the Gulgali Pass. From there you descend to the Bakharval encampment at .Permandal and the following day walk down the valley until it meets the trail from Sukunni. The stages are as follows:

Stage 1: Pahalgam-Chandanwadi
Stage 2: Chandanwadi-Sheshnag

Refer to Stages 1 and 2 of the Lidder to Sindh Valley trek via Amarnath.

Stage 3: Sheshnag-Permandal via Gulgali Pass

(Average walking time 5-6 hours)

The Gulgali route is a tough pass, particularly for your third day's trekking, with a maximum altitude of 4500 metres. A local guide should be taken early on in the season as the rough scree trail leading down from the pass is not easily detected and it is essential to follow the left-hand ridge immediately before reaching the Permandal encampment. It is possible to backpack in late May, although the pass is still under heavy snow. The advantage of taking this route is mainly economic; ponies are available in Pahalgam and unlike the Lehinvan/Ladakh trek there are no relocation costs involved.

It is worthwhile exploring the upper valley – the Sain nullah – beyond Permandal. There are many Bakharval encampments and there is a rough trail at the head of the valley which apparently leads into the Suru Valley. The walking time to the head of the valley and return to camp is six or seven hours.

Stage 4: Permandal-Humpet

(Average walking time 5-6 hours)

This stage goes down valley for five or six km, involving a ridge climb through the Bakharval encampments to about 500 metres above the main valley. The descent to the valley floor is steep down to the trail coming from Sukunni and the Warvan Valley.

The rest of this trek to Ladakh follows Stages 5, 6 and 7 of the previous trek: Humpet-Kanital; Kanital-Donara via Boktol Pass; Donara-Pannikher.

KASHMIR TO LADAKH via Margan Pass-Warvan Valley-Krishnullah Valley-Chilung Pass

On most maps of India, including *Bartholomew's*, this route is marked in preference to the Boktol route. I cannot understand why this is so, and wonder whether the Chilung Pass is mis-named, as the river which flows from the Ladakh side of the Boktol Pass to Pannikher is called the Cholong River. Whatever the reason, this route is a challenging alternative to the Boktol route.

Horses cannot complete this trek and to employ porters is difficult and expensive. The ideal compromise is to carry supplies on horses up to the head of the Krishnullah and then backpack the further two or three stages into Ladakh.

Stage 1: Lehinvan-Margan Pass-Inshin

The trek to Inshin is the same as Stage 2 of the Kashmir to Ladakh Trek 1.

Stage 2: Inshin-Yourdu

(Average walking time 7 hours)
From the *Rest House* at Inshin, cross the bridge and follow the main mule trail. There is a clearing in the forest and a camping area about halfway, just before the village of Hajikah. For those not in a hurry the walking stage to Yourdu can therefore be completed in two easy days. After approximately 12 or 13 km the trail crosses to the opposite bank, over a substantial bridge, and then remains on the right-hand bank to Yourdu.

Yourdu is the largest village in the upper Warvan and the bazaar area is a local meeting place for the Bakharval – a chance for their womenfolk to buy bangles and jewellery. Cross the bridge at Yourdu to the *Rest House*.

Otters have been seen at night, close to the bank of the river by the Rest House. It is difficult to ascertain the number of otters in these waters and it is a matter of speculation whether their habitat will be destroyed with the building of the dam immediately downstream at Hanzal.

There have been significant developments in education in the Warvan and other undeveloped areas. Yourdu is no exception and the primary school next to the Rest House is worth a visit. The classes are conducted until December when the teachers from Kishtwar and Kashmir return to their homes for the winter.

Stage 3: Yourdu-Tatopani

(Average walking time 4 hours)
From Yourdu, leave the Warvan Valley and follow the well-defined trail along the Rin Valley. The village of Anyar, where the trail splits midway along the valley, provides a shady rest stop. Ponies will have to take the upper trail as the valley track beyond Tatopani is too precarious for them. There are a number of campsites at Tatopani, including a *Forest Rest House*. For those backpacking with porters, the hot springs provide excellent therapy for weary limbs.

Logging activity here, as elsewhere in the Warvan, is controlled by the Forestry Department. There is a re-aforestation plan, although much wood is destroyed each year by spring avalanches and fire. The logging provides employment for many seasonal workers who come up from Jammu and the plains. To ensure selective felling, shutes are constructed high in the forest. The logs are then floated downstream to the roadhead at Kishtwar.

Stage 4: Tatopani-Metwan

(Average walking time 4 hours)
Follow the rocky and precipitous trail and climb over 300 metres before a steep descent back to the river. The trail remains on the left bank of the river until Metwan. Four km below Metwan there is a small waterfall where the pony trail meets the village trail again. There is a convenient camping area one km beyond Metwan. The village headman is a lively, industrious character, who still has the written testimony given to him by the French team that climbed Nun in 1953.

Stage 5: Metwan-Fariahbad

(Average walking time 5 hours)
The trail onwards is cleared by the Bakharval each spring. It is advisable to keep to the river trail as the track forks on a number of occasions. A guide from Metwan would be of use if you're going it alone. The locals refer to the camping area where the Krishnullah meets the main

valley, as Fariahbad. However, some ground survey maps refer to Fariahbad as the grazing area two stages higher up the Krishnullah Valley. From the camp it is possible to see the upper profile of Nun.

Stage 6: Fariahbad-Mandiksar
(Average walking time 7 hours)
Cross the shepherd bridge at Fariahbad, ascending the main ridge to the north for 500 metres. On occasion the ponies may have to be re-loaded. From the top of the ridge you gain the first uninterrupted views of the main Himalaya. The trail continues past scattered Bakharval encampments and there is a gradual climb to an impressive waterfall. The main Bakharval encampment at Mandiksar is one hour on from the waterfall.

In late summer the birch forest before the waterfall is the habitat of the black bear and there is considerable evidence that wild goats and ibex also frequent the area. There is also a good possibility that the snow leopard roams the upper parts of this valley.

Stage 7: Mandiksar-Sar
(Average walking time 6 hours)
You will need the assistance of the Bakharval to cross the main river valley at this point. The river gullies are fast flowing and the ponies will sink rapidly if they're not directed away from the insubstantial 'quicksand' areas of the river bed. (I nearly lost my favourite cook here on an exploratory trip.) You may need to unpack the ponies completely, especially in early summer when the water level is high.

The pony trail remains on the opposite bank for three km before a comparatively

simple re-crossing of the main nullah. There is an alternative route along the rocky exposed cliff section beyond Mandiksar which has to be backpacked. This overcomes the problems of river crossings and meets the main pony trail further up valley. The trail continues through encampments and open pastures to where the nullah reaches a narrow gorge. This is incorrectly called Fariahbad on some maps. It is the highest shepherd encampment and birchwood must be carried from Mandiksar.

Stage 8: Sar-High Camp
(Average walking time 4 hours)
Care must be taken at this stage to identify the correct adjacent valley to follow. This is particularly important as some maps completely omit one of the glacial valleys immediately below Sar, which can cause untold confusion. Climb the ridge on the left bank and continue for three km. Packponies cannot complete this section and it may be necessary to backpack if the Bakharval are not willing to act as porters. Cross the main nullah by the natural boulder bridge and ascend the open pastures for a further four or five km. Camp here below the glaciated section of the valley.

Stage 9: High Camp-Ladakh
It takes about six hours to reach the pass, which has an estimated elevation of 5200 metres. The route first takes you through moraine and then good glacial walking conditions. Descend to the Rangdum Tokpo the following day and cross the river upstream at a point below the Pensi La. There you join the Zanskar jeep track to reach Rangdum the same day.

Top: Zanskar bridge
Left: Chilung La between Kashmir and Ladakh
Right: Pass above Vishensar Lake, Kashmir

Top: Campsite in Kashmir
Left: Shepherd, Kashmir
Right: Camp cook hard at work

Jammu

The lowland region of Jammu, which lies south of the Pir Panjal range, doesn't at first glimpse give much scope for trekking. However, the former Dogra territories extended deep into the Himalaya and treks can be undertaken along the trails from Kishtwar to the Kashmir Valley, Zanskar or to the Himachal region of Chamba.

On the drive from Jammu to Srinagar you will easily understand just how the narrow gorges and steep hillsides, though barriers to communication, provided an adequate environment for the 15 to 20 hill states to retain some degree of autonomy. It wasn't until the 19th century that the Dogra – the hillmen of Jammu – were able to effectively rule these hills.

The history of the Jammu hills can be traced to the writings of the Vedas. In these sacred texts, reference is made to the Vaishno Devi cave, set in the Siwalik range north of Jammu. Pilgrims made their way across northern India to the cave and it's likely that this pilgrimage predates Amarnath. The journey to the cave involves considerably less hardship than crossing the high snow passes to Kashmir. In the cave during the spring and autumn equinox, the pilgrims paid homage to to the three mother goddesses of Hinduism.

Rajah Jamboolachan's foundation of the present site of Jammu, on the south bank of the Tawi River, came far later, in the 9th century. Thereafter the Jammu Raj held court, providing the political nucleus of the hillsmen. Jammu was included on the journeys of the Moghuls to Kashmir, following the tracks to Reasi, Rajouli, the Pir Panjal pass and Srinagar.

Following the decline of the Moghuls, Rajah Ranjit Dev secured Jammu's independence. Jammu was established as a hill state on a par with Chamba and Kangra but with the emergence of the Sikhs, Jammu relinquished its independence.

By the 1830s, ties between Jammu and the Sikh forces were beginning to loosen. The Dogra expanded their territory, but as the Sikhs held Kashmir, Ladakh was the logical objective. Led by the army commander Zorowar Singh, the Dogra moved up through the newly acquired lands of Kishtwar to the Warvan Valley and over to the Suru Valley and Ladakh. Negotiations were made with the Ladakhi king, and Ladakh became part of the Dogra empire but local revolts caused the Dogra to re-invade this mountain kingdom. The Dogra horizons expanded as their forces followed the routes over the Umasi La and through the Zanskar Valley and by the early 1840s they had taken Baltistan. By 1842 they had overrun western Tibet, but the foray was unsuccessful; the Dogra were defeated and Zorowar Singh was killed.

The Dogras still retained their hold over Ladakh and Baltistan though, and for their assistance in remaining neutral in the Anglo-Sikh wars, the East India Company gave the Dogra legitimate control over the vast region of Jammu, Ladakh, Baltistan and Kashmir. The agreement, ratified by the Treaty of Amritsar in 1846, resulted in the Dogra ruler of Jammu, Gulab Singh, being named Maharajah of this huge but ill-defined Himalayan kingdom. The British created the state, which survived intact for the next century, as part of a complex political buffer zone between their Indian empire and China and Russia.

Gulab Singh's wish was to establish Jammu as the religious centre of northern India – the Varanasi of the north. He commissioned the Raghunath Temple, in the centre of the present city, which was completed by his son, Ranbir Singh. Ranbir Singh in turn commissioned the

Rambireswar Temple, the largest Shiva temple in northern India.

The Dogra tradition continued until the partition of India in 1947, when the then Maharajah of Kashmir, Hari Singh, decided the region would remain part of India, rather than join Pakistan, so the state of Jammu & Kashmir was born.

The present heir to the Dogra title, Karan Singh, was Union Minister for tourism in the 1970 Congress government of India, and still plays an active role in the politics of Jammu & Kashmir.

Places to Stay

The main hotel area in Jammu is around Vir Marg in the centre of the city. At the bottom of the price range is the *Tawi View Hotel* (tel 47301), Maheshi Gate, which is undoubtedly the best of the bunch and popular with travellers. Doubles are Rs 31.50, with bath. Opposite the Tourist Reception Centre on Vir Marg, is the similarly priced and equipped *Tourist Home Hotel*; and another simple but clean place is the *Hotel Kashmir* where bathless doubles are Rs 30. At the railway station there's Jammu's second *Tourist Reception Centre* with doubles from Rs 25 to Rs 50 with air-con. The station also has *Retiring Rooms* starting at Rs 45 a double, or dorm beds for Rs 10.

In the middle range one of the best places is the *Hotel Jagan* (tel 42402) which has rooms from Rs 45 and an air-con restaurant. The largest hotel in Jammu is the popular *Tourist Reception Centre* on Vir Marg, with double rooms for Rs 50 up.

At the top end of the market are the *Cosmo* and *Asia* hotels with doubles in the Rs 100 and up bracket.

There are many other budget hotels but there's not much to choose between them, it's usually simply a question of which ones have available rooms. It's a good idea to find a place to stay as soon as you arrive as the competition for rooms can be pretty fierce, especially in the tourist season.

Getting There

Indian Airlines operates flights to Jammu from Delhi, Chandigarh and Srinagar. The flights are generally heavily booked, particularly during May and June, so reservations are essential. The cost from Jammu to Srinagar is Rs 210; from Jammu to Chandigarh is Rs 398; and from Jammu to Delhi is Rs 592. From Chandigarh there are direct bus/rail connections to Simla and Manali.

There are two express trains to Delhi per day and a direct daily train to Bombay. As noted in the Kashmir section, the Delhi trains arrive in Jammu in the morning and allow sufficient time to catch the bus to Srinagar that day. From Jammu there are also direct bus service to Katra, Kishtwar and Pathankot. From Pathankot there are local bus services to Dharamsala and Chamba.

TREKS OUT OF JAMMU
Vaishno Devi

This important cave is dedicated to the three mother goddesses of Hinduism. Thousands of pilgrims visit the cave every year, particularly during the four month pilgrimage season from March to July. The cave stands at 1700 metres, is 30 metres long and is reached by a very narrow entrance. A small steam, Chara Dunga, flows from under the image in the cave and devotees pass through it to the shrine.

The road terminates at the beautiful town of Katra, 48 km from Jammu, and visitors make the final, steep, 12 km on foot. There is also a road from Lower Sanjichat to the Dabba, which by-passes Upper Sanjichat and the Bahairo Ghatti, leaving you two km closer to the cave and with 300 metres less to climb. But the main pilgrimage route is good practice for later treks!

The origin of the pilgrimage is shrouded in mystery. Various legends are, however associated with the shrine. According to one, the goddess Vaishno Devi usually stayed at a place called Adkunwari (virgin since creation). The demon Bahairo wanted to marry her by force and chased the goddess, who ran all the way from Adkunwari to the cave where she took refuge after killing the demon. Pilgrims walking to the cave greet each other with the cry *Jai Mataki* – 'Victory to the Mother Goddess'.

The pilgrimage route from Katra to the cave is now lit to allow pilgrims to travel at night. Adkunwari, half-way between Katra and the cave, is a holding stage with a temple of the goddess, two sarais, a water tank, tea stalls, halwai shops and a hotel. Pilgrims may spend the night at Adkunwari or simply rest and continue on.

Katra is at the foot of the Trikuta mountains and eight km from Katra is the village of Aghar Jito, site of the annual *Kartik Purnima* or *Jhiri* festival. This is held in memory of the hero Bawa Jito whose historic struggle against tyranny is admired today as a symbol of truth and personal courage.

From Katra, at various walking stages there are *Chablis* where drinking water is available. There is a *Tourist Bungalow* at Katra, reservations for which can be made through the tourist officer at the Katra tourist bureau, the director of tourism in Srinagar, or the Tourist Reception Centre in Jammu.

There are regular and deluxe buses from Jammu to Katra. Taxis are also available from Jammu to Katra and back. Ponies, dandies and porters are available at Katra at fixed rates.

Kishtwar

It is the region of Kishtwar that provides the most interesting trek possibilities in the Jammu region and the town is well-known for its natural beauty, history and art. Kishtwar, on a plateau high above the Chenab River and below the Nagin Sheer Glacier, is also noted for the fine saffron grown in the area and for many nearby waterfalls. A marvellous sight, visible from the town, is a fall three km away which drops over 700 metres in a series of seven cascades. Saffron, a very colourful spectacle in spring and summer, grows only in a limited area and its cultivation and harvesting is accompanied by merry festivals and ceremonies.

The gorge country below Kishtwar marks the one and only breach in the entire Pir Panjal. The breach is a catchment area for a large section of the main Himalaya, providing drainage for hundreds of km from the streams below the Baralacha La in Lahaul to the tributaries immediately east of the Zoji La in Kashmir. Beyond Kishtwar is the main Himalaya, while to the north-east it is separated from the Kashmir Valley by one of the northern ridges of the Pir Panjal.

The people of Kishtwar represent a mixture of Hindu and Islamic cultures. Originally the region was ruled by the Rajputs, the Hindu warrior class. During the time of the Moghuls, the famed Muslim teacher Shah Fand-ud-Din came to Kishtwar and established Islam. Today, both religions survive, with the temples on the outskirts of Kishtwar assuming a role on a par with the main mosques in the area.

Despite Kishtwar's closeness to Kashmir, it is still administered by Jammu. Zorowar Singh was appointed the first Governor of Kishtwar in the 1820s and later the region was used as a base for the Dogra invasions of Ladakh, Baltistan and west Tibet.

At an altitude of 4000 metres, 115 km beyond Kishtwar are the blue sapphire mines of Pardar. Discovered in the 1880s the mines were originally only worked intermittently because of the difficult terrain and unscientific mining techniques. These days they're open regularly and are more productive.

Information

There is no tourist office in Kishtwar and no facilities for changing money. There are, however, prominent notices outside

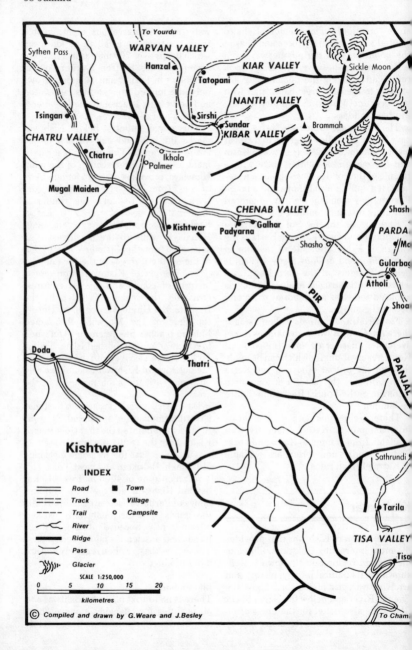

To Yourdu

WARVAN VALLEY

Sythen Pass

Hanzal

Tatopani

KIAR VALLEY

Sickle Moon

Tsingan

Sirshi

NANTH VALLEY

CHATRU VALLEY

Sundar

KIBAR VALLEY

Brammah

Chatru

Ikhala

Palmer

Mugal Maiden

CHENAB VALLEY

Shash

Kishtwar

Galhar

Padyarna

PARDA

Shasho

Mo

Gularbag

Atholi

Shoa

PIR

Doda

Thatri

PANJAL

Kishtwar

Sathrundi

INDEX

═══	Road	■	Town
═══	Track	●	Village
---	Trail	○	Campsite
～	River		
▬	Ridge		
≍	Pass		
))))·	Glacier		

Tarila

SCALE 1:250,000

0   5   10   15   20

kilometres

TISA VALLEY

Tisa

© Compiled and drawn by G.Weare and J.Besley

To Cham

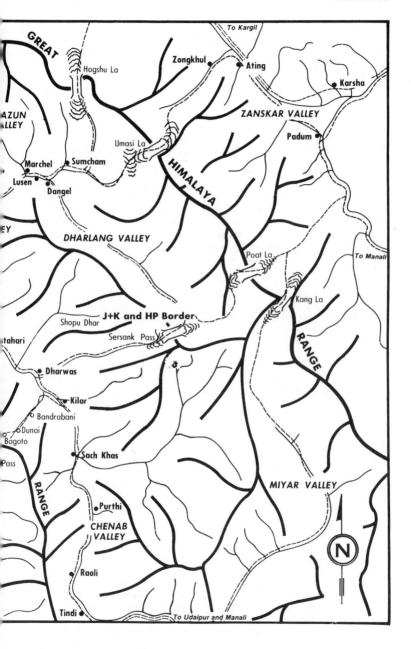

the State Bank of India building forbidding the carrying of firearms inside the bank – intended for the Bakharval shepherds rather than irate trekkers! You must therefore budget and change money before you leave Jammu or Srinagar.

Getting Ready

Supplies of kerosene, fresh vegetables, fruit, rice and biscuits are available in Kishtwar. However, it's worth bringing tinned food and oatmeal and luxury items like supplies of nuts and raisins from Jammu or Srinagar.

Besides cooking excellent chicken masala, both *chowkidars* at the Kishtwar Rest House are able to assist with trekking arrangements. Porters and horses can be ordered one day in advance so they can be ready at the appropriate trail head. The cost of horses/mules depends on where you're going. To Kashmir, budget on Rs 30-35 per animal and double that if you're going to Chamba and the approach to Umasi La. Prices in the Pangi Valley are very high, bordering on extortionate, so a reliable contact in the area is a valuable asset.

Places to Stay

Accommodation in Kishtwar is restricted to the hotels in the main bazaar – very noisy and ethnic – and the *PWD Rest House* one km away. The six rooms at the rest house cost Rs 40 each and are under the supervision of the *chowkidars* Gulam Mohammed and Wali Mohammed.

Getting There

Kishtwar is still an isolated district of the state of Jammu & Kashmir. It takes nearly 15 hours to drive from Srinagar and more than 10 from Jammu. The road to Kishtwar leaves the main Jammu-Srinagar highway at Batote and is frequently subject to landslides and monsoonal cloudbursts that close the road for days at a time. On schedule, the buses stop en route at Batote and again at Doda, the headquarters of the region, before arriving

in Kishtwar by late evening. A road has been constructed over the Sythen Pass, linking Kishtwar directly with the Kashmir Valley. It is open to jeeps and trucks for a few months (late July to mid-September) each year and will eventually be suitable for buses, cutting travelling time between Srinagar and Kishtwar by half.

Treks

The comparative isolation of Kishtwar has its advantages. It attracts only a handful of trekkers each season, which means the main trails to Kashmir, Chamba and Lahaul are fairly quiet and undisturbed. In recent years I have made two one-month treks out of Kishtwar, at the beginning and end of each season, and on both occasions met only one other trekker.

Three treks are outlined in this section:
1. From Kishtwar to Kashmir via the Marwa/Warvan valley.
2. From Kishtwar to Chamba via the Sach Pass.
3. From Kishtwar to Zanskar via the Umasi La.

Kishtwar is affected by the monsoon so the first few days of a trek in July and August may be quite wet. This should not deter trekkers from going on to Kashmir and the Zanskar as the higher you trek up the valleys the less frequently it rains. It's possible to start trekking out of Kishtwar in late May and early June, though you will still encounter snow on the passes of the Pir Panjal and the main Himalaya, especially the Umasi La. The post monsoon period is particularly fine if you're continuing on a trek to Chamba and Lahaul, and the conditions are generally stable until the end of October.

Acclimatisation does not present a particular problem out of Kishtwar. Despite the region's 1500 metre elevation, the trek-ins to the main passes take at least a week to 10 days. If this is combined with rest days en route there should be no difficulty with altitude. The trails are also well-defined from village to village and the bridges are substantial enough to make any main river crossings by foot unnecessary. Glacial crossings en route to the Umasi La could present a hazard early in the season and care should be taken if a snowfall is concealing the crevasses.

The choice of whether you trek from Kishtwar, or go the initial stage by bus or truck depends on your particular itinerary. There are short cuts you can follow, particularly to Palmer in the Marwa Valley, which provide another day to get fit before going higher.

KISHTWAR TO KASHMIR

The treks from Kishtwar to Kashmir follow two routes. The first is via the Chatru Valley and the Sythen Pass to Daksun; and the second via the Marwa/Warvan valleys and the Margan Pass to Lehinvan. These days, with road construction almost complete over the Sythen Pass, the Warvan route is the best alternative. The trek, besides revealing rural cultures reminiscent of 19th century Kashmir, also offers superb opportunities to explore some of the adjacent valleys leading into the heart of the main Himalaya. In particular, time can be spent trekking the Kiar or Kibar Valleys to the base camps of the Sickle Moon or Brammah peaks. This can be done en route to Kashmir or as part of a round trip out of Kishtwar.

Stage 1: Kishtwar-Palmer and beyond
(Average walking time 6-7 hours)
From Kishtwar you can bus or walk to Palmer village. Buses leave Kishtwar at 7 am and take about two hours. The trek short-cuts down the Kishtwar plateau and up the ridge to Palmer, and takes four to five hours. The bus service is often cancelled in wet weather and then there is no option but to trek. Facilities at Palmer are limited to a few tea stalls and confined camping areas. It's therefore advisable to continue for a few km along the road to Ikhala and a convenient camping spot by the side of the trail. It is possible to reach Ikhala from Kishtwar in one day providing you start early. There is a *Rest House* immediately below the trail, while the main village is further down the hillside. The trail to Ikhala is well-defined, a jeep track in places, with a number of tea stalls en route.

Stage 2: Ikhala-Sirshi/Sundar village
(Average walking time 6-7 hours)
A comparatively long stage. The trail winds through heavily forested gorge country with little ground for farming or camping. In this section of the valley you'll come across many mule trains carrying grains to Sirshi/Sundar, or further up valley. The supplies are subsidised by the Jammu & Kashmir government to help supplement village stocks in winter.

At the confluence of the Kibar and Kiar nullahs in the main valley, there is a substantial farming area which amply supports the villages of Sundar and Sirshi. This is also the limit of the Indian monsoon and the rice crop. Higher up the valley the rice paddies give way to corn fields. It is also the limit of the Hindu settlements; beyond here the villages are Muslim and simple shrines take the place of the village temple.

If undertaking a trek up to the Brammah base camp, stop at Sundar. The trek-in can be completed in two stages: one high above the gorge country and the second along the valley to the base camp. Porters must be hired, as horses cannot follow the narrow path into the Kibar valley.

As the crow flies it's only a couple of km from Sundar to Sirshi. For the trekker, however, the trail cuts down and up the side gorges resulting in a hot and tiring afternoon of trekking. There is a *Forest Rest House* at Sirshi, half a km before the bridge over the Marwa River. There is also a camping area just beyond the village graveyard.

If you're making a trek up to the Sickle Moon base camp then you divert at Sirshi. The trek-in will take two to three stages following the Kiar nullah up to the pastures below the main Himalaya. The initial stage from Sirshi takes four to five hours to Tatopani, the highest village in the valley. The village boasts hot springs, perfect camping areas in the nearby forest and tales of the snow leopard poaching from the villagers. The crags above the forest are an ideal habitat for the leopard during the winter months and their tracks have been followed by villagers intent on securing the skins of these highly protected animals.

Early in the season the trails from Tatopani are difficult for fully laden horses but porters can be hired to ferry supplies. The climb to the meadow at Sumbal takes about five hours, following a route not too well defined, particularly in the spring before the Bakharval have cleared the trails. From Sumbal you must ford the Kiar nullah in order to ascend to the Sickle Moon base camp. Alternatively you can continue up-valley for a further stage to the snout of the Prue glacier.

Stage 3: Sirshi-Hanzal
(Average walking time 4 hours)
This is a shorter stage, though the fit and quick can leave Sirshi early in the morning and double-stage to Yourdu higher up the valley.

The main trail crosses the main bridge at Sirshi village and then passes through farms for about three km before it re-enters the forest-gorge country. Just above the farmsteads, the summit of Brammah can be seen on a clear day. At Hanzal, plans are underway to develop the lower reaches of the river for hydro-electricity which means a dam may be built in the gorge below the village and much of the valley above Hanzal will be flooded.

There is a *Forest Rest House* beyond Hanzal or alternatively some good camping sites two to three km on where the forest trail descends to the main valley floor.

Stage 4: Hanzal-Yourdu
(Average walking time 4 hours)
A few km beyond Hanzal there is a logging site and thereafter the gorge country opens out to the rich farming settlements of the Marwa/Yourdu. It is a sizeable farming area that extends for five to six km, complete with walnut and apple orchards. At Marwa there is a rural bank and a post office – but this is not the place to change travellers' cheques or post urgent letters. Cross the bridge at Yourdu to the *Forest Rest House*.

As noted in the Kashmir to Ladakh section, these villages have only been settled comparatively recently, when the Afghans and Sikhs ruled Kashmir. The tax levied on the Kashmir villages forced many people to leave and establish new settlements here, further up the Warvan Valley. But they didn't escape all the financial demands. The traveller Vigne noted in the 1830s that there was a Sikh tax collection post at Yourdu – a week's walk from Srinagar in those days.

Just below Yourdu, the Rin nullah (which leads to the Krishnullah Valley), meets the main valley which you have been following. The valley section between Yourdu and Kishtwar is locally referred to as the Marwa Valley, while the valley beyond Yourdu is referred to as the Warvan Valley.

If undertaking a trek to the Krishnullah Valley and the Chilung Pass to Ladakh, then the trail diverges at Yourdu. The stages to the Chilung Pass are covered in the Kashmir to Ladakh trek section.

Stage 5: Yourdu-Inshin
(Average walking time 7 hours)
This stage is comparatively long, following the trail beside the Warvan Valley. After leaving the bazaar at Yourdu the trail remains on the west bank of the Warvan for about seven km. You then cross the bridge and continue on the far bank to Inshin. En route there are a number of idyllic camping spots – often frequented by the Bakharvals during their annual

migration. Inshin is the first substantial village where the trail diverges to the Margan Pass and Kashmir. There is a *Forest Rest House* on the bank opposite the village, while the village store has a supply of biscuits etc, for most of the season.

If you're undertaking a trek to the Kanital Valley and the Boktol Pass to Ladakh, then continue up and along the Warvan Valley. The stages to the pass are outlined in the Kashmir to Ladakh trek section.

Stage 6: Inshin-Lehinvan
(Average walking time 7 hours)

The ascent to the Margan Pass is quite steep, but the fine views back down the Warvan Valley are ample compensation for your effort. The pass itself is a three to four km trough through the mountainside, with a shelter hut and campsite about mid-way, and clear views towards Nun Kun and the Himalaya. The pass is one of the main Bakharval routes to and from the main Himalaya grazing areas and in mid-June and late August-early September, the shepherds with their huge flocks provide a very colourful procession. A jeep trail is being constructed over the pass, but it is not necessary to follow it on the descent to Lehinvan. The small village at Lehinvan has a number of tea stalls that provide a welcome rest before taking the bus to Anantnag and Srinagar.

Buses leave Lehinvan for Anantnag three times a day and take three to four hours. The last one leaves Lehinvan at 4 pm – just in time to miss the last bus to Srinagar, a further three hours down the highway. It's best, when all is considered, to overnight at the *Forest Rest House* at Lehinvan and go to Srinagar the following day.

KISHTWAR TO CHAMBA/ZANSKAR/LAHAUL

The treks from Kishtwar to Chamba or the Zanskar follow the same route along the Chandra and Chenab Valley as far as

Atholi. From Atholi the trail up the Pardar Valley leads over the high glacial pass of the Umasi La and into the Zanskar Valley. The trail to Chamba continues along the Chenab Valley into Himachal Pradesh and Kilar, the headquarters of the Pangi district. From there the trail goes south over the Sach Pass to Chamba.

The third popular (outlined in the Lahaul trek section) trek continues on from Kilar up the Chenab Valley to Lahaul and the Kulu Valley.

KISHTWAR TO CHAMBA
Stage 1: Kishtwar-Padyarna
(Average walking time 6 hours)

The bus from Kishtwar leaves early in the morning and takes two hours to reach Padyarna and a further hour on to Galhar at the end of the Chenab highway. Early in the season the road is subject to landslides and a 'trek day' should be reserved in your itinerary. This is particularly necessary if you're coming from Atholi as you cannot depend on local transport.

If you're trekking out of Kishtwar, the metalled road reverts to a jeep track after a few km and follows a route that cuts high above the Chenab River. Along this stage many of the villages are interspersed with Gujar settlements. These blocks of land were granted to the shepherds a few generations ago as part of the policy to encourage the Gujars not to migrate all the way back to Jammu with their buffaloes.

The walk to Padyarna is often warm and humid so the tea stalls along the way provide a refreshing and welcome relief. Just before Padyarna there is a *PWD Rest House* with a convenient camping area and in the village there are tea-stall/hotels. Grain supplies are either unloaded at Padyarna or Galhar, depending on the state of the road. The Jammu & Kashmir government subsidises this supply which provides grain for the villages at Atholi in a similar scheme to that at Sundar, Sirshi and Yourdu in the Warvan Valley.

There is no shortage of horses but most are contracted for the season. The best idea is to hire them from Padyarna or Galhar – though, with prices at Rs 70-80 per horse per day, this is easier said than done. Each villager also seems to have at least three horses and is insistent that they are all hired which is a bit of a problem if you're on your own. Another alternative is to contact a Gujar who has a horse and is willing to give it a go or arrange horses through a contractor before you leave Kishtwar.

Stage 2: Padyarna-Galhar-Shasho
(Average walking time 8 hours)
Four km beyond Padyarna is the roadhead at Galhar. Little to recommend, bar the cluster of tea stalls, although there is a *Forest Rest House* just above the village. It is onwards and upwards and downwards to Shasho. A hard stage if it is your first day's trekking. It's advisable to make the first stage a very easy one to Nunhuto, and then continue on to Shasho the following day. Nunhuto is nothing more than a *Forest Rest House* high above the road with superb views down the Chenab Valley to Kishtwar. The trail to Shasho cuts through heavily forested gorge country, similar to the lower Marwa Valley. At Shasho there is a spectacular waterfall and a campsite down through the forest by the river's edge. There is a rather dilapidated rest house above the tea-stall/hotels.

Stage 3: Shasho-Atholi
(Average walking time 6-7 hours)
Four or five km after Shasho, the forest trail begins to open out and the settlements at Kundal and Atholi can be seen at the turn of the wide fertile valley – a very picturesque setting below the snow-capped ridges of the Pir Panjal. The trail descends to the valley floor and from there on until Atholi there are a number of campsites beside the river. The farming settlements at Kundal and Atholi support both Hindus and Muslims, while on the far side of the river at Gularbargh, there are Buddhist traders who migrated from the Zanskar Valley.

The town of Atholi is set on a plateau above the confluence of the Pardar and Chenab valleys. It is the district head-quarters of the Pardar district and there is a government middle-school and a police station at the far end of the large bazaar. Biscuits and basics can be purchased in the bazaar for most of the year, as the trail to Kishtwar remains open even during mid-winter. There is a campsite and a springline by the *Forest Rest House*, about one km above the entrance to the bazaar.

Until the 1830s the Pardar district was an integral part of Chamba. In fact in 1820-25 the locals supported the Chamba forces in their invasion of the Zanskar. Allegiances changed a decade later though. After invading Ladakh and the Zanskar, Zorowar Singh led his Dogra forces back over the Umasi La en route to Jammu. The Pardar people were suspicious of the Dogra, particularly when a small body of Dogra men was left behind to 'facilitate communications' with Ladakh. In the absence of the main army the Pardar villagers killed the remaining Dogras. On hearing this, Zorowar Singh returned and in the following year (1836), the region was annexed to Jammu.

On the subject of more relevant and contemporary invasions – porters and horses are extremely expensive to hire in both Gularbagh and Atholi. The going rate is Rs 80 per horse. It's best to try some of the Buddhist donkey wallahs living in Gularbagh – still quite expensive but they're delightful trekking companions.

At Atholi bridge the trails split. The main trail continues up the Chenab Valley to Chamba or Lahaul, while the trail up the Pardar Valley goes to the Zanskar (see the next trek).

Stage 4: Atholi-Shoal
(Average walking time 3 hours)
A very easy stage, but given the absence of camping sites past Shoal, there is little alternative. You first cross the main bridge at Atholi, which was accidentally burned down during a feud in October

1984, and climb the trail quite steadily for four to five km. The trail winds above the deep gorge above Atholi before descending to Shoal village. The main trail cuts just above Shoal to a convenient campsite by the main side river, a km or so beyond the village.

Stage 5: Shoal-Istahari
(Average walking time 6-7 hours)
From Shoal the trail cuts over to the next main side valley before a steep climb for some 500 metres and four km. On the ascent out of the gorge there is a potential campsite, just above a beautiful waterfall, and a good rest stop if you're continuing. From there on the climb gets steep until the ridge top, but the view you get right back to the ridges of the Pir Panjal beyond Kishtwar is worth the effort.

From the ridge the trail drops gently, skirting the village at Thari to a potential campsite. It's a further two hours to Istahari. Note the main horse trail doesn't descend to Thari village and the direct trail to Istahari avoids further climbs. Istahari is the last main village in Jammu and Kashmir state, and from the rest house you can appreciate the ridge line – the Shopu Dhar – which marks the border with Himachal Pradesh.

Stage 6: Istahari-Dharwas
(Average walking time 4-5 hours)
Leaving Istahari it is a long haul down to the Chenab Valley. The ascent takes a couple of hours to the Shopa nullah, where there is a camping ground for the itinerant Nepalese workers who come over during the summer. The bridge over the nullah is reconstructed each year, making the trail from Atholi to Kilar suitable for horses from late May onwards.

Crossing the Shopa nullah, the trail ascends for about two km to a small cairn on the right hand side of the trail. This marks the boundary between Kashmir and Himachal Pradesh. It is two hours further on to Dharwas. a substantial village about 100 metres above the main

trail. There is a small Hindu shrine in the market place, marking the springline and the sole source of water supply to the village.

On the main trail below the village is a well kept *Forest Rest House* with an informative signpost that gives the various route stages and altitudes to the 'borders of Lahaul'. The sign, which dates from the time when British Forest Officers spent their long tours of duty in these hills, also lists the complete routes to Chamba.

Stage 7: Dharwas-Kilar
(Average walking time 2-2½ hours)
A very easy stage. In the near future it will be possible to bypass Kilar completely when a trail is completed directly across the proposed road bridge over the Chenab and the jeep trail to Dunai and the Sach Pass.

Kilar is the district headquarters of the Pangi region and government buildings here have corrugated roofs instead of the traditional village styles. Camping areas are restricted to enclosures that have little to offer. Basic supplies – rice, flour, kerosene etc – can be purchased in-season, before continuing on, either over the Sach Pass or into Lahaul.

Stage 8: Kilar-Dunai
(Average walking time 5-6 hours)
The trail from Kilar descends steeply to the gorge and a well-constructed bridge. The trail then climbs steadily before a frustrating descent to the Sach nullah. The hillsides around Kilar have suffered enormously from landslides and soil erosion in the last decade or so and the area is in dire need of a reforrestation program.

On reaching the Sach nullah the trail meets the road that will eventually link Pangi with Chamba. The construction does not seem to have progressed much over the past few years although a number of Nepalese, who live in a large shanty settlement just below Bandrabani, are employed on the road work in summer.

They come over the Sach Pass in late May and work either on road construction or on the logging projects in the Chenab Valley before returning to Chamba in mid-October.

The rest houses at Bandrabani have little to offer – they're cold and derelict and have nothing of the atmosphere of the Dunai hotels run by the Nepalese families.

The trail from Bandrabani to Dunai continues along the main valley floor – over the snow bridges in the early part of the season. Later on, after the bridges have collapsed, it's a matter of choice whether to boulder hop along the valley or follow the horse trail which climbs the ridges before descending to Dunai.

Dunai is just a collection of tea stalls – three to be precise. It is the highest shelter for porters and villagers from Kilar before the Sach Pass.

Stage 9: Dunai-Sach Pass-Sathrundi
(Average walking time 8-9 hours)
It's quite a climb up from Dunai and even in the middle of the season the snow bridges can be crossed by the horsemen. The climb to the plateau at Bagoto takes about 2½ hours. There is a superb camping ground at Bagoto with the snow faces of the Pir Panjal providing a stunning and immediate backdrop. If you're carrying a tent, then you can trek from Kilar to Bagoto in one stage, which leaves you well positioned for the Sach Pass the following day.

The climb from Bagoto to the pass is quite steep and takes about three hours. In early spring though, the soft snow conditions can nearly double that time. The trail ascends a series of glacial steps and a final ascent to the pass gives fine views back to the main Himalaya.

From the pass, the country right down to the Ravi Valley can be appreciated, while in the distance the snow ridges of the Dhaula Dhar can be seen. The descent from the pass is quite steep to Sathrundi which is another Nepalese tea house

'complex'. There is a marvellous campsite just above the tea stalls and away from the road construction in progress to the Sach Pass.

Stage 10: Sathrundi-Tarila
(Average walking time 4 hours; plus bus to Chamba)
The trail from Sathrundi crosses open meadows before following the Tisa Valley down on the right hand (west) side. En route down the valley there are a number of substantial villages, the largest being Alwas about two-thirds of the way along. There are also plenty of Gujar settlements. Deeper down the Tisa Valley it is very hot and humid in May and June, not surprisingly as the altitude drop from Sathrundi to Tarila is nearly 2000 metres.

The roadhead at Tarila has little to recommend it. There are three buses a day to Chamba, at 9 am, 1 pm and 4 pm. Double check these times with villagers on the way, as you don't want to spend the night by the side of the road. The bus takes about five hours to reach Chamba and the fare is Rs 10.

After a stay in Chamba there is a further six-hour bus ride to Pathankot, so it's possible to leave Sathrundi early and get to Pathankot in one day to connect directly that night with the train to Delhi.

If you're trekking out of Chamba to Kishtwar or Zanskar over the Sach Pass, it is necessary to allow a few extra rest and acclimatisation stages before crossing the pass. The Sach Pass is 4400 metres and the climb up from Tarila to Sathrundi would be particularly tiring for the first day on the trail. From Tarila take two stages to Sathrundi and spend at least one rest day at this beautiful camp. The climb from here over the Sach Pass will then not be too arduous, providing you make an early start. If you're carrying tents then the camp at Bagoto is recommended before descending to the Pangi region.

The pass is open to porters by mid to late May and to horses by mid-June.

KISHTWAR TO ZANSKAR

The initial stages of this trek – from Kishtwar to Atholi – follow the same route as the Kishtwar to Chamba trek:

Stage 1: Kishtwar-Galhar
Stage 2: Galhar-Shoal
Stage 3: Shoal-Atholi

From then on the climb up the Pardar Valley can be completed in five or six stages. Time must be spent acclimatising before traversing the Himalaya. Note that the pass is known as the *Pardar La* by people from Atholi and Kishtwar, and as the *Umasi La* by the Zanskaris.

Stage 4: Gularbargh-Shashut

(Average walking time 6-7 hours)

Cross the main bridge at Atholi to the village of Gularbagh. The small bazaar is populated by people of Ladakhi origin, traders who settled in the upper Pardar Valley. They own sufficient horses and mules to transport most groups for the stages up to the pass. They are canny dealers; after being engaged at above market prices (Rs 40-50 per donkey) they will then hire a few more to take their goods back to their village, and also engage in a bit of trade along the way.

Just beyond Gularbagh and directly opposite Atholi are some interesting Hindu carvings and nearby there's an elaborately carved wooden temple similar to many found in the villages of the Pardar Valley.

The trail to the Pardar Valley initially crosses the Pardar River and then winds up through small farming settlements high above the valley. There is a large logging operation about half way to Shashut and immediately beyond this there's an excellent camping area. Further up-valley the trail crosses the river before a climb to an alpine plateau just beyond Shashut village. Shashut has a tea house and a compact camping area just beside

the village temples and a *Forest Rest House* a km further on.

Stage 5: Shashut-Marchel

(Average walking time 3 hours)

An easy stage to aid acclimatisation, and the horsemens' penchant for trading. The trail is well graded, ascending some 300-400 metres with some clear views back down the valley to the Pir Panjal range beyond Atholi. Marchel lies at the confluence of the Bhazun nullah and the Pardar Valley. It is the first village in the region dominantly populated by Buddhists. Ladakhi farmers migrated to the upper Pardar Valley about five generations ago and Marchel, together with the nearby village of Lusen, support simple Buddhist monasteries which are serviced by Bardan monastery in Zanskar. Other ties with Zanskar are also maintained and marriages are arranged on both sides of the Himalaya.

There is a police check post at Marchel but it's mainly to regulate the passage of foreigners away from the Pardar sapphire mines on the far side of the mountain behind the village.

Horses are not able to cross the Umasi La, so porters can either be hired at Marchel or booked to come up from Shashut. Their availability is governed by the harvest season, but generally the rate is Rs 50 per day, per stage, plus 50% loading for the return journey. If you're travelling lightweight and are totally familiar with mountain hiking, then you can do it alone from Marchel. However, a guide/porter is highly recommended as the trail over the Umasi La is not the easiest to follow.

Stage 6: Marchel-Sumcham-Hogshu Base

(Average walking time 5-6 hours)

Two or three km beyond Marchel the Umasi La trail turns north-east up the Bhuzas nullah. (If you continue up what appears to be the main valley, the Dharlang nullah leads to the Sersank Pass and the Poat La.) It's a further three to four km on to Sumcham, the last village before the pass.

From the village the trail ascends through the terminal moraine and on to the glacial plateau some six to eight km in length. There is no shortage of camp sites or Bakharval encampments in this area. The *Hogshu Base Camp* is by a birch grove at the valley's confluence with the Hogshu nullah and the trail that leads to the Hogshu La and the Zanskar villages below the Pensi La.

Stage 7: Camp to Base 1

(Average walking time 3-4 hours)
From there on, the stages depend to a large degree on acclimatisation and fitness. The trail beyond the meadow ascends steeply to the left at the head of the valley. The climb goes above the birch tree line to a height of about 4000 metres, where the valley opens out. There is a grassy area for camping, with water coming from the glacial stream.

It is possible to continue to a higher intermediary camp by following the scree ridge to the right for a further two to three km. There is one level spot sufficient for a couple of tents and an intermittent water supply from the snow melt.

Stage 8: Base 1-Base 2

(Average walking time 4-5 hours)
The trail ascends the main scree ridge, climbing some 500 metres until it's level with the main glacial floor. The trail continues on the left hand side of the glacier and there are plenty of small cairns to guide the way. Follow the trail through the moraine until you're opposite the main ice wall coming from the Umasi La. Cross the main glacier here and climb the rocky cliff on the far side of the ice wall. The climb is particularly steep and in the soft melting snow conditions early in the season it is very tiring. The climb leads to a huge rock outcrop/cave which is the best high camp for the pass. The height is about 5000 metres.

Stage 9: Base 2-Umasi La-Nabil Camp

(Average walking time 7-8 hours)
From the high camp, the climb to the pass is not particularly arduous. The trail is again marked by cairns initially along the cliffside to the hanging glacier. Follow the glacier, avoiding the obvious crevassed areas until you reach the high plateau above the glacier floor. From here, the main Himalayan ridge line is immediately in front of you and the small col defining the pass is to the left. The total climbing time to the pass is about three to four hours, depending on the snow conditions. The pass height is 5342 metres. From the pass there are magnificent views towards the Zanskar range.

The descent from the pass is difficult. Initially it's very steep, down a snow cliff, so an ice axe or sturdy stick is essential. At the foot of the slope, descend the main glacier, again watching for the crevasses. On this day the assistance of a local guide/trader is invaluable. The trail leaves the glacier, goes across the scree to the left side of the valley and down to a natural rock bridge where you can cross the main stream emanating from the glacier. Camp here for the night.

Stage 10: Nabil Camp-Zanskar Valley

The trail heads down the right hand side of the Mulung Tokpo to the highest settlement – the Buddhist monastery at Zongkhul. The monastery, which is affiliated with Burdan and the red hat sect, is normally attended by half a dozen monks. The founding of this monastery is attributed to the sage Naropa, who wandered the Kashmir and Ladakh mountains in the 9th century. It is up to you whether to camp here or continue down, for a longish day, to the main Zanskar Valley.

From Zongkhul it is an easy day down to the village of Ating in the Zanskar Valley. From there it's a further two to three hours down to the bridge at Tungri, where you can either continue to Karsha or Padum. See the Zanskar Valley section for further treks in this region, or for catching a bus or truck over the Pensi La to Kargil.

If you're crossing the Umasi La from the Zanskar side it's advisable to camp at Zongkhul for a day or two before proceeding to the Nabil camp.

Ladakh

For most, Ladakh consists of the confines of the Indus Valley, the principal breach in the Trans Himalayan zone. It is the geological boundary between the vast Tibetan plateau and the Himalaya and has been a trading route for centuries. Early travellers and traders went far beyond the Indus Valley, crossing Ladakh regularly en route to Yarkand and Samarkand, Shigatse and Lhasa – or on to the valleys of Kashmir and Kulu on the way to the Indian plains.

Known as 'the moonland', 'little Tibet' or even more romantically as 'the last Shangri La', Ladakh is the most remote region of India, a barren, virtually rainless area. Only where rivers, running from far-off glaciers or melting snows, bring water to inhabited areas is there any plant life. These fertile, irrigated patches are lush green oases amid an amazingly beautiful landscape of shimmering, desolate, grey-brown hills and plains.

The early history of Ladakh is that of Tibet itself as it was originally a province of that kingdom. It was governed in secular matters by an independent prince, and in spiritual affairs by the Guru Lama, or chief pontiff of Lhasa.

Rock carvings scattered around the countryside indicate that the region has been used for thousands of years by nomadic tribes, including the Mons of north India, the Dards of Baltistan and the Mongols of central Asia. The Champa, nomadic shepherds who roamed the Tibetan plateau, were perhaps the first inhabitants of Ladakh but their horizons were restricted to the windswept grazing areas. It was not until the coming of the Mons, Buddhist missionaries from India, that settlements were established in the valleys; while the Dards, who made their way up from Gilgit, introduced irrigation and founded many of the fertile reaches in the upper Indus Valley.

Early rulers of Ladakh were the Thi dynasty, followed by the Che-lik and Uto-ylde kings. The Lha-chen dynasty was founded in 842 AD by Skyid-Lder-dyimagon, whose grandson Nima-gon ruled from 975 to 990, extending the kingdom far and wide by defeating invading tribes from central Asia. This victorious king built a new capital at Shey, near Leh, and constructed many forts.

The Tibetan Lamaist form of Buddhism took hold in Ladakh in the 10th century and during this time 108 gompas were built throughout west Tibet, including the Lamayuru monastery.

Between 1150 and 1324 there was a succession of kings who built palaces and promoted religious activities and during this time the famous Buddhist scriptures, the 100 volume *Kadshur* of Ladakh, were compiled.

Ladakh's golden age began in 1533 when Soyang Namgyal united the whole region, established his capital at Leh and built a palace and grand temple, decorated with Buddhist images, at Tsemo. A brave warrior, he had conquered Shigar, Kharko and other areas of Baltistan in his youth and extended his domain to the outskirts of Lhasa in Tibet. He did not depose the local monarchs but allowed them to continue their rule under his authority. His time was devoted to public works and before his death in 1555 he commissioned many of the roads and bridges in both Ladakh and Baltistan. The Namgyal dynasty of Ladakh still exists today – the Rani of Stok occupies the Stok palace and was elected to the Indian parliament.

Soyang Namgyal was succeeded by his brother Jamyang Namgyal, who immediately faced an invasion by Raja Ali Sher, the Muslim ruler of Skardu. Ali Sher's daughter, Khatoon, followed her father into battle but fell in love with the Ladakhi king. When Ali Sher became entranced by

Namgyal's daughter there was a double wedding in Leh, Khatoon was crowned queen and Ali Sher returned to Skardu.

Their son Singe Namgyal assumed the throne in 1610 and defeated the king of Baltistan who with the help of the Moghuls had tried to invade Ladakh. He also ordered the building of Hemis, Chemre and Themisgam gompas.

The golden Buddha statue in Shey was commissioned by Deldan Namgyal who ruled from 1645. His generals subjugated the Baltis and fought back the Kashmiris who were assisting them. Around 1685 the Ladakhis were unable, however, to repel the invading Mongol forces. Ladakh once again came under Tibetan influence but in order to escape this domination the Ladakhis sought military support from their former enemies the Kashmiris. The Governor of Kashmir sent troops to help the King of Leh regain his throne, but in return for this help the Ladakhis had to pay regular tribute to Delhi and erect a mosque in Leh.

In 1834 Ladakh was invaded by the Dogra forces of Zorowar Singh. The Ladakhi king Dorje Namgyal and his army managed to prevent the 5000-strong Dogra force from getting any further than Mulbec. A few months later though Dorje Namgyal was forced to surrender when Zorowar Singh led his Dogras up the Zanskar Valley, attacking Leh by way of the Zanskar ranges. Ladakh was placed under the control of various town governors appointed by the Maharajah of Jammu, who was in fact descended from Ladakhi nobility. Thus only the military was comprised of Kashmiris, the government was again in the hands of the Ladakhis. The dethroned royal family received the Stok palace, where they still live today.

Following India's independence and the ensuing conflict between India and Pakistan, Ladakh, like Kashmir, was divided between two nations. Indian and Chinese troops have been stationed on the eastern border since the 1959 Chinese invasion of Tibet; and when China occupied part of Ladakh including the Changchenmo Valley in another major conflict in 1962 the Buddhist kingdom was divided again.

Because of these conflicts, its basic strategic position and the daunting height of the Himalaya Ladakh remained isolated and virtually closed to outsiders from the end of WW II right up to 1974. Even today the main route into Ladakh is open for less than six months a year but the region is now open to all visitors – at least as far as its geography and political boundaries permit.

Little Baltistan

The valleys of Suru, Drass, Wakka and Bodkarbu lie midway between the alpine valleys of Mohammedan Kashmir and the fertile reaches of the Indus Valley and Buddhist Ladakh. The region is politically part of India, ethnically part of 'Baltistan' and geographically an integral part of Ladakh.

Geographically, there is little doubt that one has crossed the Himalayan watershed. The steep barren hills now stretch to the snowline. As the snows melt, the waters flow freely down into the heavily irrigated valleys. Here Tibetan-style settlements thrive; whitewashed mud and stone houses contrast strongly with the deep green barley fields. Mosques and minarets are the only signs that one has not yet entered Buddhist Ladakh.

When Arthur Neve wrote his book *Trekking in Kashmir* in 1911 he devoted one section to Kashmir, one to Ladakh and one to Baltistan. Unfortunately, yesterday's dreams have become today's political impossibilities. The people of the Suru Valley, together with their ethnic neighbours in the Drass, Wakka and Bodkarbu valleys, are no longer part of Baltistan. Since the 1947 Indo-Pakistan partition, the upper reaches of these valleys have become part of India and

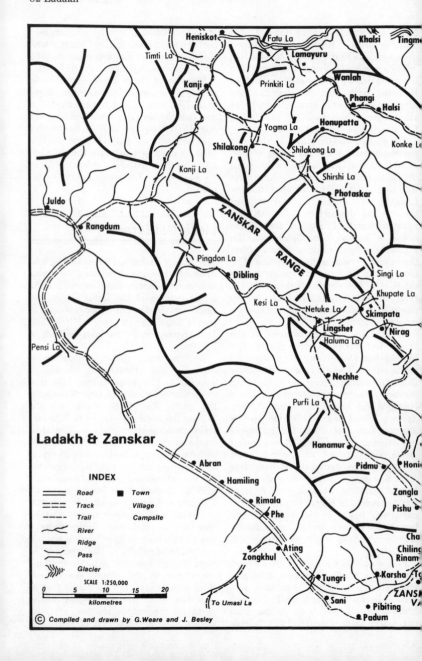

Ladakh & Zanskar

INDEX

Road	Town
Track	Village
Trail	Campsite
River	
Ridge	
Pass	
Glacier	

SCALE 1:250,000

0   5   10   15   20
kilometres

© Compiled and drawn by G.Weare and J. Besley

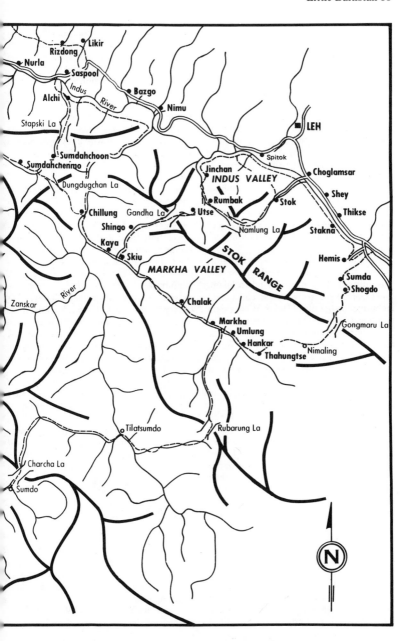

Ladakh. Being predominantly Shi'ite Muslims they are now culturally abandoned, midway between the Sunni sects of Kashmir and the Buddhist schools of Ladakh.

The earliest settlers to these isolated tributaries of the Indus were the Dards. According to the noted historian, A H Franke, the Dards were already acquainted with the Buddhist teachings prevalent in north-west India and had absorbed them into their culture some time before 500 AD. The Buddhist carvings at Drass date from this time. Later, as the Tibetan forces invaded Ladakh, much of the Dardic culture was abandoned, though isolated pockets of their heritage and language remained intact, notably at Drass.

The full cultural eclipse came far later, in the 15th century, shortly after the Kashmiris had been converted to Islam. Most Dardic groups were also converted, including the people of Drass. What exists today are Dardic groups distinct from Baltis in both language and religion – the Dards are Sunni Muslims and the Baltis are Shi'ite. To complete this cultural patchwork there are also some isolated Dardic communities, in the main Indus Valley below Khalse, which rejected Islam and are still Buddhist.

In the Suru, Wakka and Bodkarbu Valleys the cultural similarities with Baltistan are more apparent. Trade links were also strong between Gilgit and Kargil so the region's attention focussed more towards the Indus Valley rather than Kashmir. Isolated Buddhist communities still remain at Mulbec in the Wakka Valley and in the tiny kingdom of Heniskot in the upper Bodkarbu Valley.

The regions of Dardistan and Baltistan maintained a degree of independence from both the Moghul armies that held Kashmir and the Tibetan armies intent on taking Ladakh. In the 1830s however, the Suru Valley was invaded by the army of Jammu's Dogra leader, Zorowar Singh, intent on securing Ladakh. As a result of the Dogra forays, Ladakh and Baltistan came under the influence of Jammu and in 1846 became an integral part of the Maharajah's kingdom of Jammu & Kashmir. A century later the region was divided and the ceasefire line between Pakistan and India was drawn across the state of Jammu & Kashmir a few km north of Kargil. As a consequence, the politically sensitive regions down-valley from Kargil are still strictly no-go areas for foreigners.

KARGIL

To most, the region of Little Baltistan is nothing more than the town of Kargil, an overnight stop on the road between Srinagar and Leh. A place where you arrive hot, tired and dusty in the early evening, and leave at some ungodly hour the following morning. It is essentially a place of dingy hotels scattered along the main bazaar and rows of trucks lining the outskirts of town. By 8 am each day, after the trucks and buses have left taking their choking exhaust fumes with them, some sense of normality returns to the bazaar. A day or two can be spent either exploring Kargil or wandering up the Suru Valley for a glimpse of the Nun Kun massif.

Kargil was, until quite recently, an important trading centre – not just between Kashmir and Leh, but to Gilgit and the lower Indus Valley. Before 1947, the route to Leh from Kargil passed down-valley to the confluence of the Drass and Indus rivers and then up along the Indus Valley. These days political factors necessitate following the road that traverses the Narniki La to the Bodkarbu Valley and from there over the Fatu La, before descending to the Indus.

Getting Ready

The tourist office in Kargil has some trekking equipment for hire including a number of tents, foam mattresses, sleeping bags, alpine jackets, rucksacks and climbing gear.

Fresh fruit and vegetables can be purchased in the market and there's usually a plentiful supply of apricots during the season. If you're going to trek through the Suru Valley or Zanskar it's advisable to bring the majority of provisions from Srinagar, especially kerosene which is sometimes unavailable.

If you're staying in Kargil for more than one night, you can change money at the State Bank of India in the bazaar. There is also a Post Office.

Places to Stay

The Kargil bazaar is not exactly the best place for accommodation, although there is no shortage of rooms for around Rs 5 – complete with string beds, bed bugs and no water.

The *Suru Hotel*, near the bazaar bus stop, has doubles for Rs 50 but it's not all that good. The amazing *Crown Hotel* down the main street towards the river, has singles at Rs 10, doubles at Rs 15-20 and has been recommended. The *Government Rest House*, about half a km above the main bazaar, is clean and well kept and at Rs 30-40 for a double is reasonably priced though it's not terribly convenient for catching the early morning bus.

Near the bazaar are the *Greenland* and the *International* hotels – clean rooms, blankets and bathrooms from Rs 50-100 a double. Up-market, there are the *Zoji La* and *Highland* hotels, a km beyond the bazaar on the Suru Valley road. The newly constructed *Kargil Sarai* commands unrivalled views over the town (it's near the Government Rest House) and has doubles with meals for about Rs 300.

Getting There

Although Kargil is only 200 km from Srinagar it takes a full day to drive from Kashmir. The Zoji La – the road pass over the main Himalaya – is seldom clear before the middle of June, and even during the season the narrow road and precipitous edges restrict the traffic to a one-way system. The convoy from Drass to Sonamarg begins at about 8 am every day and the convoy travelling in the opposite direction, from Sonamarg to Drass and on to Kargil, leaves at about 2 pm.

The fare by A class bus, over the Zoji La, is about Rs 80 whether you're going to Kargil or Leh – there are no discounts for getting off half way. The B class bus from Srinagar to Kargil is Rs 30; while jeep hire is in the vicinity of Rs 1000-1200 one way. From Kargil there is a B class service on to Leh each day – convenient if you're going to Lamayuru or Alchi.

Transport out of Kargil and into the Suru Valley is governed by the availability of vehicles. Normally there is a daily Rs 5 bus service to Sanko; a thrice weekly service to Pannikher for Rs 8; and a weekly bus to Padam. Trucks are a useful alternative, ask in the main bazaar or around the bus station. Mr Kakpori, the Tourist Officer, will give you helpful advice on the state of the roads and trails in Zanskar and can also assist with jeep hire.

THE SURU VALLEY

From Kargil, the Suru Valley can be reached in a few hours. The principal towns of Sanko and Pannikher have simple overnight accommodation – small hotels or the *PWD Resthouse* – and from there you can either continue on foot or make a few day-treks before returning to Kargil.

When I first visited the Suru Valley it was from Kashmir over the Boktol Pass. The road from Kargil did not extend beyond Sanko, and even in the early 1970s, the mule and yak trains would ply their loads from the Zanskar right into the Kargil bazaar. These days the truck is the main means of transport, the metalled road now extends up through Pannikher and beyond to Parachik; the non-metalled road continues over the Pensi La to Padam. The road is generally open by the beginning of July, although it may sometimes not be fully operational until August, and remains open until late October.

Despite the developments of the last decade, a trek up the Suru Valley can be an exhilarating experience. It's possible to avoid the jeep trail for many of the stages beyond Sanko, and a walk-in has the undoubted advantage of assisting fitness and acclimatisation. It is infinitely better than sitting or standing in a truck with upwards of 50 people and their goats and trying to sleep along a dusty highway.

TREKS OUT OF SANKO

This region is rich in Buddhist cultural history. The statues at Drass, the Maitriya Buddha carving at Mulbec and the rock carvings beyond the village of Sanko all date from the 7th and 8th centuries when many eminent Buddhist monks were arriving from Kashmir.

Just beyond Sanko there is a comfortable PWD bungalow and in the main bazaar there are several tea-stall/hotels. Biscuits and basics are available, plus dried apricots by the boxload.

From Sanko a day-walk can be made up the valley on the trail to Drass or you can continue on to Drass itself. When I was making the trek from Sanko to Drass a few years ago, the locals in Sanko assured me that the walk could be completed in one long day. I would like to see them do it! Even after a good night's rest the trek requires two full days.

The route to the Umba La goes through some very picturesque villages and in spring the trails are lined with wildflowers. Umba is the highest village – all very friendly and excellent yoghurt. Beyond Umba is the pass at 3350 metres, which involves a steep climb but provides panoramic views of the main Himalayan range. From a camp below the Umba La you can appreciate the sunset across to the Nun Kun massif and the main Himalaya.

The Umba La traverses a subsidiary ridge to the main Himalaya and the initial descent over snow slopes is quite steep and icy. Beyond the Umba La is a series of beautiful meadows and glaciers and the valley floor contains a multitude of wildflowers – a very alpine scene, with Umba Peak at just over 6000 metres in the background. If you're not in a hurry, it's worthwhile spending a day here.

From there it's a long haul across a further ridge, which traverses the main ridge south of Drass village, and provides impressive views of the mountain range beyond Drass.

The descent in spring, when the ridge is under snow, is quite tricky down to the fields and outskirts of Drass. Stay overnight in the hotels or the *PWD Resthouse* before continuing on to Kashmir or back to Kargil.

I have not completed the trail between Sanko and Mulbec but last year I was told by the local authorities that it would take two days – so allow four. The route initially is along the Thargam Valley, then climbs steeply to the Wakka La at 4930 metres. Two camps should be made before crossing the pass. From the Wakka La there is a further pass to cross, the Sapi La, before the descent to Shergol and Mulbec, on the Kargil-Leh road, which should take a further two stages. At Mulbec there are a couple of small hotels and from here you can continue by truck to Leh or return to Kargil.

Treks

The two treks outlined in this section extend from the Suru Valley to the isolated Buddhist regions on the periphery of Ladakh.
1. From Pannikher to Pensi La in four stages. This is the easiest way to walk into Zanskar and the trek can be extended to Padam (see the section on Zanskar).
2. From Rangdum to Heniskot and Lamayuru, a challenging extension for those continuing a trek from Kashmir via the Suru Valley into Ladakh.

The trek to Padum follows the main route into the Zanskar Valley, while the trek to Heniskot is an ideal extension of a trek coming from Kashmir over the Himalaya to Pannikher (refer to the Kashmir to Ladakh trek section).

From the Suru Valley treks can also be made back to Kashmir from Pannikher, or even via Rangdum and the Chilung La – for those fit enough and suitably prepared.

Treks can be undertaken from June onwards, although both the Pensi La and the Kangi La are still under snow until July. The trekking season continues through July and August – often a time when there is a lot of traffic into the Zanskar Valley; and even in September and October the days are ideal. The first snows normally arrive by the first week of October and the main falls by the end of that month.

PANNIKHER TO PENSI LA

In Pannikher you can either stay at one of the newly constructed hotels or camp down by the Cholong River in the willow grove. If you've got time to spare it's worth making a visit to the newly constructed mosque at Namsun village; and in mid-summer wildflowers are particularly attractive along the banks of the canals that irrigate the corn and mustard fields.

Pannikher's Tourist Officer, Gulam Rasool, can help with trekking arrangements and useful hints regarding your onward journey into Zanskar.

Horses can be hired in Pannikher and the prices, from Rs 25-30 per day, are low by Ladakhi standards. Basic supplies such as dried milk, rice and biscuits are available. Fuel is *the* problem, as it is everywhere in Ladakh. Women spend many hours each day collecting juniper from the surrounding ridges, often making a round trip of five or six hours up the Cholong Valley just to collect a day's supply of wood. This is then stored in the roofs of the houses for winter.

Stage 1: Pannikher-Parachik

(Average walking time 5 hours)
From Pannikher, backtrack four km along the jeep road to Namsuru, cross the bridge over the Suru River and follow the trail towards the Lago La. The ascent is deceptively steep but there are springs to slake your thirst along the way and the climb is definitely worth the effort – from the pass there is a magnificent panorama of the Nun Kun massif. Climbing the adjacent ridge there are impressive views across the main Himalaya towards the Boktol Glacier. From the pass it's an hour's descent to Parachik; there is an open camping area before the trail descends again to the jeep track.

Stage 2: Parachik-Shafat

(Average walking time 6 hours)
Immediately after the village of Parachik the huge Nun Glacier spills out to collapse into the Suru River. There is a steady climb along the jeep track to the Lingti plains. On these grazing areas Bakharval herd their flocks through July and August. It is a matter of speculation why the shepherds bring their flocks over such harsh terrain to this comparatively scant grazing area. It may be that these areas were grazed many generations ago during the Bakharval's former migration from the north-west frontier of Baltistan.

The best camping area by far is at Shafat, opposite Shafat nullah, the approach valley to Kun Peak. The tip of Needle Peak, at the head of the Krishnullah Valley, can also be seen from here. For those without tents there is a huge rock cave just beyond Shafat where the Ladakhi horsemen, en route to Zanskar, spend the night.

Stage 3: Shafat-Rangdum

(Average walking time 5 hours)
From Shafat the trail cuts across the Lingti plains to the first Buddhist village at Juldo, a cluster of a dozen whitewashed settlements, including a tea-stall/hotel. Rangdum monastery is a further five km across the marshy plains. Don't take shortcuts – it's rather like traversing an Irish bog – stick to the trail. The monastery

was founded by the Delgupta sect about 200 years ago. It supports about 30 monks who come mainly from Tashtungtse and Juldo. However, it has close cultural ties with the villages in the Stod Valley in Zanskar and relies on them for supplies of grain after the harvest.

It is advisable to continue past Rangdum to Tashtungtse. I have enjoyed many nights of *chang* (rice beer) and dancing at this village, resulting in unscheduled rest-days. The people of Tashtungtse regard themselves as part of Zanskar, in spite of the village's location to the north of the Pensi La. Marriages between these villagers and those of the Stod Valley in Zanskar are frequent. Horses can be hired at reasonable rates from the village headman for treks on into Zanskar.

Stage 4: Rangdum-Pensi la
(Average walking time 6 hours)
From Rangdum the track winds gradually along the valley, known locally as the Rangdum Tokpo, towards the Pensi La at 4400 metres. A rather long tiring walk compensated by brilliant views across to the hanging glaciers of the main Himalayan chain. Also note the Chilung Tokpo, about five km beyond Rangdum, which leads to the Chilung Pass and the Krishnullah Valley in Kashmir.

The camping area at the head of the Pensi La overlooks the extensive Drung Drung Glacier and must be one of the most beautiful in all of Ladakh. There is a sheltered site beside a series of small glacial lakes. There is no shortage of wildlife here. Early one morning I heard the unmistakable howl of wolves from the cliff caves to the south side of the pass, and many tracks had been made through the snow the previous night. The Pensi La is normally under heavy snow for six to seven months each year and apparently the wolves make their way down to the Zanskar villages by early winter in order to take a stray yak or sheep . . . or trekker.

From the Pensi La you can reach Padum, the administrative centre of Zanskar, in three stages, described in the Zanskar Valley section.

RANGDUM TO HENISKOT/LAMAYURU
From Rangdum there is a challenging four-day trek to Heniskot via the Kanji La. The trek can also be extended to Lamayuru. For reasons of acclimatisation the Kanji La (5270 metres) should be approached slowly and this walk provides an ideal extension to a trek starting from Kashmir. The herders' camps, the stark views towards the Zanskar range and the impressive gorges provide a stunning contrast to Kashmir.

Stage 1: Rangdum-Plateau Camp
(Average walking time 5 hours)
Follow the valley to the immediate east of Rangdum. Early in the season you have to take the hillside trail but by September the river subsides and you can follow the trail along the valley floor. The yak herders en route are mainly from Rangdum and Juldo, however there are large herds brought over from the outlying regions of Lamayuru during the late spring. Abundant supplies of fresh curd are yours for the asking.

A guide should be taken from Rangdum as the trail to the Kanji Pass is not easy to detect. The 'main' trail continues up the valley to the Pingdon La and on to Lingshet, while the trail to Heniskot leads up a minor valley. The campsite at the confluence of these two valleys consists of a rocky plateau 100 metres above the main river. Just below the plateau the horses will have to be unloaded and the baggage carried to the campsite. Best to camp here for the night as there is no camping spot between here and the pass.

Stage 2: Plateau Camp-Kanji La-Camp
(Average walking time 7 hours)
From the plateau there is a gradual four hour ascent to the pass. In late spring to early summer the trail relies on snow bridges while by late September-October

the trail has been made through the loose scree. Technically, the pass traverses the Zanskar range, while to the north there are panoramic views of the Ladakh range and distant Karakoram. Care should be taken on the top of the pass as it is heavily corniced on the Kanji side. The initial descent is steep and difficult for the horses, after which the trail winds across an extensive scree ridge. There is a satisfactory campsite with water where the trail meets the valley floor.

Stage 3: Camp-Kanji Village

(Average walking time 4 hours)

Follow the valley downstream. There are many stream crossings, some quite deep early in the season after the snow bridges have collapsed. There are many bear tracks and other traces of their presence in the surrounding cliffs although I have not actually seen any wildlife in this area. The valley widens out into a shepherd encampment after five km – an alternative campsite after descending the Kanji La. The trail to Kanji village takes a another two or three hours, with more river crossings. Kanji consists of some 50 settlements and the simple gompa affiliated with Lamayuru monastery. There are campsites immediately below the village.

At Kanji the trail splits, and the road to Lamayuru climbs the valley to the north-east of the village. It takes three days, according to the locals, to cross the Yogma La, travel down the Shilakong Valley to Wanlah and then on to Lamayuru.

Stage 4: Kanji-Heniskot

(Average walking time 4 hours)

This stage offers a spectacular descent through impressive gorges, second only to those in the Zanskar Valley. The trail involves up to 13 river crossings, so take a guide to point out crossing places, and a rope is essential from late spring until mid-August. After the two initial crossings the trail follows the left bank for four or five km. The gorge then narrows and wet boots are the order of the day for the last few km to the roadhead and Heniskot.

If the water level is too high in the lower gorge there is a get-out pass, the Timti La, which leads over to Bodkarbu. It has taken me three hours to reach the roadhead by this route, as opposed to the half hour if you're able to continue straight down the gorges.

From Heniskot, a bus or truck to Leh takes about six hours; and to Kargil about four hours, depending on the convoy timings.

Leh & The Indus Valley

Leh, the capital of Ladakh, has long been a remote and fascinating outpost. At one time it was a major stop on the Asian 'silk route' and a commercial capital in its own right. The trails to Yarkand and northern India, through Ladakh were plied by traders who used Leh as a market place, while monks undertook pilgrimages to Lhasa and Bhutan across the Tibetan plateau. Indian merchants supplied tea, spices and household articles; Tibetans brought salt and Lhasa tea; and nomads from the hills brought wool for the Kashmiri merchants, who were anxious to control the shawl trade.

These days it is important mainly for its military base and of course, more recently, as a tourist centre.

Leh is about 10 km north-east of the Indus at the exit of a fertile side valley. From the town down to the Indus, the landscape is almost completely barren. Leh has a population of 20,000 and a large military camp stands between the town and the airfield, which is also down towards the Indus. There are a number of interesting places to visit in and around this fascinating town but it it equally interesting just to wander around the back streets of the old section.

The only way to explore Leh is on foot. Remember that you are at 3500 metres, so don't rush around on your first few days. When you begin to breath easier, go higher.

Things to See

Leh Palace The old palace of the kings of Ladakh overlooks the town from the south-west slope of the Tsemo hill. It has eight storeys and was built by King Singe Namgyal in the 16th century, at much the same time as the famed Potala of Lhasa – which it resembles. The damage to the palace – one side is gaping open – is a legacy of the Kashmiri invasion last century. Like the Shey Palace the Leh Palace still belongs to the Ladakhi royal family, who now live in the palace in Stok.

Few of the palace wall-paintings are worth looking at as they have been scratched and smeared over the years. The main reason to make the short, steep climb up to the palace is for the superb views from the roof, over which the coloured prayer flags wave in the wind. Beware of the many holes in the floors while you're wandering around the palace. In good weather the Zanskar range, snow covered until early summer, appears close enough to touch although it rises from the other side of the Indus.

If you can, get a monk, if one can be found, to unlock the preserved but now unused central prayer room; a dusty, spooky place with huge faces looming out of the dark and two walls lined with religious texts on rice-paper that are allegedly 600 years old.

It is open from 6 am to 9 am and from 5 pm.

Leh Town The old town of Leh, with its houses for the aristocrats and servants of the royal household, is clustered at the bottom of the hill under the palace. The new city spreads away from the hill on land which once belonged to the royal family. Due to steady growth in recent years, Leh is becoming increasingly westernised. At one time Leh had a city wall with three gates, one of which still stands close to the market – to the right and uphill towards the palace. The gate is called Kingsgate because only the king and his family were allowed to use it. The chorten above the city is the remains of a royal leisure site.

Leh Gompa The Leh Gompa stands high above the palace and also overlooks the ruins of the older palace of the king of Tagpebums. The Red Gompa (Tsemo Gompa) was built in 1430 by King Gvags-Pa-Bum-Ide and has a fine three-storey-high seated Buddha figure flanked by Avalokitesvara on the right and Manjushri on the left. The walls have recently been brightly painted and the gompa is open from 7 am to 9 am. In all there are three gompas at the top of the hill, the topmost is very dilapidated but offers extremely fine views over Leh and the surrounding countryside. To the right of the palace you can see a Buddha painted on the rocks, a remnant of an earlier monastery.

Mani Walls Near the Leh radio station there are two long mani walls. The one in the centre of the open plain is known as Rongo Tajng and was built as a memorial to Queen Skalzang Dolma by her son Dalden Namgyal about 1635. It is about 500 metres long and contains thousands of mani inscriptions carved in stone in Tibetan. At its end there is the Stupa of Enlightenment and the Stupa of Victory.

The second long mani wall, further down the hill, is said to have been built by Tsetan Namgyal in 1785 as a memorial to his father King Tsewang Namgyal, and is about 350 metres long.

Beyond Leh The surrounding valley supports a number of interesting villages. Chandspar, the village about two km outside Leh, possesses the Maitriya rock carvings of the 8th and 9th centuries. Across the barley fields is Shankar, the site of a modern Delgupta monastery, founded to service the growing villages north of Leh. This outpost is administered by the Spitok monastery and is normally attended by 15 to 20 monks. It seems surprising that Leh does not have a more impressive monastery; even the King's Dukpa monastery at the palace is entirely run-down and only attended by a single monk seconded from Hemis.

Getting Ready

Trekking provisions and supplies must be carried from Leh as tsampa, butter tea and chang is about all you can get from the villages. Pack horses can be hired at Hemis and Lamayuru with prices varying according to seasonal demand – normally in the region of Rs 50 per horse. Horses, however, are not readily available at Stok, Alchi, Spitok or Likir, especially during the main trekking season. It is, therefore, advisable to arrange them a few days ahead of time and pay in advance in order to avoid delay as they may have to be brought from outlying villages.

As in Kashmir the price for arrangements is generally much higher than it is in Nepal. There is no intense competition for work in Leh or other parts of the Indus Valley. Money has to be paid to induce a horseman to leave his village for a week to a month because it may be necessary for him to pay someone to mind his fields while he's away.

Trek equipment in Ladakh is not generally for hire so it is essential to bring your own tent, sleeping bag, down jacket and perhaps a spare sleeping bag or tent for your Ladakhi crew.

If you're going it alone, a stove and a tent are essential, because on some stages there are no villages in which to shelter. Rope should be carried, particularly in July and August, even though bridges have been constructed over the worst crossings in the Sumdah and Markha Valleys.

Trekking Agents

Unlike Kashmir, the trekking agencies in Ladakh maintain a very low profile. Agency signs hanging over windows in the main bazaar reveal simple offices manned by generally helpful staff. The Ladakhis have to some extent been overrun by Kashmiri operators but the local agents, such as Artou (Leh) and Indus Expeditions, are run by well-educated Ladakhis who are extremely knowledgeable about their monasteries and culture.

For individuals not wanting an inclusive-style trek, the Tourist Office in Leh is extremely helpful and has sufficient Ladakhi assistants on hand to provide the right introductions to a guide or cook who is ready to go. A reliable guide is very useful especially if horses have to be hired.

Places to Stay

Ladakh was officially opened to tourism in 1974 and within the first four or five years nearly 50 hotels and guest houses were built to accommodate visitors. Most are run by friendly Ladakhi families and are often an extension of their own home. They are generally clean, simply appointed and constructed in typical two-storey whitewashed fashion.

Leh is not a big place and you can easily walk around and check out a few hotels without having to hike for miles. You should be able to bargain for considerably less than the government rates outside the main season, which is late July and August; and even in season there is a surplus of accommodation.

Rooms vary depending on their age and location. In the old town, where accommodation is designed primarily to hold the warmth in winter, the rooms are simply furnished and you'll probably get a bucket of water to wash with.

In the mid-range, rooms will often have a view – usually of the snow-capped Stok mountains – and sometimes have an attached bathroom, but no running water.

The 'international' standard rooms are still simply furnished, although there will be blankets or a duvet on the bed, and an attached bathroom *with* running water (sometimes hot).

The current government rate for up-market hotels, full board, is Rs 350-400 per double; mid-range Rs 200-250 and simpler accommodation Rs 30-50 per night, room only.

Most of the simpler hotels don't provide food, unless you're living with an obliging family. But there are several good eating places in the town and for breakfast you can buy delicious Ladakhi bread from the bakeries – excellent with local apricot jam or Kashmiri honey.

In the rock bottom category you can find doubles under Rs 30 (less in the off-season) and dormitory beds at Rs 5. Some places in this bracket also provide bed bugs at no extra cost. Popular cheapies include the *Palace View Kidar Hotel*, close to the polo ground, and the *New Antelope Guest House*. The *Moonland Guest House* is in the upper-cheap bracket, the *Old Ladakh Guest House* (quite close by) is similarly priced – both in the old part of town. The *Rainbow Guest House* has doubles from Rs 15 or 20 and is run by a pleasant family who prepare good food. The *Himalayan Hotel* is friendly, with a garden and doubles at Rs 35.

In the middle price category there is the *Khangri Hotel*, just down the road from the tourist office and uncomfortably close to the diesel generator but, as in Kargil, the power goes off around 11 pm. Rooms cost from Rs 100. The side-by-side *Glacier View* and *Karakoram* have been renovated, upgraded and amalgamated to create the *Tsemo-La Hotel*. The *Hotel Yak Tail* is also in this price category and is next to the Dreamland Hotel, on the road leading to the Lha-Ri-Mo.

With rooms from around Rs 50 (none of them with attached baths), a pleasant garden and one of the best restaurants in town, the *Dreamland* is a very popular hotel choice and also very close to the centre. In a quiet area of the town, directly beneath the ruins of Leh Palace, the *Hotel Kardungla* has rooms from around Rs 120, sometimes cheaper. The upstairs doubles have attached bathrooms, thick carpets, blankets and hot water is available in the evenings. The new and clean *Kahyu Hotel* costs Rs 40/60 for singles/doubles in season; rooms have attached bathrooms. It's well away from the generator so it's very quiet, but the owners are Kashmiri so you have to be certain you know exactly what you're getting for your money – just how many buckets of water etc.

Getting Around

Buses One of the easiest ways to get around the Indus Valley is to use the local bus service. The buses are extremely crowded, run down and look as though they will never get to where you want to go but they always do. It is one of the better ways of getting close to the local people. You will share the bus with Ladakhis, Zanskaris, Dards, goats, chickens, monks, bales of hay and piles of wood. The local custom is that everyone, including women and children, stand up to give their seats to a monk.

However unreliable they may look, the buses are cheap and they usually run on time. The main problem is that there are not enough of them and there may be only one service a day to the more remote parts you want to go. Another local custom is that you need to get to the bus stop in Leh almost an hour before the bus goes if you want to get a seat. This has its advantages and disadvantages. If you are likely to be on a very crowded bus, and you are jammed into a seat by an aisle full of people, you may not be able to get fresh air. On the other hand the roofs on the buses are very low and it is impossible for an average size westerner to stand in them.

If you are not sure if you are on the right bus just ask. Ladakhis are a very friendly and helpful people and they will soon tell you what you want to know, as best they can. In season the J&K Tourist Office may offer bus tours of the area.

The main local bus services out of Leh are:

route	dist.	buses daily	fare Rs
Choglamsar	8 km	4	1.20
Chushot	25 km	3	3.30
Hemis	45 km	1	6.00
Khalsi	98 km	1	12.95
Matho	27 km	2	3.75
Phyang	22 km	3	3.10
Sabu	9 km	2	1.35
Sakti	51 km	1	6.95
Saspul	62 km	1	7.90
Shey	16 km	2	2.10
Spitok	8 km	2	1.20
Stok	17 km	2	2.85
Tikse	20 km	3	3.00

For trips further afield there are daily buses to Kargil costing Rs 39 (A class) or Rs 34 (B class). For Lamayuru (124 km) take a Kargil bus (Rs 16.10). For Lekir (54 km) a Khalsi or Kargil bus will get you there (Rs 7.10). For Karu (40 km, Rs 4.85), Alchi (65 km, Rs 8) or Nimu (36 km, Rs 4.50) you can take any of the Khalsi or Kargil buses operating along the Kargil road. The tourist office in Leh will have the full story on bus fares and timetables. Services are likely to be less frequent in winter.

Jeeps & Taxis An easy and convenient way of getting around Ladakh is to band together with other travellers and hire a taxi or jeep. Taxis are not cheap and the drivers have formed a union and now refuse to bargain, especially in Leh, but if you cannot stand the crush and endless delays of the buses, they are the only way to go. There are set fares for some longer journeys and for certain local trips but other destinations must be by negotiation.

In general, taxis charge Rs 3 per km or, on return trips, Rs 3 per km on the way there, Rs 2 per km on the way back. In most cases a loading of 30% is added for longer routes and sightseeing tours. The charge for the long tours to monasteries and places of interest usually includes a wait of one hour for which there is no charge. Beyond a one hour wait the charges are at the rate of Rs 10 an hour.

For local routes in and around Leh there will be no waiting charge for the first half hour, then Rs 5 for the next half hour and Rs 10 an hour thereafter. This is probably the most negotiable part of the taxi trip.

Overnight stays are charged at the rate of Rs 80. Where a village name is given as the route destination the fare will be to the monastery of that village. The best deal will probably be to try and negotiate a total cost for all the places you wish to visit in one day. Count on around Rs 300 to 350 for a day. You can easily visit the Shey, Thikse, Hemis and Spitok gompas in a day by jeep and split between six people the cost is not excessive. Six, however, is a bit of a tight squeeze. Four passengers fills a jeep comfortably and five is getting tight.

Airport There is a bus service out to the airport for Rs 2 and a jeep or taxi would cost around Rs 25.

Getting There

Today's journey from Srinagar to Leh by road still vies for the title of the most demanding of any in the Himalaya. The 450 km trip is generally covered in two long days. The first from Kashmir over the Himalaya to Kargil (see the Little Baltistan section); and the second from Kargil over the Zanskar range to the Indus Valley and Leh. From the time you leave the alpine meadows of Sonamarg and wind over the Zoji La until you reach Leh, the drive never fails to get the adrenalin going.

The 130 km journey from Kargil to Leh crosses cultural boundaries and passes through an amazing mountain and valley landscape of rock and rubble with its surprising splashes of green. The road starts to climb shortly after Kargil, leaving the Suru Valley by way of a small pass in the Wakka Valley. As the river valley widens, more and more irrigated wheat and barley fields appear and as you cross the religious border you see the first of the smiling Ladakhis dressed in their typical Tibetan head-gear. Just beyond the isolated Buddhist settlement at Mulbec is a seven metre figure of the Maitriya, or future Buddha, cut into the rock.

From Mulbec the road climbs up through a sandhill landscape to the 3718 metre high Namika La then down to the Mohammedan village of Bodkarbu. The descent from the pass, with its twisting and turning razorback road is, to say the least, adventurous. Further up the valley the culture changes again, the villagers at Heniskot are Buddhist. The road follows the river for a while then winds its way up to the Fatu La pass, which at 4094 metres, is the highest point on the Srinagar-Leh road. The pass marks the outer rim of the Zanskar range and from the top you get a good view back down the river valley to Kashmir; while ahead you're looking towards the Indus River valley, over several mountain ranges to Tibet.

The road from the pass to Khalsi is one of the most fascinating along the whole route. About 15 km from the top of Fatu La stands the old Tibetan monastery at Lamayuru, on a crumbling mountain below the road.

If you have time it is worthwhile leaving the road and walking down the pilgrim trail, past the ancient chortens and mani walls, which date from the monastery's foundation in the 10th century. In the 16th century Lamayuru gompa was declared a holy site in which even criminals could seek sanctuary. For that reason it is known to Ladakhis as *Tharpa Ling*, 'Place of Freedom'. There a a few small hotels if you decide to break your journey here.

The road from Lamayuru drops nearly 1000 metres and involves nearly 30 switchbacks in the 25 km to Khalsi and must surely be a record for road building anywhere in the world.

Khalsi, a charming village set among apricot orchards, is a rest stop for buses and has many restaurants on the main road. Beyond Khalsi the former royal highway follows the road to the village at Nurla and then branches up valley to Tingmosgang. From there the trail once

followed a higher ridge to Likir and Bazgo, but these days it follows the banks of the Indus and the road is hewn out of the mountainside as far as Saspool. This is a beautiful area and Saspool, on a bluff above the Indus, is a good place for a stopover. From there you can get to Rizdong, Alchi, and Likir by bus, jeep or on foot.

From Saspool to Nimu even the Indus gorges are too steep for contemporary road-builders, so the road bypasses the village and monastery at Alchi and climbs the Rongdo La to Bazgo.

As you approach Bazgo it's not hard to see why it was of such strategic importance to the Ladakhis. It was here they were able to hold back the invading Balti and Mongol forces for years at a time. Just above the dilapidated Bazgo fortress, which commands the only route into upper Ladakh, the new trail rejoins the old.

About 2.5 km beyond Nimu the Zanskar River flows into the Indus through *Nimu Gyasho*, (the Nimu Gateway), a large cleft rock. The red-brown, shimmering Indus Valley floor broadens considerably for the final 35 km to Leh. It is flanked by the Stok range to the south, the Ladakh range to the north and tucked into one of the sheltered side valleys is Leh – the capital of Ladakh.

The buses stop just below the main bazaar and it is left to you to approach the bazaar on foot – not so unlike the traders and pilgrims of a generation or more ago.

The Srinagar/Leh highway is only open for about six months each year, as soon as the Zoji La is cleared of snow, normally by mid-June. The pass generally remains open until mid-November.

The cost one way for the 'A' class bus is Rs 90, and for the 'B' class is Rs 60. 'A' class buses leave from the Tourist Centre in Srinagar and 'B' class buses from Lal Chowk. Jeeps can be hired but are expensive – Rs 3000 one-way Srinagar/Leh and Rs 2000 Leh/Srinagar – however you have the advantage of being able to stop and sightsee on the way. Trucks are a viable alternative later in the season with the charge approximately the same as the bus.

For those who want to take the journey more slowly there are plenty of places to stay en route. Besides the hotels in Kargil there are government *Rest Houses* and tea-stall/hotels in Drass, Bodkarbu, Lamayuru and Khalsi. Food and accommodation are basic yet adequate; sleeping bags, as elsewhere in Ladakh, are a must.

There are regular Indian Airline flights into Leh from Srinagar, Chandigarh and Delhi which makes Leh accessible to visitors throughout the year. It should be borne in mind that the flights are generally heavily booked and are sometimes cancelled in bad weather. The flight path from Srinagar to Leh is a spectacular half hour's flying and well worth taking at least one way during your stay in Ladakh. The cost is Rs 257, one-way.

Treks

Three treks are outlined in this section:
1. From Stok or Spitok to Hemis via the Markha Valley: a trek beyond the kingdom of upper Ladakh.
2. From Likir to Rizdong, north of the Indus Valley, encompassing the lower Ladakh kingdom.
3. From Alchi to Lamayuru via the Sumdah Valley to the south of the Indus, including the initial stages of treks going further afield into the Zanskar region.

Acclimatisation is the most important consideration on these treks. The Stapski La, above Alchi, is over 5000 metres, the Namlung La, above Stok, is around 4500 metres and the Gongmaru La, two stages beyond Hemis, is 5030 metres. A good acclimatisation program in Leh is imperative, and the initial stages of the trek should be taken very slowly. Remember that Leh (3500 metres) is the same height as Thyangboche in Nepal, an acclimatisation

camp en route to the Everest base camp.

It is possible to trek from early June and even May, although snow plodding will be necessary over the passes. July and August can be very pleasant, although the temperatures often soar into the mid-20°Cs. It is worth considering a very early start and completing each trek stage before midday. Dehydration in this intensely dry area is a problem and fluid levels must be kept up. River crossings still constitute a problem, although not as hazardous as in Zanskar. September is ideal as the weather is settled and in October the days are generally clear, making it a good trekking month providing you have sufficient warm clothing to endure a cold spell.

STOK/SPITOK TO HEMIS via Markha Valley

There are two approaches to this trek: a walk-in via Stok and over the Namlung La to Rumbak; or, a walk-in to Rumbak via Spitok, across the Gandha La to the Markha Valley. The Stok walk-in visits the royal palace en route before a steep climb over the Namlung La (4570 metres). This takes a minimum of two days, preferably three, and should not be followed unless you are fully acclimatised.

Spitok

From Leh it is a short drive past the airport to Spitok. Spitok is the oldest Delgupta monastery in the Indus Valley, dating from the 15th century. It is interesting to note that the Delgupta monks created the precedent of building monasteries on hilltops, rather than on valley floors. This follows the Tibetan notion that the higher the monastery site, the closer it is to the gods. There was certainly no political significance attached to its strategic siting at the time. Nowadays Spitok administers Shankar monastery in Leh and also the Stok village monastery.

Stok

It's one hour's drive from Leh to Stok village. Dominating Stok is the royal palace. It was built in the 1840s after the Ladakhi royal family was deposed by the Dogra invasion and is now occupied by the Rani of Stok, the former Member of Parliament for Ladakh. The last king of Stok died in 1974 and the eldest son, now in his teens, will ascend the throne in his early 20s, the auspicious date being set by the high lamas of Hemis monastery where the queen's brother is treasurer.

The present Rani has assumed personal responsibility for the maintenance and reconstruction of the Ladakh palaces in Stok, Leh and Shey. The museum in Stok palace is a show-piece for the royal *tankas* (rectangular paintings on cloth) while the collection of turquoise head-dresses, worn only for royal weddings, is the most impressive in Ladakh. Eventually it is hoped to move the museum pieces to Leh palace, when sufficient funds are available for its renovation.

SPITOK WALK-IN

Stage 1: Spitok-Rumbak

(Average walking time 8 hours)

From Spitok cross the new bridge and proceed across the barren trail to the south-west of the Indus. This undulating trail extends for seven or eight km until it reaches the Jinchan Valley and the first shade! From here it will take four or five hours to climb to Rumbak, going through Jinchan village en route and will involve frequent river crossings in the gorge country below Rumbak village.

It may be advisable for the first day out to camp below Jinchan and the next day continue past Rumbak to Utse.

STOK WALK-IN

Stage 1: Stok-Shepherd Camp

(Average walking time 5 hours)

From Stok follow the main trail to the outskirts of the village. The climb through the gorges is straight-forward for the first three or four km, after which care should

be taken to pick the correct gully, as the trail peters out in places. It's a very steady climb to the shepherd's camp and a sensible distance for the first day's walk. The shepherds are women from Stok who graze their angora goats during the summer months. Beyond their huts is a meagre stream and camping area.

For those needing to spend additional time acclimatising, the first stage could be limited to the meadows at the outskirts of Stok village. Camp here for the night and then continue to the shepherd camp the following day.

Stage 2: Shepherd Camp-Rumbak

(Average walking time 4 hours)

It is a steep ascent to the Namlung La (4570 metres), with breath-taking views back into the Indus Valley. It takes two hours to descend to the barley fields of Rumbak where you can camp on the village outskirts. Some years ago one of our ponymen burst into tears upon reaching a family at the village. Given that he had been comparatively cheerful before, it was only afterwards that I learnt the cause of his distress: it is customary for a relative, however distant, to show grief on visiting a family where death has recently occurred.

Stage 3: Rumbak-Utse-Camp

(Average walking time 5 hours)

From Rumbak the trail ascends to Utse. This village is in the side valley about three km above the Jinchan valley and is essentially one large household. The family is extremely hospitable and many a day's trekking has been unavoidably postponed due to an over-indulgence of chang. For those who emerge from Utse with a clear head, a steady ascent towards the base of the Gandha La, where there's a spring and level camping area, takes a further two hours.

Stage 4: Camp-Gandha La-Shingo-Skiu

(Average walking time 6 hours)

A steady 90 minute climb to Gandha La

provides views towards the Zanskar range. The descent to Shingo village takes a further 90 minutes, followed by three more hours through a wooded ravine to Skiu where the trail meets the Markha Valley. Skiu is a small settlement one km up the trail towards Markha, and a sheltered if rather marshy campsite is located below the main house.

From Skiu it's recommended to make a half-day walk to the impressive Zanskar gorges. The village of Kaya en route provides a rich harvest of apricots and some extremely hospitable families. Kaya gompa is typical of Ladakhi village gompas and belongs to the Drukpa sect, administered by Hemis. The resident monk spends a three year period here, on loan from the Markha monastery.

Stage 5: Skiu-Markha
(Average walking time 7 hours)
The route from Skiu to Markha takes a full day. After two and a half hours the trail crosses the river by a newly built bridge, then re-crosses upstream at Chalake. Beyond this settlement there is an impressive line of chortens and a huge mound of goat horns, probably to ward off any evil spirits trying to enter the valley.

There is a wolf trap several km before Markha – a circular stone enclosure, slightly overhanging at the rim. A goat kid would be left to attract marauding wolves who, after jumping in after the bait, are unable to get out. The villagers then, en masse, stone the animal to death. By doing it together they are not breaking any Buddhist tenets because no 'individual' has actually taken the life of another creature. This practice is also common in the Zanskar Valley.

A medieval fort silhouetted on the hillside is the first indication that Markha is close at hand. There is an ideal camping area in the open meadow a km beyond Markha and a camp inspection will be made by the old women and children of the village. There is plenty of wood and water and the people are friendly.

Stage 6: Markha-Hankar-Thahungtse
(Average walking time 5 hours)
Three km beyond Markha the trail meets the Chacham Valley coming from the Rubarung La and Zanskar. The Markha gompa, set high on the cliff face, lies just beyond this junction. The gompa is affiliated with Hemis monastery and is the most important in the valley. The keyholder to the monastery lives in the village and the monastery is usually only open at early morning prayer times.

The main trail follows the valley through Unlung village to Hankar and the site of more impressive fort ruins. The small gompa below the fort was constructed in favour of a former ruler. From Hankar the trail diverts from the main valley and follows the Nimaling stream to Thahungtse and a good camping area. En route, in late autumn, we were fortunate to see a herd of wild sheep as they made their way down from the high grazing areas.

Stage 7: Thahungtse-Nimaling
(Average walking time 4 hours)
The trail climbs quite steeply to the plateau, offering impressive views of Nimaling Peak (6000 metres), and passing a number of mani walls en route to the open plains. Nimaling supports shepherd encampments with goat and yak herds from Hankar and Markha. During my various treks to Nimaling between July and October it has never failed to snow, so be well prepared when setting out on this trek.

There are some challenging climbing options along the ridges opposite Nimaling peak. A full day can also be spent climbing the grazing pastures to the head of the Nimaling Valley.

Stage 8: Nimaling-Gongmaru La-Sumda
(Average walking time 6 hours)
The climb to the Gongmaru La (5030 metres) takes almost two hours, so make an early start before the clouds obscure the views across the Stok Ranges and down to the Indus Valley and Martselang

village. The descent through the gorges to Shogdo, the first village, takes some three hours, with many stream crossings. Take extra care if you're descending after heavy rainfall as the stream becomes a torrent in no time, causing considerable destruction to the trail. This has happened several times over the last three or four years. The camping ground at Shogdo is in the 'garden enclosure', opposite the main cluster of houses. Alternatively, continue down valley for three km and camp at Sumda village.

It has become fashionable among younger continental trekkers who are 'going it alone' on this trek to buy their own donkey. But don't fall into this trend. On this stage to Hemis a few years ago I came across a young Frenchman tugging a rather disobedient donkey behind him. He asked me the way to Manali and I pointed straight up the valley. My Ladakhi companions informed me later that this unfortunate explorer had taken two days to reach Shogdo from Hemis, having to virtually carry the donkey over every river crossing. The donkey was sold at a greatly reduced price to a local villager and that, I believe, was as far as the donkey and the Frenchman got.

Stage 9: Sumda-Hemis
(Average walking time 4-5 hours)
Descend the valley, crossing the river several times until the trail meets the Leh/Manali jeep track. Turn left (west) by the large chorten above Martselang village, from where it takes about one hour to ascend the rather dusty trail to Hemis. There is a camping ground just below Hemis monastery where meals can be purchased.

If you take this but follow a reverse itinerary (from Hemis to Stok), it's advisable to allow a few days in Hemis for acclimatisation, or at least three days before crossing the Gongmaru La.

Hemis
The position of Hemis monastery, lying in

a small isolated valley south of the Indus belies its importance. As headquarters of the Drukpa (old Buddhist) order, it administers monasteries throughout the whole of Ladakh – from the Indus to the Zanskar Valley and from the Markha to the Sumdah Valley. Hemis was established at the behest of Senge Namygal in the early 17th century and since then has enjoyed the patronage of the royal family of Ladakh. It provides monks as caretakers for royal monasteries at the Bazgo, Leh and Shey palaces.

The former head lama of Hemis was brought from Tibet as a young scholar. He returned to Tibet for further studies but was unable to return to Hemis because of the Chinese occupation of Tibet. It wasn't until 1975 that a new lama was appointed a 12 year old boy brought from Dalhousie near Dharamsala. He will assume full religious authority over Hemis when his training is complete.

Each year Hemis comes alive during its famous festival in June, attracting monks and their families from throughout Ladakh and Zanskar. Masked dances are held in the main courtyard, above which hangs a tanka depicting Padmasambhava, the sage who introduced Tantric Buddhism to the Himalaya. Once every 11 years a huge tanka, one of the largest in the Tibetan world, is revealed. The next showing is due in 1991.

To fully appreciate the extent of the Hemis complex and also gain some insight into the meditative practices still pursued by the monks it is a good idea to climb to the hermitage, about one hour above the monastery.

From Hemis it is about 50 km back to Leh by road. Jeeps have to be pre-ordered from Leh but there is also a daily bus service.

To complete the circuit of the upper Ladakh kingdom it is essential to visit Shey and Thikse on your return.

Shey
The former palace of upper Ladakh

efore Leh was established, this site ommanded an important vantage over ne Indus Valley. Since 1834 however, fter the royal family moved to Stok, much f the palace and fort fell into disrepair; ven the marshland immediately below 'as once a clear lake.

Some restoration has been carried out ecently though, particularly on the two-torey Sakyamuni Buddha, originally ommissioned by Senge Namygal and owadays attended, as with Leh, by the)rukpa monks from Hemis.

Immediately to the east of Shey are xtensive grounds studded with many hortens. These have been built not only a memory of the principal monks and oyalty but also for the villagers from main amilies in both Shey and Thikse who egard this area as most favourable for remation.

hikse

)ne of the most imposing monasteries in ne Indus Valley, Thikse was part of the riginal Delgupta order in the 15th entury. The monks' quarters stretch ight the way along the hillside beneath ne main assembly hall. The library at 'hikse is supposedly one of the finest in adakh and a multi-denominational gompa as recently been constructed – proof ndeed of the continuing vitality of luddhism in Ladakh.

Across the valley from Thikse, on the ar side of the Indus, is the Drukpa nonastery at Stakna, built at the same ime as Hemis.

IKIR TO RIZDONG & TINGMOSGANG

'his easily graded trek follows the former rade route to the north of the Indus 'alley then goes up-valley to the fortress f Tingmosgang and across the plateau bove the Indus to Likir. From Likir the oute continues across the Rongdu La, inally meeting the new road just before lazgo.

The highway dates from at least the 5th century – the era of the Tibetan saint Tsongkapa who founded the Delgupta sect in Ladakh. The 'modern' construction of the Bazgo and Tingmosgang forts also dates from this period. This trek provides one of the richest historical courses in the Ladakh region.

The altitude on this trek never rises above 3800 metres, a rarity in Ladakh. It can also be completed in the space of a few days, a combination which makes it very attractive to those who haven't time or energy to go further afield. The trail extends beyond the one km limit north of the Leh/Srinagar road and the Tourist Office in Leh should always be consulted in advance. However, given that Likir, Rizdong and Tingmosgang can be visited without special permission the trek should be open.

I have not completed the entire trek, and my initial familiarity with the area was through visits to Rizdong and Likir and then from mention of the trail by one of my Ladakhi guides. I didn't believe there was any trail in Ladakh devoid of strenuous ascents and descents until I was able to appreciate the terrain from the south side of the Indus when climbing the Stapski La. The villages in the sheltered valleys above the present Indus highway appeared to be linked across a broad plateau about 500 metres above the Indus – which was the route before modern machinery was able to carve a road along the banks of the Indus.

Horses must be hired from Saspool, and overnight accommodation is possible in the monastic quarters. You can either jeep it to Likir or catch the local Saspool bus which stops a few km below Likir. As always, supplies must be brought from Leh.

Likir

Founded at the same time as Spitok and Thikse, Likir is recognised as the foremost Delgupta monastery in the Ladakh region. Its head lama is the younger brother of the Dalai Lama, which possibly explains the apparent prosperity of the monastery.

Nowadays, besides presiding over the monasteries at Lingshet, Karsha and Phugtal in Zanskar, it also gives them some financial support. Likir also assumes responsibility for Alchi gompa, in the nearby Indus Valley.

From Likir it takes two stages to reach Rizdong. Two low pass crossings are necessary with a convenient camping site halfway on the Wuleh Tokpo. The path down to Rizdong diverges from the main trail, not surprisingly as Rizdong was founded only in the last century – one of the most recent Delgupta monasteries. Still attended by nearly 100 monks, the monastic grounds exude an air of prosperity. The monastery is also noted for its monks' commitment to their studies, a contrast to many of the more lapsed orders in other localities.

From Rizdong the trail downstream leads to the Uludrokpo on the Leh/Srinagar road. To follow the former trade route you have to retrace your steps and climb another none-too-demanding plateau-pass before descending to Tingmosgang. The fortress of Tingmosgang is on equal standing with Bazgo. It originally subscribed to the Delgupta order before being colonised by the Brugpa order, the King's order from Hemis, in the 17th century. Beyond the palace is the Maitriya Temple, dating from the time of Tsongkapa, which is maintained by the monks from Likir.

From Tingmosgang it is a few km's descent to Nurla village on the Leh/Srinagar road, midway between Khalsi and Saspool.

If returning to Leh then a visit to Bazgo is necessary to complete an appreciation of the lower Ladakh kingdom.

Bazgo

The fort commands an imposing view over the only route into the Indus Valley. Even after the royal family moved from lower Ladakh to Leh, Bazgo was maintained with at least some relatives of the royal family living there – which ensured the care and maintenance of the Maitriy. Temple beside the fort. Bazgo was als. the site of the famous siege in the late 17t. century when the Tibetan-Moghul force. had set their sights on invading the Indu. Valley and Ladakh. It was only after thre. years that the Ladakhi army was relieve. by the Moghuls, sent from norther. India.

LAMAYURU TO ALCHI

Although Lamayuru is nearly 600 metre. higher than Alchi, it is still preferable t. trek from Lamayuru to Alchi. This wi. give adequate time for acclimatisatio. before crossing the Konke La (457. metres) to the Sumdah Valley. If th. approach is made from Alchi a steep clim. is required on the first day and a half an. according to my altimeter, the Stapski L. is in excess of 5180 metres.

When I first completed this trek it wa. from Alchi. The horseman from Saspo. assured me we would cross the Stapski L. and reach Sumdahchoon in one da. Unfortunately his two horses and thre. donkeys had other ideas and we were 'be. nighted' on a very cold and windy pas. However, the sight of dawn over th. Ladakh range was suitable compensation.

If undertaking this trek from Lamayur. it is advisable to get off the Srinagar-Le. bus there, rather than going to Leh an. returning later. Bring all your supplie. from Kashmir and schedule a day or so fe. camping at Lamayuru to arrange horse. and explore the monastery.

Lamayuru

The ideal way to approach Lamayuru. via the old caravan trail that diverges fro. the road at the Fatu La. Descending fro. the pass the full dimensions of Lamayur. monastery are first seen beyond th. impressive line of mani walls and chorter. leading down to the village. Legend has. that Lamayuru valley was once filled by. lake which was drained by the sag. Naropa to permit the foundation of th. monastery. What is certain, is tha.

Top: Hemis festival, Ladakh
Left: Lamayuru Gompa, Ladakh
Right: Autumn traverse of the Bodgpatri pass in the Pir Panjal range

Top: Kashmiri shepherds
Left: Old Ladakhi man
Right: Ladakhi woman

Lamayuru, built in the 10th century, is the oldest monastic site in Ladakh. One of the original temples is still standing just beyond the main assembly hall and is now being extensively renovated. The monastery belongs to one of the old Tibetan schools, the Kargyupa/Drukpa school. For many of the outlying monasteries beyond Lamayuru the distinction is merely technical; the monasteries in Wanlah, Phangi and Halsi, although affiliated with Lamayuru, also have a close cultural tie to the main Drukpa monastery at Hemis.

Stage 1: Lamayuru-Phangi
(Average walking time 5 hours)
The only camping area at Lamayuru is in a shady grove just below the monastery. From here the trail heads down the valley for two km before turning east towards the Prinkiti La. The climb to this pass (3506 metres) should take less than an hour and from there you can appreciate the lie of the land across to the Konke La. Descend the barren gully to the Shilakong Valley two km above the village of Wanlah. Shortly after Wanlah the trail crosses the Yapola Chu and climbs gradually to the village of Phangi.

Two things of interest along the stage from Wanlah to Phangi (which takes about two hours), are the huge fields of boulders which were brought down by a landslide about 18 years ago, and the ingenious irrigation canal which extends for some three or four km from just below Phangi village. This system of cultivation was passed down from the original Dardic settlers.

Stage 2: Phangi-Camp below Konke La
(Average walking time 5 hours)
From Phangi follow the trail up the Ripchar valley. Frequent river crossings are necessary until you reach the village at Halsi. From Halsi the trail is more defined, continuing through small settlements for about 2½ hours to the grazing areas which support the village summer

camps. From the high camp you are only a few km below the base of the Konke La.

Stage 3: Camp-Konke La-Sumdahchenmo
(Average walking time 5-6 hours)
The climb to the Konke La, although steep, should take no more than two hours from camp. From the Konke La (4570 metres) Sumdahchenmo village can be seen in the distance, while further off, beyond the Zanskar River gorge, you can see the Stok mountains. The trail winds across the ridges down to Sumdah Chu, by no means an easy trail to follow if you're coming from the opposite direction.

Having crossed the Konke La you are now in the Hemis/Drukpa catchment area. There is a relatively modern gompa and a number of summer encampments above Sumdahchenmo and a sheltered campsite by the river below the main village. A huge wooden Buddhist statue of the Maitriya Buddha and many smaller statues have been left standing in the open in what was the original monastic site at Sumdahchenmo.

Stage 4: Sumdahchenmo-Sumdahchoon
(Average walking time 7 hours)
This stage must be undertaken with a local guide. The trail descends the Sumdah Chu for three or four km before splitting – one trail heading up the ridge to the Dungdugchan La and the village of Chillung on the Zanskar River, the other to Sumdahchoon, further down the wooded Sumdah Valley.

It takes one day, according to the locals, to reach Chillung village where much of the copper work for the Leh market is made.

From Chillung you could return to the Indus Valley by following the trail downstream to the confluence of the Zanskar and the Indus Rivers and then on to Alchi. Alternatively, you could cross the Zanskar River by the pulley bridge above Chillung and then continue to the Markha Valley. If you're doing this you would have to arrange new horses on the Markha side as the animals are unable to ford the Zanskar River between late spring and very late autumn.

The trail descending the Sumdahtokpo is quite hazardous and the horses may need to be unloaded, especially during the many river crossings. About three hours below Sumdahchenmo there is a direct trail to Sumdahchoon which climbs the ridge above the river. Don't miss it, because if you do you'll have to continue downstream to the confluence of the river (emanating from Stapski La and Sumdahtokpo) which is very difficult for horses and by no means easy for trekkers, especially when the river is in flood during mid-summer.

There are a number of suitable camp-sites at Sumdahchoon, including some very pleasant spots about two km further along towards the Stapski La.

The monastery at Sumdahchoon was built by Rinchen Zangpo at the same time as Alchi. The assembly hall, although not in as good a condition as Alchi, displays similar wall paintings and wooden carvings. There is also an impressive statue of the Maitriya Buddha in the adjoining temple.

During late autumn, herds of urial make their way down from the high ridges to the valley pastures beyond Sumdahchoon. They have also been seen at this time below the Rubarung La and above Hankar village in the Markha Valley.

Stage 5: Sumdahchoon-Stapski La-Alchi
(Average walking time 7-8 hours)
Leave Sumdahchoon early to complete the tiring climb to the pass before the heat of the day. If you camp above the village, closer to the base of the pass, so much the better. The climb should take approximately three hours. From the pass there are panoramic views across the Ladakh range and right down to the Indus Valley, some 2100 metres below. From the pass the trail descends quite steeply for the first km to the herdsmen's camp and from there it takes a further two or three hours to reach Alchi. There is a regular campsite at Alchi, close to the monastery grounds where food can be purchased durin season.

Alchi
The monastic complex at Alchi was buil in the 11th century. Its sheltered position in the Indus Valley, off the main trails to Leh, is probably the major reason why i survived wars and abandonment to th elements. It is the best surviving example of the era and is notable because it wa built down in a valley instead of on a hil top or mountainside.

Rinchen Zangpo under the patronage o a local Tibetan king, was responsible fo founding Alchi. The Tibetans, newl converted to Buddhism, did not then have the ability to construct and decorate the temples; consequently, artists and monk from Kashmir and north-west India were employed, resulting in a typically Indo Buddhist style.

For a complete survey of the Alch temples and a detailed illustrated histor of other monasteries in Ladakh, get hol of Snellgrove & Skorupski's *Cultura History of Ladakh*.

The Zanskar Valley

Zanskar, the region between Kishtwa and Manali in the south and Kargil an Lamayuru in the north is an ideal trekkin area. Surrounded by the main Himalaya on one side and the Zanskar range on the other, it is the most remote district o Ladakh and there are few inhabite valleys in the world that are so isolated.

Zanskar consists of two populate valleys, the Stod (Doda Chu) and th Lunak (Tsarap Chu), which converg below Padum. The Zanskar River flow across the plains from Padum to Zangla where it penetrates the huge Zanska range en route to the Indus, creating som of the most spectacular gorges in th Himalaya.

The valley is about 300 km long and is unusual in that access is only by high passes from the sides. A unique feature of the Zanskar area is the twin peak of Nun and Kun.

The entire Ladakh region is extremely arid but the Zanskar Valley gets more snow than other areas, with snow falling for seven months of the year. The people spread gravel on it to make it melt. Passes are often under heavy snow for more than half the year and winter temperatures of -20°C and below, make Zanskar one of the coldest places in the world. In the depths of winter all the rivers freeze over. Even the Zanskar River freezes on the surface and the Zanskaris walk along it to reach the Indus River near Nimu – an otherwise inaccessible route.

Until a few years ago it took villagers a week or more to reach the roadhead out of the valley but these days there is a jeep track linking Kargil and Padum. Despite this link with the outside world life in the valley has changed little. Yak trains still plod their way over the wild and remote passes to Lahaul, Kulu and the Indus Valley.

The new road over the Pensi La from Kargil to Padum has brought some of the trappings of civilisation to the Zanskar capital but one severe winter proved how tenuous a connection that road is. You won't find hotels in Zanskar but neither will you find the military installations and soldiers so common in the rest of Ladakh. The most you'll come across is a mounted patrol or pony-caravan of the J&K Police. As for foreigners, they are still few and far between in this far 'off the beaten track' Himalayan valley.

Zanskar's uninterrupted Buddhist heritage is principally due to its extreme isolation and can be traced from a time when the Buddhist monks first crossed the Himalaya from Kashmir. While the Mohammedan influence stretched right through Baltistan to the northern borders of Zanskar, Islam did not spread over the Pensi La. There are Mohammedan communities in Padum, but these mainly date from the time of the Dogra invasion in the 1830s.

The foundation of Sani in the 11th century is recognised as the earliest monastic siting, while the original sites at Phugtal and Karsha are also attributed to this period. In many respects the development of Buddhist sects was on par with Ladakh. The Delgupta order was established in the 15th century and the later foundations of the well-preserved monasteries at Karsha, Lingshet and Mune date from this period. The Drukpa order established Bardan and Zangla and 'colonised' the monastery at Sani in the 17th century.

Today the Delgupta monasteries have established ties with Likir monastery, the head lama being the younger brother of the present Dalai Lama. Similarly, Bardan, Sani and Zangla have administrative and financial links with the monastery at Stakna in the Indus Valley.

Zanskar became an administrative part of Ladakh under Senge Namygal. He had three sons whom he installed as rulers of Ladakh, Guge, and Zanskar and Spiti, respectively. After Ladakh's war with Tibet this order gradually fell apart and Zanskar's royal families split, one assuming jurisdiction of Padum and the other Zangla. This continued until the Dogra times when both families were reduced to nominal powers. This was a period of great unrest in Zanskar and the records testify to wholesale destruction of many of the villages. Thereafter Zanskar's political history was again very much intertwined with Ladakh.

Getting Ready

Trekking in Zanskar is not easy. The trails are often rough, the river often deep and the passes always high. This is not a place for beginners. But careful preparation will make a Zanskar trek an easier proposition.

Basic supplies such as kerosene, rice, flour, dried milk and biscuits are normally available in Karsha and Padum but only later on in the season. In the small villages along the trail it is not always easy to buy even *tsampa* meal. Anyone intending to trek in Zanskar should, therefore, be completely outfitted in Srinagar or, at the latest, Kargil. Most important you must take sufficient kerosene (and ensure the containers don't leak!) as there is very little fuel for burning.

For those wanting a night out of tents there are also a number of dormitory-style hotels in Karsha and Padum.

On arrival, or during your visit to Padum, you must register at the Tourist Department. The Tourist Officer in charge can also help to arrange horses. The Government Development Officer at Padum – son of the King of Zangla – is extremely helpful in finding horses when they are not immediately available.

Prices for horses vary greatly with the season but are always costly, particularly at harvest time. If ordering three or four horses then expect to pay about Rs 50 per horse. If you're ordering one horse during the harvest time then Rs 60-70 or more must be budgeted for. Porters are also available should you be going lightweight to Lamayuru or Leh. However, only porters can go on the trek over the Umasi La to Kishtwar and should be hired at the village of Sani.

Getting There

Although a jeep trail extends along the Stod Valley to Padum, a walk into Zanskar is recommended, to assist both fitness and acclimatisation, particularly if you intend to undertake an extended trek later on.

The trek in to Zanskar, from the Pensi La to Padum, is an extension of the stages described in the Pannikher to Pensi La trek in the Ladakh section. From Padum you have the choice of taking any of the three principal treks outlined.

If you're trekking in over the Pensi La it is worthwhile to make Tungri – where the bridge crosses the Stod Chu – your base for a few days, rather than Padum. It is

then possible to visit Karsha for a day should you want to continue on to Manali or the Markha Valley to Leh. Alternatively a visit to Sani and Padum can be completed in one day should you continue on a trek to Lamayuru.

Treks

There are four treks described in this section:

1. From the Pensi La to Tungri and Padum.
2. Down the Zanskar Valley and over the Singi La to Lamayuru.
3. Across the Zanskar range via the Charcha La and the Rubarung La to the Markha Valley and Leh.
4. Along the Lunak Valley and over the Shingo La to Lahaul and Manali.

The three principal treks in this section all go through some wilderness areas, particularly the route to the Markha Valley and Leh. The trails are often ill defined and a good guide is necessary. The Zanskar area is no different from the Indus area when it comes to river crossings. In late spring (May-June) the rivers are affected by the spring snow melt, and during summer (July-August) are subject to flooding. Trekking schedules must be flexible, and alternative routes may sometimes have to be followed.

It is interesting that the easiest summer route out of Zanskar and on to Leh – over the Pensi La – becomes the most difficult after the first heavy falls of snow. The Zanskaris then choose the alternative and harder trail to Markha and Leh over high passes which are not subject to heavy snow during early winter and late spring. In the middle of winter an even simpler route is open to the villagers. From late January and February, when the Zanskar River is frozen over, the villagers descend straight down through the Zanskar gorges, a route involving no passes or snow drifts. A journey to Leh can then be completed in a week.

ENSI LA TO PADUM

he road between the Suru Valley and
anskar is generally under snow until
rly June. So a trek to Padum at this time
ll be free of vehicles. By late October the
st snows cut Padum off from the Pensi
a and I recently spent 10 very satisfying
ys trekking through the snow from
adum to Kargil. At this time a sense of
e old world seems to return to this part
Zanskar with yak trains and lamas on
rses plodding their way from village to
lage.

age 1: Pensi La-Abran

verage walking time 5-6 hours)
scending from the campsite the trail
oids the jeep track until it meets the
de plains of the upper Stod Valley. A
etalled bridge has been constructed
er the Pholoki River and the trail cuts
ross the undulating pasture land and
wn to the first main village of Abran. On
ny sections of this route you can short
t the jeep track and follow the lines of
ni walls which mark the former pony
il.

For those not carrying tents, there is a
ge cave shelter up a side valley about
o km beyond the base of the Pensi La.
owever, during the season it is generally
cupied by shepherds from Abran.

age 2: Abran-Phe

verage walking time 4-5 hours)
is is an easy stage so, if you're feeling
, you can easily continue to Tungri the
me day. But why hurry? The day's walk
sses through a number of interesting
lages, Hamiling being the largest. The
lagers are remarkably friendly as most
urists do not actually stop en route
less their truck breaks down. The wide
cial valley is one of the most fertile in
nskar. Opposite Phe is the Bardan
lley and the route to Umasi La and
shtwar. To reach this valley, however,
u must continue to the bridge at Tungri
d return on the opposite bank.
An alternative walk-in is to ford the

Stod River above Abran, a crossing that
can be completed safely in late autumn.
From here continue down the opposite
bank to the Bardan Valley and Tungri.
The crossing at Abran can also provide
immediate access to the difficult Hagshu
Valley trail to Kishtwar.

Stage 3: Phe-Tungri-Karsha/Padum

From Phe it is a three hour trek to Tungri,
where the trail splits to Karsha and
Padum. It's a further three hours to each.
The camping site at Tungri beside the
Stod River is an ideal base for a round trip
to either Karsha or Padum. Tungri can
also be used as base for a day's trek up the
Bardan Valley and a visit to the Zongkhul
monastery. The monastery's foundation
is associated with the Indian sage Naropa,
who meditated in the surrounding caves.
The monastery belongs to the Drukpa
order and supports about 20 monks.

Continuing to Padum the trail crosses
the Tungri bridge and cuts across the
undulating alluvial plains. Halfway to
Padum you pass the village of Sani and the
ancient monastery built at the same time
as Alchi in the 11th century. Like Alchi,
the gompa complex is set in an open
valley, instead of using a cliff site like
other monasteries in the region. Legend
has it that Naropa meditated at Sani at the
site of the impressive Kanika chorten,
which may even pre-date the monastery.

Padum, apart from being the administrative centre of Zanskar, holds little
interest. Incongruous government buildings
are being constructed and the atmosphere
is definitely not as serene as in the
outlying villages. It is advisable to camp
below the village, beside the Lunak River
(Tsarap Chu). Valuable fodder is grown
here and horses must be taken further
afield for grazing.

There is a sizeable Muslim community
in Padum, and the original families are
related to the royal family at Zangla.
Most, however, settled during the 1830s,
during the time of Zorowar Singh's
invasion. A ruined fort below the village of

Pibiting is a reminder of the Dogra invasion in Zanskar.

KARSHA TO LAMAYURU

This demanding trek traverses seven passes en route to Lamayuru, five of which are over 4500 metres, the highest being the Singi La at 5100 metres. It is a rugged route by any standards but is the only way to see the incredible gorge country in this western extremity of the Tibetan plateau. Many permanent villages and settlements manage to eke out an existence in these wilderness areas and provide an attractive dimension to the trek. A minimum of 10 days should be allowed to complete this trek.

Karsha

The monastery, the largest in Zanskar, is occupied by nearly 100 monks who live in the labyrinthine quarters below the gompa. The monks come from Karsha village and the outlying areas between Padum, Pibiting and Abran, and return to their villages each autumn to receive contributions of grain and donations for the monastery. The festival at Karsha takes place in late January and provides a colourful relief from the bleak winter conditions. The monastery site was founded in the 11th century during the time of Rinchen Zangpo. The construction of the main monastery complex was completed later in the 14th century as the Delgupta order consolidated itself in Ladakh and Zanskar.

In order to reach Karsha directly from Padum you must cross the Stod River. There is a raft for hire below Karsha for a nominal sum, or by mid-September you can wade through the none-too-warm waters. Should the raft be unavailable you will have little option but to go via the bridge at Tungri and from there down valley to Karsha. There is no camping area in the immediate vicinity of Karsha and the closest spot to pitch a tent by clear waters is on the plains a few km below the main village.

Stage 1: Karsha-Pishu

(Average walking time 4-5 hours)

From Karsha the trail descends across t windy plains to the village at Rinam; th follows the course of the Zanskar River Pishu. It's an easy stage, which allow time to detour to the Zangla 'twig' bridg visit Zangla and return to Pishu evening. There is a campsite below Pish village on open grazing land by the riv

Stage 2: Pishu-Hanamur

(Average walking time 4-5 hours)

Another level stage with the trail frequen skirting the banks of the Zanskar. T village of Pidmu is halfway and there i river bank campsite below the sm sheltered settlement of Hanamur. T villages of Pishu, Pidmu and Hanamu together with Chazar and Honia on t opposite bank, 'belong' to the form kingdom of Zangla. Zangla is not overly large kingdom and Hanamur is t last village you encounter in Zanskar.

Stage 3: Hanamur-Nechhe

(Average walking time 5 hours)

A difficult stage for horses which m have to be unloaded as the trail win steadily up to the Purfi La. There a many conifer roots on the steep ban beyond the trail as this area was qu extensively forested till villagers a erosion denuded the area.

From the Purfi La there is a steep 50 metre descent down the juniper hillside the Zingchan Tokpo. Halfway down the is a campsite and springline sufficient a small party.

The bridge over the Zingchan Tok marks the boundary between Zanskar a Ladakh, another potential campsite. It i further two or three km over the ridge the settlement at Nechhe. The settleme consists of a small system of shelte burrowed into the ground. The subsister farmers are most hospitable and c provide goat curd, tsampa and salt t The campsite is below the settlement the end of the willowgrove.

age 4: Nechhe-Haluma La-Lingshet

(verage walking time 5-6 hours)
he trail from Nechhe ascends the valley,
hich is a tributary of the Zingchan
okpo. Expect delays in July and August
high water in the gorges often destroy
e trails. If unduly delayed there are
me shepherd encampments where you
n camp below the pass.

A climb from Nechhe to the Haluma La
800 metres) should take three to four
purs and is by no means steep. The
ward is a wonderful view towards the
ngi La and the distant snow covered
ok range to the north-east. Lingshet
onastery can be seen in the distance.

From the pass it's a steep 750-metre
escent and a ridge crossing over to
ngshet – a very tiring climb if you're
ming in the opposite direction. The
mping area at Lingshet, complete with
rings, is just below the main trail about
e km before the monastery.

The monastery complex at Lingshet is
ry similar to Karsha, with the monastery
d monks' quarters, set on a hillside,
ominating the village below. It was
unded by the Delgupta order in the 14th
ntury, although the original monastery
e, first used in the 11th century, is
rther down the valley. The ruins indicate
at it may have been one of the 108
onasteries Rinchen Zangpo is reputed
have founded in west Tibet.

There are normally 20 or 30 monks in
tendance at Lingshet and the monastery
rvices the outlying villages at Nirag,
ilchang and Skumpata.

From Lingshet there is a trail across
untry to Rangdum. It crosses the Kesi
a, immediately north of the Haluma La,
en the Pingdon La and goes down valley
where the trail meets the track from the
anji La. The local horsemen informed
e that it takes three days to Rangdum
th horses by this route.

age 5: Lingshet-Camp below Singi La

verage walking time 5-6 hours)
though the monks trek to Photaskar in
one stage, it would be a killer for all but the
super-fit, so camp below the Singi La. The
trail from Lingshet winds over the Netuke
La and the Khupate La and then on to the
base of the Singi La. Between these two
minor passes is the settlement at Skimpata.
Two or three km before reaching camp a
trail diverges down past the lone yak
herder's camp at Yulchang, to the Zanskar
River and the settlement at Nirag.

The adequate, albeit rocky campsite
below the Singi La is beside a springline
which eventually cascades down to the
Zanskar River, 1500 metres below.

Stage 6: Base of Singi La-Singi La-Photaskar

(Average walking time 5-6 hours)
The climb up the rather steep scree slope
takes about two hours. Frozen waterfalls
from the limestone cliffs are an impressive
sight above the trail. The Singi La (Lion
Pass), at 5100 metres, is the highest en
route to Lamayuru. Heavy snowfall on this
pass prevents movement between winter
and late spring. From the pass you can
appreciate the lie of the country across to
the Shirshi La beyond Photaskar.

The trail down takes three or four
hours, a gradual descent to the Photang
Valley and a campsite at one of the grazing
areas upstream from Photaskar village.

At Photaskar, just above the village,
there are two small gompas, both of the
older Tibetan Kargypa orders.

Stage 7: Photaskar-Shirshi La-Honupatta

(Average walking time 6 hours)
From Photaskar it's a long and tiring haul
to the Shirshi La. The views towards the
main Zanskar range are ample compensation though and the climb is especially
well worth making in the early morning.
From the top of the pass there is a possible
trail to the upper Shilakong Valley and
then over the Yogma La to Kanji and
Heniskot.

In summer the descent to Honupatta
takes 2½ hours, through a wilderness area
that supports abundant wildlife.

In late autumn it's possible to descend directly from the village of Photaskar to the gorges of the Photang Valley. This route by-passes Honupatta and continues direct to Phanji village. However local advice must be sought before taking this route.

Stage 8: Honupatta-Wanlah
(Average walking time 5 hours)
From Honupatta the trail descends three or four km until it meets the Photang Valley. Some river crossings may be necessary. From the confluence the river cuts a deep gorge for two or three km making the valley trails difficult in times of high water. Over the last few years the trail has been up-graded in places to overcome this problem. The valley opens out about two or three km above Phanji, and from there it is a further five or six km to Wanlah (as per the Alchi-Lamayuru trek).

Stage 9: Wanlah-Lamayuru
(Average walking time 3-4 hours)
From Wanlah follow the Shilakong Valley upstream for two km to the gully turn-off to the Prinkiti La. The gully entrance is marked with prayer flags and small chortens. It is recommended to complete the gradual two hour ascent in the early morning while the gully is still in shade.

The descent to Lamayuru from the pass takes about one hour – to the camping area immediately below the main village. The simple hotels that have been constructed in the village and at the monastery serve *thupa* and even cold beer.

PADUM TO LEH
This demanding trek crosses three 5000-metre passes. Between Zangla and the Markha Valley the trail winds through spectacular gorges and across windswept ridges, way beyond the limit of human habitation. It has become a natural reserve for goat herds, bears and wolves. A naturalist could spend many weeks here studying the wildlife migration – and it's an ideal area for national park designation. A

local guide is essential on this trek as the trails are by no means easy to follow. you're doing this trek in July and Augu great care must be taken with the nume ous river crossings.

Stage 1: Padum-Zangla
(Average walking time 7 hours)
From Padum the trail to Zangla cross the main bridge over the Tsarap Chu ar follows the well graded track to Tongd Overlooking Tongde is an impressi monastery affiliated with Karsha. Th trail then passes Chilingkit and Chaza There is a marshy campsite one km befo the main village of Zangla.

Four km above Zangla is *the* twig brid of Zanskar. The original rope suppor span nearly 40 metres across the turbule Zanskar River. Crossing it on windy da is out of the question and ponies a prohibited at any time.

Ladakh and Zanskar are famous f dogs, big and small. The first sign royalty in Zangla is the two regal co dogs lurking around the kings's palac The King of Zangla, now in his mid-70s, most hospitable and chuckles away behi his heavy framed glasses while he co ducts audiences in his quarters. He trac his family line from Ladakh, and althou the royal lineage was split between Padu and Zangla, it continued until the time Zorowar Singh's invasion. While the Ki of Padum would not submit to Dogra ru and was killed, the Zangla family reache a compromise and were allowed maintain nominal rule over the near villages. The head lama at Spitok related to this family, and also presid over the Zangla monastery, located on th cliff just beyond the village.

Stage 2: Zangla-Sumdo
(Average walking time 3 hours)
Follow the trail beyond the chortens ar up past the former palace, high above th Zumlung Chu. The trail climbs this valle crossing the river many times. There is campsite eight km along where the vall

pens out on to a wooded grazing area. ere the trail splits; the route to the harcha La follows a side valley, while the ain valley continues to the Ningri La and n to an upper tributary of the Tsarap hu.

tage 3: Sumdo-Charcha La-Camp
Average walking time 6 hours)
ollow the trail to the immediate west of e campsite for two km, then ascend the de valley to the north. The climb to the ass is quite strenuous for those not fully cclimatised. The huge glacial steps every 00 or 300 metres make the going a little asier before a final steep ascent to the ass at a height of 5200 metres. The verage time to the pass is about four ours. The Charcha La is marked with a bstantial chorten and the view extends cross the range beyond Zangla to the ain Himalaya. The descent over the pass the first campsite takes two hours.

tage 4: Camp-Tilatsumdo
Average walking time 6 hours)
are must be taken when making the umerous river crossings. Six hours is the verage autumn walking time. In mid-ummer the many crossings may mean aving to allow an extra day. It may be ecessary to exploit the lower river onditions in the morning and camp by id-day at the latest. There are plenty of ntermediary campsites, easily disting-ished by the thousands of sheep roppings around them, a legacy of the erds taken this way in late autumn by the nepherds en route to Zanskar to trade ool for grain.

There are many wolf and bear droppings n the trail also and it isn't hard to imagine ears sheltering in caves high in the rocky utcrops. One particular limestone cave ve km before Tilatsumdo is of special nportance because of its *lingam*, or hallic image of Lord Shiva. Local tradition ays that barren women should prostrate nemselves on this rocky mound in order regain their fertility.

Warning On some maps and guide books there is a trail marked going down the Khurna River from Tilatsumdo to the Zanskar River then on over to the confluence of the Markha Valley. This track is probably an alternative winter trail connecting Zangla to lower Zanskar and the Indus. There is *no* summer trail along the Zanskar River between the junction of the Khurna River and the Markha Valley.

Stage 5: Tilatsumdo-Camp below Rubarung La
(Average walking time 5-6 hours)
The trail climbs alongside the Khurna River for one hour to Khurnasumdo, then diverges along the left-hand gully to a narrow gorge which marks the ancient border between Zanskar and Ladakh. Ponies may have to be unloaded for about one km. The trail to Rubarung La extends up the valley for a further seven or eight km to a camping area some two km below the base of the pass.

You may encounter Champa nomads, employed to graze a herd of horses from the villages in the Rupshu region. The Champa may be directly related to the Tibetan shepherds who originally pop-ulated the Ladakhi hillsides. They still live without permanent settlement in tents made of yak hair, and rely on the produce of their herds of yaks, goats and sheep. They either barter or sell their services for grain, exploiting their ability to roam the mountain pastures from season to season.

Stage 6: Base Camp-Rubarung La-Markha
(Average walking time 6 hours)
The climb to Rubarung La takes two hours, up through a gully which opens out just below the pass. To the north the Stok range is clearly visible. Three km below the pass there is a springline and a possible campsite for trekkers coming in the opposite direction from Markha.

The descent to the Markha Valley takes up to four hours down the Chacham Valley through impressive gorge country and huge limestone outcrops. Markha village is a further two km downstream from where the Chacham Chu meets the Markha River.

From Markha the trek to Leh can be completed in three or four stages, either by continuing down the Markha Valley to Skiu and then crossing the Gandha La and the Namlung La to Leh; or ascending through Hankar to Nimaling and then crossing the Gongmaru La to Hemis and Leh. Details as per the Markha Valley trek in the Ladakh section.

PADUM TO DARCHA

A decade ago this trek extended through Lahaul and over the Rhotang Pass to Manali and would have taken a minimum of two weeks. Nowadays, with a road through to Darcha, the trek can be completed in a week. A trek up the Lunak Valley provides some rich examples of Zanskari village life before the trail traverses the main Himalaya at the Shingo La – at a height of 5300 metres.

Stage 1: Padum-Reru
(Average walking time 6 hours)
The trail follows the Tsarap Chu along the dusty foundations of the jeep track through the villages to Trakkar and Bardan. There is a campsite and spring just after Bardan monastery if a late start is made from Padum. The monastery is attached to Sani and most of its 30 monks live at Sani during the summer. It belongs to the Drukpa sect and was built in the 17th century shortly after Hemis monastery. It is now affiliated with Stakna gompa from which it receives some financial aid. The monastery is at present being reconstructed and renovated; the original wall paintings, in particular, are in a poor state of repair.

From Bardan to Reru the trail is under reconstruction. En route is the Mune gompa, founded by the Delgupta order and dating from the 15th century. Below Mune there is a springline, large enough to support a small camp. However, there is better campsite four or five km further c beside the Reru Chu. A detour can b made on the way, to the village of Re which is off the main trail.

Note The difficult trail to the Poat La an the Chandrabhaga Valley follows th Temasa Valley from just below Mune.

Stage 2: Reru-Purni
(Average walking time 6 hours)
From Reru the trail descends steeply the main river valley and the village Ichar on the opposite bank. For thos coming from Bardan there is a campsi and spring below Ichar village. The tra between Ichar and Sule goes throug some impressive gorge country and ther are few campsites. You could cross th rope bridge and camp at Char, howeve ponies will have to continue to Pur where there is a better campsite at th junction of the Tsarap Chu and Kargy Chu.

Stage 3: Purni-Phugtal-return
(Average walking time 4 hours return)
A side trip to Phugtal monastery is a mus The monastery, one of the most impressiv in Zanskar, has been carved right out the mountain wall and set in a hug limestone cave. The monastic site date back to the 11th century, though th present structure was developed on pa with Karsha during the 15th century. normally has over 50 monks in attendanc and the monastery administers many the smaller Delgupta gompas betwee Reru and Kargya. In the monastery ther is also an inscription to the Hungaria Tibetan scholar, Coso dre Koros, wh studied at Phugtal for a year in 1825/2

Stage 4: Purni-Kargya
(Average walking time 6 hours)
Re-cross the bridge over the Kargya Chu The trail continues through Testa an Kuru before re-crossing the river by th bridge below Tanze. A trail diverges from

here to the Phitse La and the Baralacha La. The main trail continues for four or ve km to Kargya, the last village en route ● the Shingo La. Camp beside the river mmediately below the impressive row of ●hortens.

If you have time, explore the valley nmediately opposite Kargya. An extended eriod could be spent exploring the glacial ystems at the head of this valley which xtend into the main Himalaya range.

Stage 5: Kargya-Lakong
(Average walking time 5 hours)
The trail to Lakong stays on the east side ● the Kargya Chu, winding across yak astures used by the herdsmen till late utumn. After four hours the trail crosses ●e upper reaches of the river and a short :eep climb takes you to the base of the ●hingo La. The only shelter here is a small :one yak herders' hut, sometimes ccupied.

Stage 6: Lakong-Shingo La-Rumjack
(Average walking time 6-7 hours)
The climb to the Shingo La should take ●vo to three hours, with the trail ascending :eeply before traversing the main ridge ●elow the pass. You are now in the heart of ●e great Himalaya, amid hanging glaciers ●nd unclimbed 6000-metre peaks. The ●escent traverses the glacier immediately ●elow the pass, crossing lateral moraine to goat track 500 metres below. Continuing ●own the goat track, Rumjack provides a ●easonable shepherd campsite. Alternat-●ely, you could descend further to the ●nfluence of the Shingo stream and the ●arai River.

Stage 7: Rumjack-Darcha
(Average walking time 6-7 hours)
●rom Rumjack the trail descends to the ●arai River. It is possible to cross the river ●y snow bridge early in the season; ●owever, by July/August extreme caution

should be exercised in crossing this swift flowing river. The trail then descends to the far side through boulder fields and grazing land with the occasional silver birch tree. After 10 km the trail re-crosses the river, this time by a stone bridge. It is then four or five km down valley to Darcha.

At Darcha there is a police checkpost and also some small hotels that sell biscuits and basics. There is a regular bus and truck service to Manali via Keylong and the Rhotang Pass, but it's not for the faint hearted.

For those undertaking a trek out of Manali it is essential to approach the Shingo La very slowly. Two stages should be allowed to reach the Barai River crossing and a further two higher camps before crossing the Shingo La. To push your itinerary harder would invite the problem of high altitude sickness.

Himachal Pradesh

The state of Himachal Pradesh, in its present form, only came into being in 1966 following the partition of the Punjab into Punjab and Haryana. Essentially a mountain state, Himachal Pradesh is the transition zone from the plains to the mighty Himalaya and in the trans-Himalayan region of Lahaul and Spiti it actually crosses that high barrier to the Tibetan plateau. It's a delightful place to visit especially during the hot season when people flock to its hill stations to escape the searing heat of the plains.

The main attractions of Himachal Pradesh include Simla, once the 'summer capital' of British India and still one of India's most important hill stations; and the lush green Kulu Valley, without doubt one of the most beautiful places on earth with the snow-capped Himalayan peaks as a backdrop and the sparkling Beas River running through it. Then there's Dharamsala, home-in-exile for the Dalai Lama, a host of other mountains, hill stations, lakes and walks and in the far north of the state the snow melts for the brief summer to allow visitors to explore the Tibetan culture of Keylong in Lahaul and Spiti.

There is a wide variety of trekking possibilities in the region which, as yet, have barely been exploited. The Himachal Pradesh Tourist Office can supply a booklet titled *Trekkers' Guide to Himachal Pradesh* which concentrates on treks in the Kulu and Manali area and they also have three excellent large scale maps of the whole state.

Equipment and provisions will depend very much on where you plan to trek. In the lower country of the Kulu and Kangra Valleys, or around Simla, there are many rest houses and villages. On the other hand the sparse population and more severe conditions in Lahaul and Spiti mean you will need to be much better

equipped in terms of cold weather gea food and equipment. There are a gre number of *Forest Rest Houses, PWD Re Houses* and other semi-official accom modation possibilities along the Himach Pradesh trekking routes. Enquire at loc tourist offices about using these place before setting off.

The treks out of the Kulu Valley a Himachal Pradesh's answer to Pahalga and the Lidder Valley. The immediacy the mountains in the Kulu Valley mak trekking a logical extension of any visi and from Mandi, Jagatsukh and Naga treks can be made to Beas Kund an Chandertal as well as over the Pir Panj passes to Lahaul.

Lahaul, the barren region to the north Kulu, is often regarded as a transit area f trekkers en route to the popular trails the Zanskar. Yet Lahaul has possibilitie in its own right, both to the Baralacha L or down the Chenab Valley to Kishtwar Chamba. Lahaul also has one advantag over its immediate neighbours; the regio is beyond the influence of the monsoo and enjoys an uninterrupted trek seaso from June onwards.

The states of Chamba and Kangra bot reflect a rich cultural heritage and som thing of this can be appreciated on the h trails. Kangra state is known to man because of the hill station of Dharamsal the home of the Dalai Lama. From ther treks are made over the Dhaula Dhar t the Ravi Valley and Chamba.

From Chamba the choice is open. Trai continue over the Pir Panjal to Kishtwa and Lahaul while extended treks leadin on to the Zanskar Valley and Ladak regions can be undertaken with wel equipped parties. These regions, togethe with Kulu, come under the monsoon influence and the ideal time for trekking i Himachal Pradesh is during the pos monsoon period of September-October.

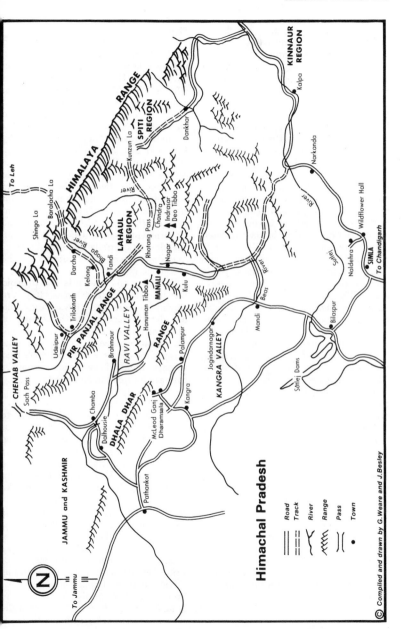

Himachal Pradesh

	Road
	Track
	River
	Range
	Pass
•	Town

© Compiled and drawn by G. Weare and J. Besley

KINNAUR REGION

SPITI REGION

HIMALAYA RANGE

LAHAUL REGION

To Leh

Shingo La

Baralacha La

Kunzun La

Dankhar

Narkanda

Wildflower Hall

SIMLA

To Chandigarh

Bhaga River

Chandra River

Rhotang Pass

Indrasor Deo Tibbo

Darcha

Kelong

Tandi

Nagar

Kulu

Beas River

Sutlej River

Naldehra

Bilaspur

Mandi

Sutlej Dams

Triloknath

Udaipur

PIR PANJAL RANGE

RAVI VALLEY

Hanuman Tibba

MANALI

RANGE

Jogindarnagar

KANGRA VALLEY

CHENAB VALLEY

Sach Pass

Brahmaur

Chamba

Dalhousie

DHALA DHAR

McLeod Ganj Dharamsala

Palampur

Kangra

Pathankot

JAMMU and KASHMIR

To Jammu

N

Many interesting day walks can also be made out of Simla, while treks can be undertaken from the Sutlej Valley over to Kulu during the early spring and late autumn when other passes in Himachal Pradesh are under snow.

SIMLA

In the days before independence Simla was the most important British hill station and during the hot season became the 'summer capital' of India.

It was first surveyed by the Gerald brothers, two Scottish military officers, in 1817. Immediately prior to this, Simla and the nearby hill states had been over-run by the Gurkhas. The local Rajahs requested assistance from the British, which resulted in the Gurkha wars of 1814-15. The Simla hill states were annexed by the British and returned to the local Rajahs, though Simla was later purchased by the British political agent. The first permanent house was built in 1822 but it wasn't until years later that Simla became the semi-official capital. As the heat built up on the plains each year, first the memsahibs, then the sahibs, or at least those who could escape, made their way to the cool alpine air of Simla. The high flown social life of Simla in the summer was legendary and even today the town still has a distinctive British air about it.

The British lost little time in surveying mountain trails across the Punjab Himalaya. Guide books of the time detail the various trekking stages out of Simla to Kulu, Dharamsala and Leh, and it was not considered out of the ordinary to walk for months on end, either on a tour of duty or vacation.

Following independence, Simla became the headquarters of the Punjab administration until the creation of Chandigarh. In 1966, when the Punjab was broken into the Punjab and Haryana, Simla became the capital of the newly formed state of Himachal Pradesh.

Places to Stay

There is no shortage of accommodation in Simla; there are now over 100 hotels, mostly in the vicinity of The Mall and main bazaar. The Himachal Pradesh Tourist Offices in The Mall and at the bus station can help you find a place during the peak domestic tourist seasons from April to June, and in September and October.

Simla's two most famous hotels are the *Cecil* and the *Grant*, both operated by the Oberoi chain. Cecil's is currently being renovated. Other up-market hotels include the *Woodville Palace*, about one km beyond The Mall, and the nearby *Grant Hotel*. The Himachal Pradesh Government *Holiday Home* is pushed hard by the Government Tourist Office. It's clean, friendly and centrally located but it lacks the atmosphere and character of the Woodville Palace.

For peace and quiet it is best to avoid the busy Mall/bazaar areas. If you're staying for more than a few days it would be ideal to check into a cottage or timbered house similar to those at Manali. This, however, is easier said than done, as many of the concrete flats on Simla's best vantage points have become summer cottages for rich Indian tourists.

Getting There

To get to Simla by rail involves a change from broad gauge to narrow gauge at Kalka, a little north of Chandigarh. The narrow gauge trip to Simla takes nearly six hours. Add on two or more hours to change train at Kalka plus the trip from Delhi and you'll find it much faster to take the bus. On the other hand the train trip is great fun! The fare from Delhi to Simla is Rs 287 air-con class, Rs 150 first class, and Rs 30 second class.

The deluxe bus from Delhi to Simla takes eight to 10 hours and costs Rs 80-120. There are also deluxe and local bus services between Chandigarh and Simla. From Simla there are also deluxe buses to Manali (via Mandi) daily throughout the season, twice weekly at other times. If you're continuing on to Dharamsala you must change local buses at Mandi, while for Kashmir it is quicker to return to Chandigarh and get the night train to Pathankot and Jammu.

Treks

With the development of roads along the Simla ridge it is no longer recommended to trek direct from Simla. Nevertheless, there are many day walks in and around Simla. The Simla hills are comprised of Jakhu Hill to the immediate west of The Mall, and Summer Hill and Prospect Hill to the east, where the the ridge splits into two spurs. Following the bridle trails is no problem.

To climb Jakhu Hill, follow the trail behind the cathedral, up to Jakhu Temple. Dedicated to the monkey god Hanuman the temple is at an altitude of 2455 metres near the highest point of the Simla ridge. This spot is renowned for its fine views, especially at sunrise, of Simla, the surrounding valleys and out to the snow-capped peaks of the Himalaya. The temple is a 45-minute walk from The Mall. The walks to Prospect and Summer Hills take about half a day and there are fine views back down to the plains. If you have time a visit to Chadwick Falls, beyond Summer Hill, is also recommended. The falls are 67-metres high and are at their best during the monsoon.

Beyond Simla day walks can also be undertaken from Wildflower Hall, Naldehra and Narkanda.

Wildflower Hall, 13 km beyond Simla and at 2593 metres was the former residence of Indian commander-in-chief, Lord Kitchener. The present huge mansion surrounded by pines is not the original one built for Kitchener though. Naldehra, 23 km from Simla, was Lord Curzon's escape from the dispatch boxes of Simla, while Narkanda is 64 km from Simla along the Tibet/Hindustan road. It is this road you take to reach the Sutlej Valley and the treks to the Kulu Valley. Spending a few days at Narkanda is highly recommended;

the views are superb, while for trekkers a climb to the nearby Hattu Peak is a convenient way to get fit and acclimatise for the days ahead.

Accommodation at Wildflower Hall is at the hall itself, now a Himachal Pradesh government hotel, while both Narkanda and Naldehra have comfortable Rest Houses. Bookings can be made from the Tourist Office in Simla. Wildflower Hall costs Rs 100-150; while Narkanda and Naldehra are Rs 40-60, room only.

From Narkanda the highway winds down to the Sutlej Valley and continues to the Kinnaur and Spiti regions. Both regions are subject to inner line restrictions, and permission is needed to proceed beyond the town of Rampur.

Bearing this in mind there are two treks into the Kulu Valley. One trail over the Jalori Pass has been made into a fair-weather jeep/minibus road, while the second trail over the Bashleo Pass is an ideal four-to-five-day trek from Rampur. The trek has an additional advantage; it can be undertaken both in early spring – March/April, and also in late autumn/early winter until mid-December.

The trail to the Bashleo Pass is not steep and the pass height at 3600 metres should not present difficulties. The ridge divides the region of Inner and Outer Saraj, a subdivision of the Kulu administration. The walking stages are conveniently set between the villages, and the *Forest Rest Houses* ensure that a tent isn't essential. The pass is crossed normally on the third day, from where it is a further two stages to the Banjar/Largi road. From there you can either return to Simla by minibus, or continue to Largi, where there are regular buses to Kulu and Manali.

The Kulu Valley

The original name for the Kulu Valley was *Kulantapith* – the end of the habitable world. It is a narrow alpine valley drained

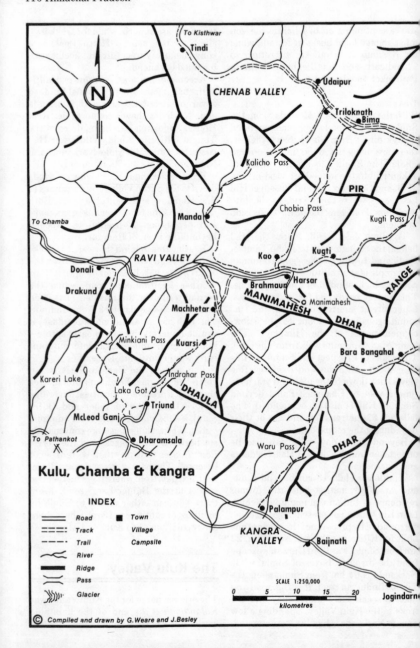

Kulu, Chamba & Kangra

INDEX

Road	■ Town
Track	Village
Trail	Campsite
River	
Ridge	
Pass	
Glacier	

© Compiled and drawn by G.Weare and J.Besley

SCALE 1:250,000

0   5   10   15   20

kilometres

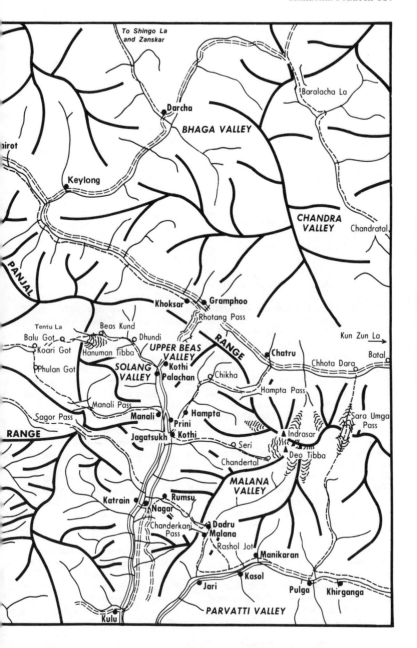

by the Beas River and enclosed by the Pir Panjal to the north, the Bara Bangahal range to the west and the Parvatti range to the east. The Rajahs who ruled the valley preserved Kulu's rich cultural heritage. Each mountain, stream and river confluence in this beautiful valley is sanctified to honour the numerous Hindu gods so it is hardly surprising that Kulu has been known as the Valley of the Gods.

For centuries the Kulu kingdom was restricted to the upper Beas Valley, with the original capital at Jagatsukh. The Kulu Rajahs' influence extended between Sultanpur (Kulu) and the Rhotang Pass and it was not until the 15th century that the Kulu boundaries extended south beyond the Largi gorge to Mandi. During the 17th century the capital was transferred again from Nagar to Kulu and the kingdom's boundaries extended north to Lahaul and Spiti, and east as far as the Sutlej.

The Kulu Rajahs held the important trade route from the Indian plains to the Himalayan state of Ladakh and beyond. It was contested by both Sansar Chand from Kangra, and later for the Sikhs during their brief periods of power. After 1847 Kulu, along with the other Punjab hill states, came under British authority and was administered from Dharamsala.

The British appointed a District Officer, and communities from Simla and beyond began to settle in the valley. The routes over the Jalori Pass were followed from Simla, while the principal route from the plains and Kangra was via the Dulchi Pass to the south-west of the Kulu Valley. The first road into the valley, up the Largi Gorge, was not completed until 1927. For many of the British settlers this was the beginning of the end of the peace and serenity of the valley, and many of the established families were on their way home before 1947.

The Kulu Valley today is still beautiful and a welcome haven after the long, tiring bus ride from Delhi. The valley's size enhances its popularity; the bazaars at Kulu and Manali can be easily explored on foot, while the outlying villages at Jagatsukh, Nagar and the nearby Parvatti Valley can be reached in an hour or two from Kulu or Manali.

Getting Ready

Most provisions for the trek can be bought in Kulu or Manali, while stocks should also be purchased here if you're going on to Lahaul and Zanskar. Kerosene shortages are sometimes a problem in the Manali bazaar and a trip to Kulu may be necessary.

Horsemen at some trek-off points such as Palachan and Jagatsukh are in great demand so they should be arranged in advance out of Manali. Their rates are quite high, about Rs 50, but could be cheaper if you're taking three or four horses.

If you're travelling light, a local porter is a logical alternative as the usual daily rate is Rs 30-40 per day with some food provided by you. If the trek is going higher and involves a pass crossing, then Rs 40-50 is the going rate. The rates for guides and cooks varies between Rs 50-100 per day; cooks are particularly expensive as they may be in demand in the hotels or on the lucrative treks through the Zanskar.

Trekking Agents

Trekking organisation in the Kulu Valley is not as developed as in Kashmir. There are no pony-wallah unions, or set government rates for trek stages. There is also a lack of camping equipment for hire or purchase so tents and sleeping bags must be brought with you. Finding a good guide or cook is still a matter of wandering the bazaar, or enquiring at your hotel until someone turns up.

The Mountaineering Institute is a helpful intermediary, and a mine of information about local conditions. The staff can organise a complete trek outfit for you but they tend to be quite expensive if you're on a strict budget. Private agencies include West Himalayan Holidays, to all accounts a professional organisation; and International Trekkers and Kulu Expeditions which are both run by locals with guides, porters and allied staff.

Places to Stay

Although the Kulu Valley is a popular resort for the domestic tourist escaping the Indian plains in April and May, there is still no shortage of accommodation. The Himachal Government have built a number of hotels in the last decade in both Kulu and Manali. Besides these, the normal retreat is to one of the many guest houses, complete with verandah, open fire and often in the grounds of an orchard. It is a compliment to the valley authorities that no multi-storey hotels have been constructed and that what has been built, fits into the character of the valley. In the vicinity of the main bazaar there is cheaper basic accommodation for a few rupees a night.

In Kulu and Manali, the Government Tourist Offices seem, like their counterpart in Simla, to strongly recommend the government-run hotels. However, there are plenty of hotel 'card wallahs' in Manali, both outside the Tourist Office and at the bus stand, to help expand the selection. Neither Kulu nor Manali are large places and a short walk around town should turn up something to your taste and pocket.

Price-wise, rooms are more expensive from April to mid-June and from September to mid-October, particularly during the Dussehra festival time. Up-market hotels/ guest houses are about Rs 250 per double, full board, while in the middle range they are about Rs 80-100 per double with breakfast. On a budget, basic hotel rooms go from Rs 20 upwards and *Government Rest Houses* in outlying valley areas range from Rs 20-80 room only. Like Kashmir and Leh, many hotels are family-run and it's difficult to recommend a specific guest house or hotel. They all have their own attractions and are ideal for a rest before undertaking a trek.

Getting There

There are daily bus services – deluxe, super-deluxe and super-deluxe with video – from Delhi to Manali, or Kulu. The service normally takes 18 hours (about the length of four or five Hindi movies) and costs Rs 100 to Rs 180 per seat, depending on the facilities and the season.

It's an equally long journey from Kashmir to Manali. It can be completed in 16 hours travel time – the first day to Pathankot and the second from there to Manali, with stops everywhere along the way.

From Dharamsala there are regular bus services to Mandi and from there to Kulu, where you change for Manali. There is a non-stop deluxe bus service between Simla and Manali, taking the road via Mandi, while the road from Simla to the Kulu Valley via the Jalori Pass is suitable only for jeeps.

From Kulu to Manali there are regular local bus services to the various trek-off points. The bus fare from Manali to Nagar is about Rs 3. Taxis are a convenient alternative, particularly if sharing with a few people, and can cut the travelling time to a third. The taxi rates are about Rs 70-80 from Mandi to Nagar, while from the airport at Bhuntar to Manali the cost is about Rs 150.

Vayudoot have a regular flight between Delhi and Kulu to Bhuntar. The flights are daily during the peak seasons of April, May, September and October, and three times a week during the summer monsoon. The flight from Delhi costs Rs 425. Book well in advance in the high season. The flights are cancelled occasionally during the monsoon.

Treks

The treks out of the Kulu Valley are a superb introduction to trekking in India. There are spectacular camping possibilities after only a day or two's walk along the popular and well-defined trails up the Solang Valley or to Chandertal. If nothing else, these treks are an excellent fitness and acclimatisation exercise before going on to Ladakh and the Zanskar, while for those looking for an alternative to Kashmir, the Kulu Valley is a perfect choice.

Four treks are outlined in this section:
1. From Manali to Beas Kund and Hanuman Tibba.
2. From Jagatsukh to Chandertal to Deo Tibba base.
3. From Manali to Hampta Pass and Lahaul.
4. From Nagar to Malana and the Parvatti Valley.

Although it's possible to attempt the initial trek stages in May, heavy snow conditions are regularly encountered from late May right through June and possibly early July. June is generally a reliable pre-monsoon month, but you must be well prepared if going higher to cross the Pir Panjal or Bara Bangahal passes. This is especially true with the Hampta Pass into Lahaul. However, the Rhotang Pass – the road over the upper Beas Valley from Kulu to Lahaul – is normally open to vehicles by mid-June.

If you have no alternative but to visit Kulu in July and August then you'll just have to put up with the rain. It is heavy but seldom lasts for more than a few hours a day and the rewards at this time of the year include the summer flowers on the alpine slopes over 3000 metres.

The post-monsoon period from early September through till late October is the most reliable season for trekking. Pass crossings can then be made in relative comfort and extended treks can be completed well before the onset of the winter snows. Late season treks can also be undertaken over the Jabri Pass or the Dulchi Pass through till December, providing one of the few trekking opportunities in the Indian Himalaya at this time of the year.

The starting elevation for most treks out of the Kulu Valley is no more than 200 metres. It is therefore quite a climb up to the passes and days should be reserved to adjust and acclimatise before going higher. You would certainly be going too high too quickly for adequate safety if you went over the Hampta Pass (4200 metres) or Tentu Pass (just under 5000 metres) after just a few days of trekking.

The rivers and streams can be a particular problem in the early season from mid to late June, during the main snow melt. In the absence of snow bridges or newly constructed shepherd bridges, care must be taken with all crossings, and the deepest ones should be negotiated by mid-morning.

Another local hazard is the bears, who settle in the forest areas during the warmer months, so take extra care on these forest trails especially if you're moving at night. If in doubt make as much noise as possible and any bear *should* get off the trail.

MANALI TO BEAS KUND & THE SOLANG VALLEY

This is the most popular trek in the Kulu Valley. The three stages cover some magnificent scenery en route to the base of Hanuman Tibba. An extra day should be reserved at Beas Kund for exploring the upper Solang Valley. This trek can be extended by going over the Solang Pass and returning to the Kulu Valley via the Manali Pass, or by returning to the camp at Dhundi and circling the ridges of the upper Beas Valley to the road leading to the Rhotang Pass.

Before leaving Manali a day or two should be spent getting fit. An easy option is to cross the Manasulu nullah and explore the large village of Manaligarh and its ruined fortress.

The present site of Manali was originally called Dana, which means fodder, as it was once the last place horsemen could obtain supplies of fodder for their animals before crossing the Rhotang Pass. Later the area was known as Duff Dunbar in honour of the Scottish forest officer who did much to improve the bridges in the Kulu Valley in the 1850s and '60s. He also built Dunbar House, near Dunghri Temple. The temple itself is well worth the climb up through the forest. It is dedicated to the goddess Himma Devi who figures prominently in the Mahabharata and is one of the most influential goddesses in the valley.

Stage 1: Manali-Dhundi

From Manali there is a regular bus service to Palachan village on the main Manali/Rhotang road. The climb to Dhundi is a gradual ascent up a well-marked trail.

Stage 2: Dhundi-Beas Kund

Beyond Dhundi the Solang Valley narrows and the steep cliff sides force you to make a number of crossings over simple Gaddi bridges. The last two km involves a steep climb to the meadows and small lake of Beas Kund at 4100 metres. From Beas Kund there is an uninterrupted mountain panorama, including Hanuman Tibba, Ladahi peak and Mandi peak. Well worth a rest day here.

From Beas Kund a climb can also be made to Lady Lake, crossing the ridge to the east of the campsite. This affords even better views of Hanuman Tibba, while Indrasar and Deo Tibba can also be seen. From Beas Kund the trip to Lady Lake can be completed in a couple of hours. Alternatively, the descent direct from Lady Lake to the Solang Valley can be made to Bhaga thatch and from here on down to Dhundi, without returning to Beas Kund.

Stage 3: Beas Kund-Return

The return from Beas Kund to Palachan can be completed in a morning with a same day return to Manali. An alternative is to return to Dhundi and continue north, usually to Murhi and the upper Beas Valley below the Rhotang Pass. Two stages should be reserved for this return to Manali.

The ascent to the Solang Pass (commonly known as the Tentu La) is demanding. The three to four hour climb is steep and in the early part of the season there's plenty of soft snow and you'll have to boulder-hop up through the narrow gully. From the pass there are magnificent views of the Kulu Valley and the Parvatti Range. The descent to Balu Got, 10 km, makes for a longish day. Balu Got is a popular base camp beneath the west ridge of Hanuman Tibba.

You'll need a local guide to continue on from Balu Got back over the Manali Pass. Trail-finding is not easy and an intermediary camp is necessary before the pass crossing. The trail from Balu Got goes down valley initially to the Gaddi camp at Koari Got and from there up the adjacent valley to the meadow at Phulan Got. The following day you should get to the base camp at the snout of the glacier below the Manali Pass. The Manali Pass is not heavily crevassed and will not present problems to experienced trekkers. From the pass the normal camp is at Rani Sui, while the final stage involves a steep descent down through the forest at the outskirts of Manali.

JAGATSUKH TO CHANDERTAL

As with the Beas Kund trek, the walk to Chandertal can be completed in three comparatively easy stages. Additional days can be spent exploring the adjacent valleys, and the trek can be extended by returning to Jagatsukh and heading for the Hampta Pass and Lahaul.

It's about one hour by bus from Manali to Jagatsukh where again a day can be spent exploring this former capital of the Kulu Valley. Jagatsukh, under its original name Nast, was the capital prior to Manali at a time when traders from Spiti and Lahaul still held influence over the Beas Valley. The dilapidated fortress is a testimony to that era. The origins of the town can be traced back to the 8th century and the original foundations of the Sandya Devi Temple are also from this period. The temple was rebuilt sometime in the 15th century, and some of the carvings can still be appreciated.

Stage 1: Jagatsukh-Chikha

The first day's walk involves a steady climb, of three to four hours, up the well-defined forest trail to the alpine plateau of Chikha. There is no shortage of camping spots in this scenic area.

Stage 2: Chikha-Seri-Chandertal

From Chikha the trail levels out for about eight km climbing about 600 metres. The camp at Seri is in a spectacular setting beneath the south-west face of Deo Tibba (6001 metres). Seri is also famous for the rich array of wildflowers which bloom during the summer months. Using Seri as a base, the climb to Chandertal takes a further two to three hours. In the spring, the lake is still iced over and the snow underfoot makes for heavy going until late June-early July.

Stage 3: Seri-Return

From Seri the return trek to Jagatsukh can be completed in time to get the bus back to Manali the same day. Alternatively, the rest of the day can be spent preparing for the trek to the Hampta Pass.

MANALI TO LAHAUL via Hampta Pass

Although this trek is not physically challenging, the trail on the far side of the Hampta Pass is, in stages, steep and difficult to follow. A guide or experienced horseman is highly recommended, particularly with the spring river crossings on the far side of the pass. From the Chandra Valley at Chatru the trek can return over the Rhotang Pass, or continue up the spectacular Chandra Valley to the Baralacha La.

Stage 1: Manali-Hampta-Chikha

The initial stages involve some steep sections up through the settlements of Hampta village, about two to three hours beyond the roadhead at Prini. Above Hampta village there is a Tibetan settlement, Settan, established by Khampa refugees. Camp in the vicinity or continue above the tree-line to one of the many alpine camping areas, one of which is known as Chikha. Not to be confused with the Chikha camp on the Chandertal trek.

Chikha means 'the place of bears'.

Stage 2: Chandertal-Hampta Pass-Camp

It's a gradual climb up to the Hampta Pass and a camp below the pass is recommended if this is the first trek out of Manali. The upper valley leading to the col is a former glacial valley defined by huge rock spires and boulders. From the pass there are panoramic views towards Hanuman Tibba, the Lahaul Valley and the north face of Indrushan (6221 metres). From the pass, the trail descends very steeply and an ice axe or sturdy stick is a prized possession. After 300-400 metres descent there is a flat area with not too much scree that would be OK for camping.

Stage 3: Camp-Chatru

The descent to the Chandra Valley initially crosses the main nullah coming from the Indrushan glacier. Do not remain on the left bank. The trail descends steeply down over scree to the valley floor where you re-cross the main nullah by the Gaddhi bridge just above the confluence of the Chandra River. From there it is a further 1½ km to Chatru.

From Chatru you can drive back to Manali over the Rhotang Pass. Alternatively, the walk up to Gramphoo, essentially a summer work settlement for Nepalese road workers, is 16 km. The trail then ascends to the Rhotang Pass – 'the Pass of Bones'. This pass, like so many of the Pir Panjal passes, is noted for extremely high winds and severe snowfalls. The trek from the pass takes you straight down the upper Beas Valley, 2000 metres to Rahla where there is a basic shelter, or to Kothi and a comfortable Dak Bungalow before a short drive back to Manali.

NAGAR TO MALANA & THE PARVATTI VALLEY

A trek to the Malana Valley provides an

opportunity to visit a community which has remained isolated from the culture of the rest of the Kulu Valley. From the village of Malana the trek can continue to the Parvatti Valley, with its Hindu heritage, before returning to Kulu and Manali.

From Manali it takes about two hours by bus to Nagar. With its commanding position across the Kulu Valley, this town was once the main capital of the valley. Nagar castle has now been adapted as a comfortable tourist bungalow and a day or so can be reserved to explore the village. Nagar's principal attraction today is the Roerich gallery, where samples of the work of the famous painter and philosopher, Nicholas Roerich, are displayed. His reputation as one of the avant garde post-1917 Russian painters was enhanced during his stay in Kulu during the 1930s and '40s when he made Nagar his home.

Stage 1: Nagar-Rumsu-Camp

Depending on your itinerary it is a tiring climb up through Nagar to Rumsu village and then on through the forest trail to camp. There are many camping sites above Rumsu, and the choice depends on whether you want to cross the pass the following day, or take an additional stage and camp closer to the pass. The latter is recommended if this is your first trek.

Stage 2: Camp-Chanderkani Pass-Dadru Village

The trails above the villages cut through heavily forested terrain. There are many forest trails so don't lose the main path. At the pass the trail follows the Chanderkani ridge for a km or so and there are some superb views down the Kulu Valley. From the top of the pass there is a direct route that locals follow to Malana village. The descent is about 1500 metres, a treacherous trail when wet and not recommended. The horse trail is well-defined down to Dadru village. There are possible campsites above the village.

Stage 3: Dadru to Malana

Malana is a closed society with a separate language and different customs from the rest of the Kulu Valley. The villagers do not marry outsiders and until recently you needed a permit to enter the village.

The origin of the village is difficult to trace. The language is said to include some Tibetan words, yet in all probability these people came from the Indian plains many centuries ago. It was, for a long time, the custom in Malana to settle disputes before a local tribunal of priests who passed judgement in the name of the local god *Jamlu*.

When entering the village you must remain on the paths. Visiting the temples is prohibited, as is the wearing of leather in the village, and that includes leather walking boots.

From Malana there are two ways of trekking to the Parvatti Valley. The first involves a steep descent down the Malana gorge to Jari. At Jari there is a *Forest Rest House* and from there you can wander up-valley to Manikaran, or drive directly back to Kulu. The alternative route is to trek over a further ridge, the Rashol Jot at 3248 metres. It's a steep ascent and takes about four hours, with a descent to the Parvatti Valley and the villages of Kasol and Manikaran the following day. A day can be spent visiting the local temple and hot springs at Manikaran before catching the regular bus service back to Manali via Ghuntar and Kulu.

Lahaul

North of the Rhotang Pass the geography of the Himalaya changes. From the alpine valleys of Kulu the mountains of Lahaul appear bare and rugged, the valleys devoid of forest and lush vegetation. It is a

land which would have appeared to the ancient traveller as being beyond the habitable world; a land which marks the southern limit of the Tibetan plateau.

Geographically, Lahaul is divided into two regions: Upper Lahaul consists of the Chandra and Bhaga Valleys; Lower Lahaul is the land below the confluence of the Chandra/Bhaga Rivers in the Chenab Valley, which flows west through the Pangi district and on to Kishtwar. To the east of Lahaul are the sparsely populated valleys of Spiti and Kinnaur. The region is bounded by Ladakh to the north, Kulu to the south and Tibet to the east.

Only 117 km from Manali this Tibetan region is quite unlike the Kulu Valley. As in Ladakh, little rain gets over the Himalayan barrier so Lahaul and Spiti are dry and mostly barren. The air is sharp and clear and the warm summer days are followed by cold, crisp nights. Beware of the sun in this region – you can get burnt very quickly even on cool days. The heavy winter snows from September to May close the passes, isolating the region for all but the brief summer months.

In many ways, Lahaul's historical background runs parallel with that of Ladakh. Accounts recall how sages crossed the Rhotang Pass, the Kun Zun La and the Baralacha La en route to Ladakh and Kashmir. In the 10th century upper Lahaul was united with Spiti and the Zanskar as part of the vast Lahaul-West Tibet kingdom. Ladakhi influence at this time stretched to the upper reaches of the Kulu Valley and for centuries the Kulu Rajahs paid tribute to Leh.

However following Ladakh's defeat by the Mongol-Tibetan armies in the 17th century Lahaul was gradually separated into two regions. Upper Lahaul came under the influence of the Kulu Rajahs and Lower Lahaul from Triloknath to Pangi came under Chamba's jurisdiction. Trade agreements evolved between Kulu and Ladakh from that time with Kulu trading iron and Ladakh sulphur. Lahaul was considered neutral territory and trade negotiations between Kulu and Ladakh were carried out on the vast Lingti plains.

The Sikh forays into the Kulu Valley also reached Lahaul, and for a time the whole territory was under the influence of Ranjit Singh. In 1847, Kulu and Lahaul came under British administration as a division of the Kangra state. Spiti at the time was linked to Ladakh and the newly formed Maharajah's Kingdom of Kashmir, but in the same year was exchanged for other territory and administered by the Kangra authorities.

Under British jurisdiction, Lahaul's trails were up-graded and bridges constructed along the main trading highways. This meant bringing construction materials into the region to build substantial bridges to provide a reliable trade route between Lahaul and Kulu. Even as late as 100 years ago, logs were hauled over the Rhotang Pass by upwards of 200 porters while forced labour was the only means of improving the roads.

The Hakurs of Lahaul consolidated their position and secured trade agreements with Kulu and beyond. The Rhotang Pass was the lifeline to the Indian plains and only in midwinter was Lahaul truly cut off from the outside world. Lahaul traders entrenched themselves in the business of the Kulu Valley, a situation that has remained unchanged to the present day.

Getting Ready

Apart from the abundance of potatoes during the late autumn harvest, there is rarely any surplus food in Lahaul. It's advisable to bring all provisions , especially kerosene, with you from the Kulu Valley. Some meat (goat or lamb) can be bought from the villages, as can biscuits and basics if you're only undertaking day-treks. Horses can be hired from most villages, although you may have to wait a day or two as they are often grazing higher up the valleys. Prices vary enormously particularly in the main trek season in August when many horsemen head towards

Zanskar. This is certainly true at Darcha, the main trek-off point for the Shingo La, where prices can be as high as Rs 80 per horse. You may be fortunate to meet horsemen returning empty to Padum in which case the negotiated price will be lower. However, it would be foolish to budget for this occurrence.

Places to Stay

Along the roads are a number of *PWD* or *Forest Division Government Rest Houses*, which can generally be opened without prior reservation. The *chowkidar* normally lives in a nearby village and is quite amenable to visitors. The rooms are generally simply furnished and cost Rs 20-50 (executive style) per night. In a number of villages such as Darcha, Keylong, Udaipur and Khoksar there are small hotel/tea shops that cope with seasonal demands. In all of these places you must have your own sleeping bag.

Getting There

The 3915-metre Rhotang Pass is the only access into Lahaul and is normally open to vehicles from the end of June until the end of October. Well prepared traders and trekkers however can tackle the pass from late March till early December by ascending the pass in the early morning before the snow softens.

During the short season it is open there are regular buses from Manali to Keylong. The Tourist Office operates a daily Rs 45 bus up to the pass, mainly for tourists 'to see the snow'. It's a very spectacular trip over the pass.

In the last decade roads have been constructed along the main valleys to Lahaul so it's now possible to drive down the Chenab Valley to below Udaipur. This road will eventually be extended to Pangi and Kishtwar.

All of Spiti, Kinnaur and a large part of Lahaul are off-limits to visitors without permits. A road is operable over the Baralacha La and along the military road to Leh but tourists are not allowed to go further than the Baralacha La as permits do not extend along the road to Leh.

Although you cannot continue up the jeep road from Keylong to Leh you can make the long and difficult trek from Keylong to Padum in the Zanskar Valley and from there to Ladakh.

Similarly Spiti is still a restricted area because of its proximity to Tibet. The 4500-metre Kunzam Pass connects the Lahaul and Spiti valleys and although it may be open by mid-May a safer date is mid-June. It's 475 km from Manali to Lehi via Keylong, the bus trip takes eight hours and costs about Rs 25. But you need special permission to use this road.

Most of the Kinnaur region, in the valley of the Sutlej River, which extends towards the Tibetan border, is also off-limits unless you have special permission from the Ministry of Foreign Affairs in New Delhi. You can only go as far as the Wangtu Bridge, just beyond Nachar without a permit.

Treks

With the development of the roads into the region, Lahaul has become, to some extent, a transit point for trekkers from the Kulu Valley en route to Zanskar and Ladakh. But there are possibilities for trekking both in and beyond the Lahaul region itself.

Three treks are outlined in this section:
1. Up the Bhaga Valley to Darcha and on to Zanskar via the Shingo La.
2. Up the Chandra Valley to Baralacha La and on to Zanskar via the Surichun La or Phitse La.
3. Down the Chenab Valley to Pangi and Kulu or Chamba.

Because it is outside the main influence of the Indian monsoon, Lahaul is an ideal alternative for trekking during July and August. The trek season across the main Himalayan passes is from mid-June until mid-October. However, the trails down the Chenab Valley are normally suitable for trekkers by late May/early June – an ideal time to explore Lahaul before it becomes 'motorised' for the season. To undertake a trek at this time of the year you must allow time for the trek-in over the Rhotang Pass.

DARCHA TO ZANSKAR via Shingo La

From Manali it takes a full day by bus or truck to reach Darcha which is a small village at the confluence of the Bhaga River and the Zanskar nullah. From Darcha it is possible to cross the Shingo La in three stages to the upper Zanskar Valley. The first walking stage is to the confluence of the Zanskar nullah and the Shingo nullah (the Jankhar Sangpo), which is crossed by a flying fox/pulley system. The second stage is to the base of Shingo La and the third over the pass to camp at Lakong. Strong walkers could even reach Kargya, the highest village in Zanskar, on the third stage.

Acclimatisation on this walk-in is vital. The Shingo La is over 5000 metres and should not be tackled in a hurry. Ideally a week or more should be reserved before the pass crossing. Even if you're on a tight itinerary, it is strongly advisable to have rest days at both the first camp and also at the camp immediately below the pass. For these stages, a tent is essential. The stone shelters at Palamo, en route along the Zanskar nullah, and at Rumjack, are hardly adequate for inclement weather and it is a very long stage from Rumjack over the pass and down to shelter in the Zanskar Valley. You should have no trouble following the correct route. The trail is well trekked by both locals and trekkers during the season, and it's simply a matter of following the cairns. The terrain on the pass is hardly crevassed and any misleading photographs in recent travelogues should be taken with a grain of salt.

LAHAUL TO ZANSKAR via Baralacha La

For trekkers with more time at their disposal, an ideal alternative is to walk in via the upper Chandra Valley and the Baralacha La. This route covers much of the magnificent scenery of Lahaul and at the same time allows more stages to acclimatise. The initial stages of the trek-in are from Manali, over the Hampta Pass to Chatru village in the Chandra Valley. (See the Kulu Valley treks for details.) Alternatively you could drive from Manali over the Rhotang Pass to Koksar and from there catch the once-a-day local bus to Chandra.

Although the initial part of the trek from Chandra is along a dirt road, similar to the road into the Zanskar Valley, there are many compensations. The 32 km walk takes two stages providing excellent views of the Bara Shingri glacier which, at over 30 km in length, is one of the largest in the Himalaya.

There are *Rest Houses* conveniently placed at the camping sites of Chota Drara and Batal. Tea stalls selling basic food are set up after mid-June.

From Batal the trail diverges from the road, which continues on up to the Kun Zun La and Spiti, so you have two choices before you. One is to take the road to Kun Zun La and then traverse around the mountain ridge to Chandratal; the other is considerably easier and goes direct to the lake – an ideal place for a rest day. From Chandratal it's a further three stages to the Baralacha La, about 35 km in total. En route the walk may be extended to avoid crossing the worst of the swift-flowing side torrents. Ideally a rope should be carried particularly after the spring snow-melt between late June and mid-August.

From the Baralacha La there are two alternatives. You can descend in two easy stages to Darcha and then continue by road to the Kulu Valley. Or you can continue over the Surichun or Phitse passes to the upper Zanskar Valley.

If you're taking the latter route then good horsemen are essential to assist you at river crossings, particularly when crossing the upper headwaters of the Tsarap River. From the Baralacha La, the

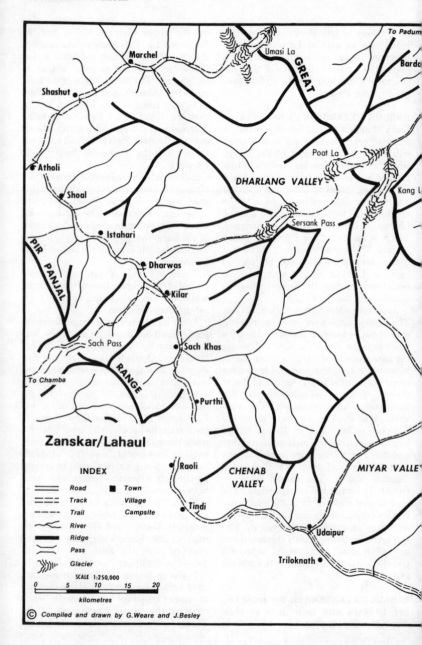

Zanskar/Lahaul

INDEX

═══ Road	■	Town
══ Track		Village
- - - Trail		Campsite
∿ River		
▬ Ridge		
⌣ Pass		
⑅ Glacier		

SCALE 1:250,000

0   5   10   15   20

kilometres

© Compiled and drawn by G.Weare and J.Besley

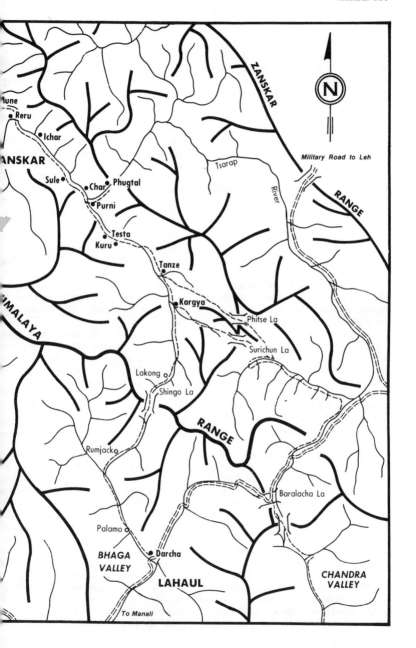

upper Zanskar Valley can be reached by four stages. Three to the base at Chumik Marpo, from where the trails diverge to the Surichun La or Phitse La. Neither ascent is difficult by Zanskar standards and the views to the north are magnificent. Both passes involve steep, rocky descents; the trail from the Surichun La reaching the upper Zanskar Valley at the village of Kargya; while the trail from the Phitse La goes further down-valley to the village at Tanze.

LAHAUL TO PANGI & CHAMBA/KISHTWAR

The other trekking alternative in this region is to explore lower Lahaul and the Chenab Valley. This involves a full day's drive from Manali over the Rhotang Pass to Khoksar and from there down-valley to Triloknath or Udaipur.

Here a day or two can be spent visiting the local temples, which were founded in the 8th century, when both the Buddhist sage Padmasambhava and the Hindu philosopher Sankaracharya wandered these valleys in search of converts. It was also a time when the Kashmir kingdom had considerable influence over the west Himalaya and many a sage or trader would have trekked beside the Chenab River en route to the Kashmir Valley.

From Triloknath there is a local bus to Udaipur, the last main village in the Lahaul region, and a place where horses and porters can be arranged. From Udaipur the roadworks have extended into the gorge country as far as Tindi.

The trail below Udaipur en route to the next main village at Tindi takes two stages and is not for the faint-hearted. The cliff trail is extremely narrow in places, sometimes just a ledge, and footholds must be chosen with care to avoid the sheer drop into the Chenab River. With the roadworks in progress, this trail section will soon be superseded by a road big enough for horses and jeeps, and within a season there should be a bridge across the river to Tindi. At present the flying-fox/pulley

system means you need porters for this stage.

Down-valley from Tindi the trail is similar to that experienced and described in the Jammu/Chamba sections. Deep gorges, plenty of ups and downs to negotiate the side valleys, and in some cases, very basic bridges which improve as you move towards Kilar.

For the trek from Udaipur to Kilar you should allow seven stages. Two to Tindi, two on to the village at Shaun, and a further two or three on to Kilar. You'll meet up with many Nepalese workers employed by the PWD and Forestry Department along this route and there is no shortage of tea shops – just like trekking in Nepal!

It's advisable, as always, to carry a tent as the *PWD/Forest Rest Houses* are located in the villages and those closer to Udaipur are heavily booked. There are some magnificent campsites en route to Kilar with no shortage of deadwood for camp fires.

From Kilar there are two choices. One to continue down the Chenab Valley by a further six or seven stages to Kulu; the second to climb the Sach Pass to Chamba – see the Jammu trek section.

Kangra Valley

The beautiful Kangra Valley begins near Mandi, runs north then turns east and extends to Shahpur near Pathankot. Situated between the Siwalik hills and the snow-capped Dhaula Dhar, the Kangra Valley controlled access between the plains and the hills and was once second only to Kashmir in importance in the West Himalaya.

There is little to see in the ancient town of Kangra today but it was at one time a place of considerable importance. Strategically it was dominated by the fort which prompted the local saying 'He who holds the fort, holds the hills', and was always fiercely contested by the Rajahs of Kangra. Culturally, the famous temple of Bajreshwari Devi was of such legendary wealth that every invader worth his salt took time out to sack it. Mahmud of Ghazni carted off a fabulous fortune in gold, silver and jewels in 1009. It was plundered again in 1360 by Tughlaq, recovered again and during Jehangir's reign was paved in plates of pure silver.

It was a turbulent time during Mahmud of Ghazni's brief occupation of Kangra, following his invasion of the north-west plains of India. Many of the artists from Kangra fled across the hills to Kulu and Chamba to find new patronage. During the Moghul period Kangra again submitted, but in the post-Moghul period the Rajahs re-established their hold over the fort and under Sanser Chand set their sights on Chamba, Manali and Kulu.

It was a period of prosperity for the kingdom, one which attracted many of the artists no longer secure in their positions on the plains. This migration led to the formation of the Kangra school of painting and the technique of depicting many of the Rajahs and the followers of Vishnu in miniature. Their inspiration and design was clearly Moghul in origin, but it was a design later popularised throughout the Himalayan foothills from Jammu to Kulu.

Sanser Chand's ambitions were never fulfilled. He was defeated by the combined hill states and the Gurkhas, and driven back to Kangra. In Kangra his kingdom was subjected to Sikh occupation which lasted until the Treaty of Amritsar.

In 1847 the Kangra Rajahs hoped they would gain the autonomy previously granted to the Tehri Garwhal, the state east of the Sutlej River. This was not to be. The British established a new administration in the nearby foothills at Dharamsala in 1848. Kangra experienced the inevitable decline and even the fort was destroyed by an earthquake in the spring of 1905.

DHARAMSALA

Dharamsala was the district headquarters of the British administration of Kangra, Kulu and Lahaul until 1947, and many of the buildings still retain a colonial character. In nearby McLeod Ganj is the Church of St John in the Wilderness, where the Viceroy of India, Lord Elgin, was buried after his death in 1863, while on a tour of duty from Simla. In those days the hill tracks would have been delightful, four or five stages from Simla to Dharamsala and a further two across the forest ridges of the Dhaula Dhar to Dalhousie. Travel today is of a different order, but driving from Simla to Manali and Kulu and then on to Dharamsala, Dalhousie and Chamba is an ideal way to explore the foothills in late March/April before the onset of the trek season, or after the passes have closed in November/December.

Of course these days Dharamsala has an added attraction. Since the early 1960s it has been the residence of Tibet's government in exile, headed by the Dalai Lama. The Tibetan settlement at McLeod Ganj provides a focus for the refugee camps that have been established in Himalayan regions as far apart as Ladakh, Kulu, Nepal and Darjeeling. The Dalai Lama has frequently visited these communities and the major monasteries in order to maintain Tibet's cultural traditions.

Getting Ready

Trekking supplies can be purchased in Dharamsala/McLeod Ganj. From reports, it is possible to cross the Dhaula Dhar without a tent – just. There are a number of *Forest Rest Houses* and in the absence of these, local shepherds' huts and caves are sufficient for the night. However, if you have a tent with you in Dharamsala, bring it along. Inclement weather is no less a problem here as elsewhere in the Himalaya. Forest Rest Houses can be booked in Dharamsala in advance and the Tourist Office in Dharamsala can assist you regarding accommodation at Triund and Kareri.

Places to Stay

For most, a stay in Dharamsala means a move up the hill to McLeod Ganj, close to the Dalai Lama and the Tibetan community. It's a regular little freak centre, full of colour and energy with lots of Tibetan-run hotels and restaurants – almost a little Kathmandu. There are a number of ashrams and Buddhist viharas in the vicinity, and for the bona fide trekker there are plenty of hotels and guest houses. Finding a good room in March or April may involve a bit of searching but there is still no shortage of accommodation. The prices, at Rs 30-40 per room, are very reasonable and most places have an uninterrupted view of the Indian plains.

Down the hill at Dharamsala there is a very comfortable government hotel, the *Dhaula Dhar*, next to the bus station. Prices here range from Rs 60-120 per room and the food is excellent.

Getting There

To reach Dharamsala or Kangra involves a three or four hour bus trip from the Himachal bus station at Pathankot. Pathankot is connected by overnight train from Delhi and was the former railhead before the line was extended to Jammu in 1971. Dharamsala can also be reached in a day from Kashmir by flying from Srinagar to Jammu, connecting with the local bus to Pathankot (three hours) and the last bus to Dharamsala, which leaves Pathankot at about 5 pm. If travelling from Kashmir to Dharamsala by road you will have to overnight in Jammu. Coming from Kulu/Manali or Simla you need to change buses at Mandi. To visit Kangra it is probably best to stay at Dharamsala and make a day trip as there is a regular bus service.

Buses run frequently between Dharamsala and McLeod Ganj, though to keep fit, the shorter hill trails are recommended. It is about one hour up the hill to McLeod Ganj from where you make interesting excursions to the temple at Bhagsu, o further to Triund at the foot of the Dhaula Dhar.

Treks

A trek out of Dharamsala, in many respects, requires a minimum of preparation. The Dhaula Dhar rise immediately behind McLeod Ganj and you can start walking then and there. A popular alternative is to combine a trek to the Ravi Valley with a visit to Brahmaur, Chamba and Dalhousie, before returning to Dharamsala by road, or trek back over an alternative pass.

Two treks over the Dhaula Dhar are outlined in this section:

1. Over the Laka or Indrahar Pass to Brahmaur/Ravi Valley.
2. Over the Minkiani Pass to Brahmaur, Ravi Valley.

The treks can be undertaken from the beginning of June, providing you have prepared for snow conditions over the passes. By mid-July and August the passes are free of snow, but the rain dampens trek possibilities. Early September through October is the ideal time to trek, before the onset of the winter snow, although if you're well-prepared, it is possible to trek in early November.

It's a long way up to the passes. The average elevation is around 4500 metres so a few extra days should be allowed en route for acclimatisation. The trails particularly in June, are under some snow Even in the post-monsoon period they are sometimes a little hard to follow and you may need to get some directions from the Gaddi shepherds.

The Kangra and Chamba districts are the home of the Gaddi – the colourful Hindu shepherds who tend their flocks on the Dhaula Dhar and the Pir Panjal during the summer season. Each spring they bring their animals from the Kangra foothills, over the Dhaula Dhar to the Ravi

Top: Kashmiri horsemen
Left: Sach Pass, Himachal Pradesh
Right: Bridge crossing in Himachal Pradesh

Top: Bridge crossing in Himachal Pradesh
Bottom: Chamba, Himachal Pradesh

Valley. From there they go higher across the Pir Panjal to the main Himalaya and on to the rich grazing areas that stretch from the Lingti plains beyond the Baralacha La, across to the high ridges that mark the border between the states of Jammu & Kashmir and Himachal Pradesh.

The Gaddi can be distinguished from the local people by their *chola*, a warm, knee-length, woollen cloak which is tightened at the waist. The origins of these shepherds dates back to the time when the first Rajput settlers made their way to the Himalayan foothills, although it was in the late Moghul period that some of the Gaddi families chose to settle in Brahmaur and Chamba. Today, the Gaddi migration, like that of the Bakharvals in Kashmir, means they have to reconstruct bridges, and clear the mountain trails. Their annual task ensures their own safe passage over the mountains and is crucial for anyone undertaking a trek in Himachal Pradesh.

DHARAMSALA TO RAVI VALLEY via Indrahar Pass
by Manmohan Singh Bawa

This is the most popular trek over the Dhaula Dhar, crossing the Indrahar Pass (also known as the Laka Pass) at 4610 metres. The climb from Dharamsala is steep and one rest day at least should be reserved before the pass crossing.

Stage 1: McLeod Ganj-Triund

The journey to Triund is a pleasant 11 km trek through pine and rhododendron forests. The first half of the trail climbs gradually, but steepens towards Triund. There is a Rest House at the peak of the three ridges, popular with those spending a day or two out of Dharamsala.

Stage 2: Triund-Laka Got

This is a short stage of seven km along a rocky path through deodar and oak forests. Laka Got (3350 metres) is at the

snout of a small glacier. There is a number of small cave shelters here and another cave two km further up the track by the side of the Laka glacier.

Stage 3: Laka Got-Indrahar Pass-Chatra Parao

It's quite a long haul to the pass, particularly in soft snow, and an early start is vital. The view from the pass takes in the Pir Panjal in the distance and the Ravi Valley below. The descent to Chatra is gradual and there is a log hut to spend the night.

Stage 4: Chatra-Kuarsi

Following the valley downstream to Kuarsi involves many ups and downs across intermediary ridges, a stage of some 16 km. Kuarsi is a Gaddi village with a Shiva temple, where you can shelter for the night.

Stage 5: Kuarsi-Brahmaur

The route descends by a steep forest trail. There is a further ridge crossing at Jhanouta where you can camp, or go further down to Machhetar. From there you can either follow the newly constructed road to the main Chamba-Brahmaur road, or cross the river and then cross the Manimahesh Dhar on foot to Brahmaur. A day can be spent at Brahmaur before the four-hour bus ride to Chamba.

DHARAMSALA TO RAVI VALLEY via Minkiani Pass

by Manmohan Singh Bawa

This trek is an alternative to the Indrahar Pass and can be completed in a minimum of five stages. The approach to the Dhaula Dhar is more gradual, but involves a number of ridge crossings. A rest day near Kareri Lake is recommended.

Stage 1: McLeod Ganj-Kareri Village

Follow the road towards Dal Lake out of McLeod Ganj. The trail descends for a while before a steep climb of three hours, then a gradual haul for four km to Kareri village. There is a *Forest Rest House* at the end of the village.

Stage 2: Kareri Village-Kareri Lake

A 14 km stage to the base of the Minkiani Pass. From the *Forest Rest House* the trail turns left along a thickly wooded ridge. After three km it turns right at (not over) a turbulent stream and climbs steeply up through an oak forest for another four km until it meets the stream coming from the pass. Follow this stream for a further seven to eight km up to Kareri Lake. Both Gaddi and Gujar shepherds camp here in the summer. At Kareri Lake there is a Shiva temple, used by local villagers during the season, which can be used as overnight accommodation.

Stage 3: Kareri Lake-Minkiani Pass-Minkiani Got

The trail follows a snow gully at the extreme left of the lake. You will need a shepherd's assistance to locate the trail particularly in the pre-monsoon period, when the ground is under heavy snow. From the pass at 4314 metres, it's a gradual three km descent to the next camping area where there is a possible rock shelter.

From Minkiani Got a day trip can be made to a series of lakes; Lam Dal about three km, Nag Dal a further three km, and beyond that a third named Chanderkup. The lakes are held sacred by the local people and make an interesting excursion after the spring snow-melt.

Stage 4: Minkiani Got-Drakund

Follow the main Donali stream down through the alpine pastures to Gaddi Got and continue on through the forest until the *Forest Rest House* at Drakund.

Stage 5: Drakund-Donali-Brahmaur

The trail continues down the right bank of the Donali stream through a number of villages until the Ravi River meets the Chamba-Brahmaur road. There is a regular bus service down to Chamba (28 km) or Brahmaur (37 km). The last buses leave Donali in the late afternoon.

As with the Indrahar trek a visit to

Brahmaur is recommended before going to Chamba. Alternatively, you could trek out of Brahmaur to Chanaota and from there complete the round-trip to Dharamsala by five stages.

Chamba

The Ravi Valley is bounded to the north by the Pir Panjal, to the south by the Dhaula Dhar and to the east by the Bara Bangahal Range. Chamba is perched on a plateau overlooking the Ravi River, at the point where it turns south and forges its way through the Dhaula Dhar to the Indian plains. Founded in the 9th century, at about the same time as Jammu, Chamba has often been likened to a mediaeval Italian village and is famous for its many temples.

The Ravi State was historically known as 'the Middle Kingdom'. Its position beyond the Indian plains and the Kangra hills made it an important link to the Pangi Valley and the trans-Himalayan trails between Lahaul and Kashmir. Until the 9th century the state capital was at Brahmaur, 65 km further up the Ravi Valley and for a time Brahmaur was regarded as second only to Kashmir as a cultural centre in the west Himalaya. It was a time when craftsmen wandered the high passes from Pangi and Lahaul in search of commissions.

With the establishment of Chamba, the culture of the Ravi Valley flourished. Many of the Chamba temples, including some of the important Lakshmi shrines near the Rang Mahal, date from the town's foundation. In fact Chamba has, with a few exceptions, maintained an uninterrupted cultural tradition. The state paid only nominal tribute to the Moghuls and its most famous Rajah, Prithi Singh, saw to it that Chamba's borders extended far beyond the Ravi Valley. A later Rajah, Umed Singh, was responsible for the Rang Mahal, 'the palace of colour', a fortress inspired by Moghul architecture. It was extended by his successors in the late 18th and early 19th centuries.

Following the Sikh wars, Gulab Singh from Jammu was granted control of all the country between the Ravi and Indus Rivers, including Chamba. A deputation was sent to Sir Henry Lawrence in Calcutta and it was agreed that the Chamba region, which at the time included the Pangi Valley and lower Lahaul, would come under British administration.

In 1851 it was proposed to establish a sanatorium for Europeans somewhere in the Dhaula Dhar. The site was chosen near Chamba and founded by Lord Dalhousie in 1868, as a hill station on a par with Simla. At this time, Chamba, like the region of Lahaul and Kulu, had totally inadequate roads and forest trails. Trek stages were defined, altitudes and spot heights checked and forest areas surveyed as the PWD and Forest Departments moved up-country. Even today the *PWD/ Forest Rest Houses* are well maintained with ordered gardens.

Getting Ready

Supplies, provisions and kerosene should be bought in Chamba, before continuing on to Brahmaur. Generally, cooks and assistants must be brought with you from Kashmir or Kulu. Horses and local guides may be hired at the roadhead, but allow a day or two for negotiations. This is particularly true at Tarila where the mule trains are usually busy during the summer months, with contractors carrying a wide range of goods to the Pangi Valley. For crossing the Chobia and Kugti Passes, porters can be hired at Brahmaur but will normally only go as far as the highest village. At Kugti village, for instance, porters will have to be engaged for the pass. Porter rates are about Rs 35-40 per day.

Places to Stay

Accommodation in Chamba is virtually restricted to the *Akhand Chandi*, behind the Rang Mahal, where the rooms range from Rs 30-60 per night. The staff are very helpful and can organise jeeps or cars if you're tired of Himachal Pradesh public transport. In Brahmaur there is a comfortable *Government Rest House* which can be booked in advance from Chamba.

In Dalhousie, hotel rooms vary depending on the season. It's a choice between the up-market Indian hotels and the rather sad, dilapidated Raj-era guest houses which have certainly seen better days. The rest houses at nearby Khajjiar are a convenient alternative.

Getting There

To get to Chamba from Delhi means taking the overnight train to Pathankot and then a long six-hour bus trip the rest of the way. Chamba and Dharamsala are quite close as the crow flies, but it still involves a complete day's drive. There's a direct bus service from Dharamsala and one via Pathankot, but there is little difference between the two, as the direct bus labours along on unclassified roads.

From Kashmir, Simla and Kulu it is also

ecessary to go via Pathankot – a tiring
ourney, which explains why Chamba has
emained off the main tourist map for so
ong.

There are two roads for trekkers out of
Chamba. One is to Tarila at the roadhead
efore the Sach Pass, a six hour drive
hrough marvellous hillside scenery. The
us costs about Rs 15. The other 'highway'
oes to Brahmaur, a further 65 km. It's a
ve-hour bus trip and you can spend a day
r two exploring the important temples
efore trekking off.

reks

he treks over the Pir Panjal between
Brahmaur and Lahaul cross some of the
nost remote territory in this mountain
ange. If this isn't sufficient attraction
here are some superb extensions, either
o continue down the Chenab Valley and
ack to Chamba via the Sach Pass (see the
ahaul section), or to continue from
Dharamsala over the Dhaula Dhar (see
he Kangra section).

A general assessment of the three main
rek possibilities from Brahmaur over to
ahaul is given in this section.

The trek over the Sach Pass from
Chamba/Tarila is described in the Jammu
ection.

Treks out of the Ravi Valley can be
ndertaken from early June onwards,
lthough most of the passes are well under
now until July. An exception is the Sach
Pass, the main highway to the Pangi
alley, which is crossed by locals from
arly May onwards.

Chamba does come under the influence
f the monsoon but the rainfall is not as
eavy as in Dharamsala and the Kangra
alley. So a trek can still be undertaken
cross the Pir Panjal at this time of the
ear, particularly if you're going on to the
ahaul or Zanskar regions. As with other
reas of Himachal Pradesh the ideal
rekking season is in September and
October before the onset of the winter
nows.

TREKS FROM CHAMBA TO LAHAUL

There are three main passes over the Pir
Panjal – the Kalicho, the Kugti and the
Chobia Passes – linking the upper Ravi
Valley with Lahaul. You must allow at
least five days out of Brahmaur to cross
these passes. They are all around 5000
metres and involve a pretty tough ascent
and an even steeper descent on the
northern ridges down to the Chenab
Valley.

All the trek-ins initially follow the
Budhil River, the principal tributary of
the Ravi that flows through Brahmaur,
and the trails through the villages are well
defined. The initial approach to the Kugti
Pass, through Brahmaur and Harsar to
Kugti village, takes two stages, while the
Chobia Pass route through Chobia and
Kao village takes one stage out of
Brahmaur. In the villages there are *Forest
Rest Houses* or a schoolhouse for accom-
modation, but from there on a tent must
be carried.

It takes a further two stages from the
highest village to the base of the passes
ascending through the forest to the alpine
encampments of the Gaddi shepherds.
Here the trails often criss-cross between
the various grazing areas, and the support
of the local porter or guide is valuable. The
alpine areas are rich in wildflowers during

August and are an ideal location for a couple of days rest and acclimatisation.

You have to traverse a small glacier en route so take care, especially early in the season. There are clear views of the Himalaya to the north and misty perspectives of the Chenab Valley immediately below. One night's camp is necessary on the far side of the pass, and the following day involves a steep descent down to the Lahaul villages. It is easy to see why it is not recommended to cross the pass from the Lahaul side unless you're already experienced and very fit.

On reaching the roadhead, you can spend some time visiting the temples at Triloknath and Udaipur before catching a bus or truck over the Rhotang Pass to the Kulu Valley.

There is confusion over place names in this region. The name *Got* simply refers to an alpine pasture which may or may not support a Gaddi encampment. The name *Alywas* or *Alias* is the local name for the camp below the base of a pass where there are usually rock caves for shelter. In the valleys there are *Forest Rest Houses*.

Immediately above the villages there is normally a small shrine, such as the temple six km beyond Kugti village, where prayers are made to the god of Keylong for a safe passage over the pass.

While in the Brahmaur district a three day trek can be undertaken to Manimahesh Lake. The trail starts from Harsar village 16 km east of Brahmaur, and ascends the Manimahesh range (a subsidiary range between the Dhaula Dhar and the Pir Panjal) to a sacred lake revered as resting place of Lord Shiva.

On the first day the trail follows the Manimahesh stream to the alpine meadow above. On the second day pilgrims cross the Bindar Ghat, or 'monkey ridge', and then on to Bharron Ghat where the trail is literally carved out of the rock face. Manimahesh Lake is dominated by the equally sacred Manimahesh peak. The two rock formations on the mountain resemble human figures and according to local legend are the bodies of a Gaddi shepherd and a sadhu who tried to reach the summit. There are small shelter huts along the way and at the lake.

Uttar Pradesh

In terms of population Uttar Pradesh is the largest state in India and is one of the country's great historical and religious centres. The Ganges River, which forms the backbone of Uttar Pradesh, is the holy river of Hinduism and a number of towns along the river are of great importance to pilgrims. There is Rishikesh and Hardwar, where the river emerges from the Himalaya and begins its journey across the plains, and Varanasi, the most holy city of all. Buddhism also has its great shrine in the state as it was at Sarnath, near Varanasi, that Buddha first preached his message of the middle way.

The region has also been centre stage for great historical events. Over 2000 years ago it was part of Ashoka's great Buddhist empire; more recently it was part of the Moghul Empire and for some years Agra was the capital.

Uttar Pradesh also has great social and geographical variations. Most of it consists of the great Ganges plain, an area of awesome flatness subject to disastrous flooding during the monsoon. The people of the region are predominantly backward farming peasants who scratch a bare living from the overcrowded land. Yet Garwhal Himal, the north-west corner of the state, is part of the soaring Himalaya, with beautiful scenery, excellent treks and India's highest mountain.

GARWHAL HIMAL

The mountains in the Garwhal region are more immediate and impressive than in any other region of the Himalaya and it's easy to understand why the range is considered to be the abode of the gods.

The entire region is revered but there are many specifically important Hindu pilgrimage sites such as Yamunotri, Gangotri, Kedarnath and Badrinath. Gangotri is recognised as the source of the holy Ganges River, though the actual source is at nearby Gaumukh, at the base of the Bhagirathi peaks. Kedarnath is the divine resting place of Shiva, while Badrinath is similarly assigned to Vishnu.

Although the Garwhal Himal is little known as a trekking region it boasts a number of famous peaks, including Trisul and India's highest mountain, Nanda Devi. (At least it was the highest until Sikkim, and therefore Kanchenjunga, was absorbed into India.) The soaring Himalaya are complemented by glistening glaciers and the trekking routes pass through rich green forests and across beautiful meadows, which in summer are carpeted in flowers.

The Nanda Devi Sanctuary, surrounded by nearly 70 white peaks which form a sort of natural fortress, is dotted with meadows and waterfalls. The sanctuary has a perimeter of nearly 120 km and covers an area of 640 square km. Clustered between the glaciers of Gangotri and Milan are some of the most outstanding peaks of the central Himalaya including the camel-humped, 7818-metre Nanda Devi itself.

Actually the term Garwhal Himal is something of a misnomer. There is only Garwhal – the Himal is an incorrect addition. Garwhal and Kumaon are neighbouring cultural provinces known under the combined name of Uttarakhand.

Until the Gurkha invasion in the late 18th century, the region of Uttarakhand was ruled by the local Rajahs. These included the Chand Rajahs of Kumaon and the Panwars of the Garwhal. During the Moghul period there were frequent border skirmishes with the Tibetans. The Tibetans were accused of harassing Indian pilgrims en route to Mt Kalaish, a sufficient motive for the local Rajahs to intervene and secure the important trading rights along the passes into Tibet.

The right to control the passes was never fully resolved, even during the

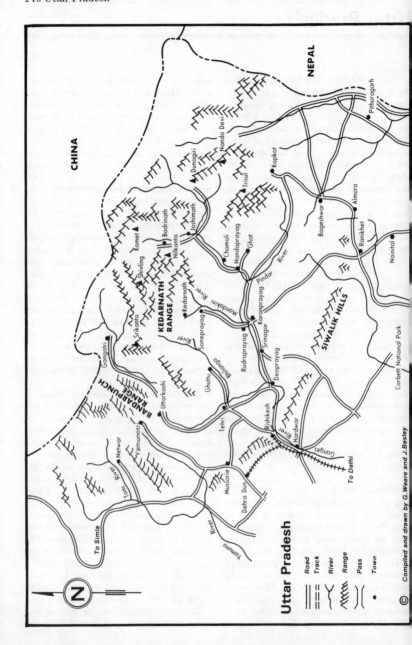

Uttar Pradesh

Road
Track
River
Range
Pass
Town

Compiled and drawn by G. Weare and J. Besley

British period, but nowadays the main passes through the Himalaya are regarded as the boundaries between India and Tibet (China).

Following the decline of the Moghuls, the Gurkhas of Nepal lost little time in expanding their borders but their ambitions were not fully realised until 1803 when they defeated the Garwhal army at Dehra Dun. The Gurkhas kept pushing their borders further through the Simla hill states to the Sutlej but it was an uneasy situation. The Gurkhas were ambitious and so were the Sikhs, the new rulers of the Punjab Himalaya, and the British feared a collision between the two. Also a huge Himalayan empire from Kashmir to Sikkim would put paid to any British ambition. A neutral British territory was necessary, and after the British/Gurkha wars, the Treaty of Sagauli in 1815 fixed the Nepal border back to the Kali river, the present boundary between India and Nepal.

The British gained the districts of Almora, Nainital, Kumaon and Dehra Dun, and the eastern district of the Garwhal. The western districts were restored to the local Rajah who established his capital at Tehri – now known as Tehri Garwhal. Hill stations were built to accommodate the British, notably at Dehra Dun, Mussoorie, Almora, Nainital and Ranikhet, both as retreats from the plains, and as administrative centres. Nearby Simla, in Himachal Pradesh, had been established by the 1830s and by 1864 became the summer capital of India. PWD and *Forest Rest Houses* were constructed along the hill trails, and the bridle paths between the hill stations provided an ideal introduction to trekking the Himalayan foothills.

The British regions were initially included under the Presidency of Bengal, then became part of the North-West Frontier Province, and finally came under the United Provinces. In 1947-49 the entire region became part of the state of Uttar Pradesh.

The mountain pilgrim and trekking routes followed cliff trails where a slip would be fatal and which were subject to annual avalanches. It is only relatively recently, in the post-war years, that metalled roads have been constructed into the mountain regions and walking stages to the sacred sites have been greatly reduced.

Gangotri is now linked by road; it is only one stage from the road to Kedarnath or Yamunotri; and you can drive all the way to Badrinath. Pilgrims now gain merit by going higher into the mountain valleys, or following the routes across the ridges of the Garwhal from one river valley to the next.

En route to the Garwhal it is recommended to spend a few days at Rishikesh or Hardwar and visit the temples that line the banks of the Ganges. After completing a trek, another perspective of the region can be drawn by visiting the famous hill stations at Mussoorie, Dehra Dun or Nainital.

Getting Ready

The best times to trek in the Garwhal Himal are May-June and September-October. Some places, like the Valley of Flowers and the high altitude *bugyals* (meadows), are at the best during the July-August rainy period.

Most supplies can be purchased from the bazaars at Joshimath and Uttarkashi. If you're not trekking off from there, then supplies should be brought from Rishikesh or Mussoorie, as there isn't a wide range of goods at some of the smaller roadheads.

Porters can generally be hired from Utarkashi and Joshimath. The best are usually in demand for the regular mountaineering expeditions, so again, that local contact is necessary. If you're going with a small party direct to the roadhead, then you will always find some willing hands at Ghuttu or Kapkot. However, anything more elaborate, particularly with guides, will involve some contact with the Uttar Pradesh trek organisation.

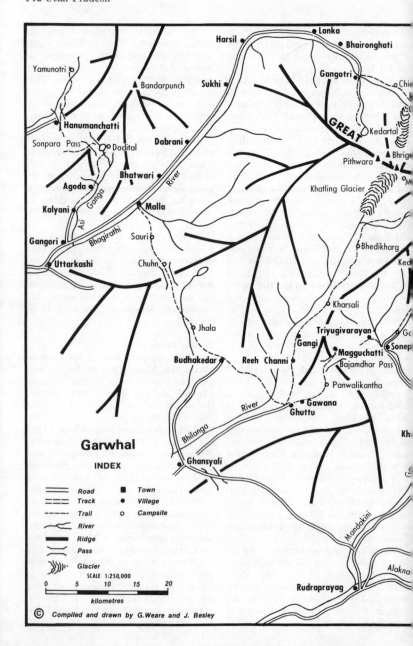

Garwhal

INDEX

═══ Road	■ Town
═══ Track	● Village
─ ─ ─ Trail	○ Campsite
River	
▬ Ridge	
Pass	
))))) Glacier	

SCALE 1:250,000

0	5	10	15	20

kilometres

© Compiled and drawn by G. Weare and J. Besley

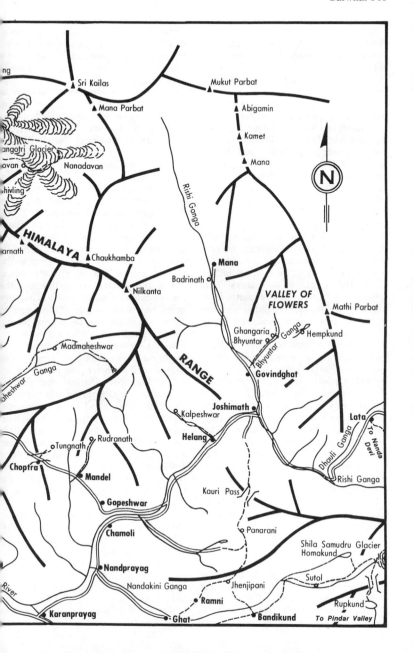

If bargaining on your own, spell out your requirements clearly. 'We are going to . . . and we are taking six days.' If you don't, then the stages will be shortened to make the journey easier but longer and therefore more costly.

Local regulations however are enforceable regarding the guide and porter rates. A guide will about Rs 65-70 per day, and a porter about Rs 35-40. These rates may vary depending on whether you provide food. If you do a slightly lower daily rate is possible. Food in this instance is rice, dahl, vegetables and the daily cigarette allowance.

Trekking Agents

The Garwhal Mandal Vikas Nigam, run by the Uttar Pradesh Government, can organise tours, accommodation and guide services, either from their offices in New Delhi, Dehra Dun or at Uttarkashi. In other districts, such as Joshimath, there are similar contractor/agents who can organise porters, guides and basic equipment.

There are several agencies in Delhi which cater for organised inclusive treks and specialise in organising mountaineering expeditions in the Garwhal. Equipment can also be hired from Delhi and some respectable climbing gear has been acquired over the years from foreign expeditions. The Delhi Mountaineering Association and the Indian Mountaineering Association in New Delhi can help in this regard and recommend a good local contact in areas not covered directly by the Uttar Pradesh Government undertaking. The Mountaineering Division, located in the Tourist Bungalow in Rishikesh, can also provide information on trekking in the Garwhal Himal.

Places to Stay

Accommodation in Uttar Pradesh falls into three sections. The hotels in the hill stations for stays before and after a trek; the government accommodation at Rishikesh and Hardwar, the 'gateway' to the Garwhal; and the up-country assortment of PWD/Tourist Bungalows/Rest Houses which provide a comfortable alternative while trekking or visiting pilgrimage centres.

In Dehra Dun, Mussoorie and Nainital there is a wide variety of accommodation from the ex-colonial hotels such as the Savoy at Mussoorie and the Grand Hotel at Nainital, to the simple Tourist Cottages and Youth Hostels which are often booked by Indian trekkers en route to and from the Garwhal.

At Hardwar and Rishikesh there are the Uttar Pradesh State Government Tourist Bungalows – room only for Rs 25-30. The Tourist Bungalow at Rishikesh, about eight km from the bus and railway station is particularly recommended. Food is available there and you can relax in the pleasant garden. The bungalow at Hardwar is less conveniently situated across the river from the main part of town. There are many hotels nearer the station, and of course the railway station retiring rooms providing you have a prior reservation.

In the mountain districts, apart from locally run hotels, there is a comprehensive network of government-run places. There are PWD Rest Houses and Tourist Bungalows at Deoprayag, Rudraprayag and Karanprayag, while at Joshimath, Badrinath, Soneprayag and Kedarnath there are Tourist Bungalows and PWD Inspection Bungalows. At Uttarkashi and Hanumanchatti (below Yamunotri) there are Tourist Bungalows and Forest Rest Houses; at Gangotri there is a Forest Rest House and a Tourist Rest House; and at Yamunotri, a Forest Rest House.

Accommodation can be pre-booked at Uttarkashi for Gangotri; at Mussoorie for Yamunotri; at Joshimath for Badrinath; and at Soneprayag for Kedernath.

Further into the mountains there is a comprehensive system of Forest Rest Houses and chattris (pilgrims' rest houses), but a tent is also an invaluable asset to ensure you have some independence and flexibility.

Getting There

From Delhi there are regular bus services to Hardwar and Rishikesh, from the inter-state bus terminal. There is also a frequent bus service to Dehra Dun and Mussoorie, as well as to Nainital, Almora and Ranikhet. Deluxe buses are also operated by the Uttar Pradesh Government, and bookings can be made at their offices in Janpath, New Delhi, or through one of the many private operators whose boards are displayed at the corner of Janpath and Connaught Place.

To continue on to the trek-off points, there are regular Uttar Pradesh buses from Rishikesh to Uttarkashi (for Gangotri), Soneprayag (for Kedarnath) and Joshimath (for Badrinath). You will need an additional stop in Uttarkashi or Joshimath before going on to the roadhead. It is not recommended to drive from Rishikesh to Gangotri, or to Badrinath, in one long day.

The Uttar Pradesh bus service is very comprehensive, but there are also many private bus charters – worth it for the additional room and comfort. One peculiarity of buses in Uttar Pradesh is that there is a toll tax, and a rupee or two is collected.

Train reservations from Delhi to Hardwar, Rishikesh and Mussoorie are always tight, so the tourist quota is the best bet. There is a branch line service from Hardwar to Rishikesh. From Dehra Dun there are frequent bus services to Rishikesh, and daily deluxe and local buses on to Simla and Himachal Pradesh.

Vayudoot run a flight from Delhi to Dehra Dun three times a week. The cost is Rs 205. Bookings are very heavy in the pre-monsoon season.

Treks

The treks outlined in this section represent only a sample of the many possibilities for trekking in the Garwhal region. The treks covered follow routes which do not require special permission or cross terrain where any technical difficulties are en-countered. Neither do the treks present huge organisational problems, as many of the walks are only a few stages from basic supplies and the nearest roadhead. It should be noted that treks into the Nanda Devi Sanctuary and the Valley of the Flowers are now regulated, and all entry to the Sanctuary has been banned for a trial five-year period.

Each of the trek regions described have their own attraction. In particular, the treks in the Yamunotri, Gangotri, Kedarnath and Badrinath regions are of immense religious significance, and combine the rich Hindu heritage of India with the spectacular scenery of the main Himalaya.

For the go-it-alone trekker, the treks out of Uttarkashi and Joshimath are appealing. The treks to Gaumukh and the Gangotri Glacier can be completed with little difficulty as can the treks to Dodital and Kedartal. From Joshimath, the treks to Hempkund and the Valley of the Flowers are easily organised, while the treks from Malla to Ghuttu and then on to Kedarnath are along the former pilgrim trails – comparatively easy to follow and with local tea stalls en route.

Lower altitude treks that do not involve pass crossings can be completed from mid-May onwards. However, for extended walks June is more suitable and will generally avoid the worst of the snow plodding.

Trekking in the monsoon months of July and August is possible, but heavy rainfall and the resultant muddy conditions may make the going a little sluggish. Nevertheless, the wildflowers are at their best in August, and a short clear spell is all you need when trekking the Valley of the Flowers, or the flowered *bugyals* beyond Kedarnath. The monsoon period in the Garwhal clears earlier than in Himachal Pradesh. The rains begin to clear by mid-August which hastens an ideal trek season which usually lasts until the end of October.

Acclimatisation is not the acute problem it is in other Indian regions as you are not crossing the main Himalaya range, only approaching it from various valleys. While the trails rarely go over 4500 metres, the approaches to the alpine plateaus are very steep and physically demanding so you still need to be fit and ready.

YAMUNOTRI

Yamunotri is the source of the Yamuna River, where it emerges from a frozen lake of ice and glaciers on the Kalinda Parvat at an altitude of 4421 metres. There is a temple dedicated to the goddess Yamunotri on the left bank of the river and, just below the temple, there are several hot springs where the water emerges at boiling point. Pilgrims boil their rice and potatoes in the spring water believing that they are then 'food from the gods'.

Treks

There are two treks outlined in this section:
1. The pilgrim trail from Hanumanchatti to Yamunotri.
2. From Yamunotri to Netwar via Har-ki-Dun.

TO YAMUNOTRI

It takes at least three days to reach Yamunotri from Delhi. The first day to Mussoorie or Hardwar and the second by bus to the roadhead at Hanuman-Chatti. From there you trek the 14 km to Yamunotri.

As with the other popular pilgrim treks, there is no shortage of tea stalls, camps and rest houses en route to service the large number of pilgrims, so a tent is not essential. The main temple is six km below the glacier.

Although the direct trek-in to Yamunotri is of rich cultural interest, a trek-in from the nearby valleys of Uttarkashi or Har-ki-Dun, is highly recommended.

The following trek through some spectacular scenery, to the Har-ki-Dun Valley is of special note, as it links the two main upper valleys of the Yamuna river. (The alternative trek from Uttarkashi via Dodital to Yamunotri is dealt with in the next section.)

YAMUNOTRI TO NETWAR via Har-ki-Dun

From Yamunotri there is a short steep climb to the alpine plateau of Damni, inhabited by the local shepherds from mid-June onwards. The following day involves another hard climb to the Yamunotri Pass at 5172 metres – not to be undertaken until fully fit and acclimatised. The views from the Yamunotri Pass to Bandarpunch (6387 metres) and Swargarothini (6252 metres) are worth the climb.

From the pass it's a short steep descent to the rock shelter at Thange. The next stage is comparatively easy to Rushar Tal. The trail winds across the alpine plateau to the base camp for climbing Swargarothini.

It is recommended to spend a few days in the vicinity to explore the surrounding glacial country and appreciate the peaks. The descent to the Har-ki-Dun Valley can be completed in a long day, down the forest trails and through small villages to the *Forest Rest House* at Seema, just above Osla village.

From Osla a detour can be made up-valley to Har-ki-Dun, with its fine alpine views, before continuing down-valley by two stages to Taluka and Sankri. From Sankri there is a jeep trail to the roadhead at Netwar.

Netwar is a sizeable town at the confluence of the Rupin and Supin tributaries which form the Tons River. There is a *Forest Rest House* and local hotel accommodation. The bus from Netwar to Dehra Dun takes about 10 hours.

GANGOTRI

It takes two days by bus to reach the source of the Ganges from Delhi – the first to Rishikesh or Mussoorie and the second to Gangotri. From Rishikesh it takes five to seven hours to reach Uttarkashi where you can stop for the night to hire porters or guides if necessary. From Uttarkashi on to Gangotri can take up to a full day, depending on the state of the road. The section between Lanka and Bhaironghati was destroyed by an avalanche in the early '70s and is only now near completion.

Gangotri, at 3140 metres, is in a spectacular setting and marks the confluence of the Kedar gorge and the Bhagirathi River, which eventually becomes the Ganges. The Bhagirathi River at this point flows for a while in a north-west direction giving the town its name, Gangotri or 'Gange turned north'. Many pilgrims visit the temple of Gangotri, which is dedicated to the goddess Ganga. The shrine of Bhagirathi was built by the early 19th century Gurkha commander in the Garwhal, Anan Singh Thaypa. The temple remains open from May till October when the priests take the temple offerings back to Uttarkashi.

Treks

There are four treks outlined in this section:

1. Gangotri to Gaumukh and the Gangotri Glacier.
2. Gangotri to Kedartal.
3. Uttarkashi to Dodital and Yamunotri.
4. Gangotri to Ghuttu.

TO GAUMUKH & GANGOTRI GLACIER

The first stage beyond Gangotri is to Bhujbasa, a convenient overnight camp from where pilgrims visit Gaumukh, the source of the Bhagirathi River. Most return through Bhujbasa to Gangotri the following day.

The path to Bhujbasa is a very well-defined bridle path which cuts up through the pine forest to the alpine plateau at 3800 metres. The 11 km climb of nearly 300 metres takes about four to five hours.

There's a *Forest Rest House* at Chirbasa, midway between Gangotri and Bhujbasa, and many tea stalls along the route. At Bhujbasa there is an ashram where both pilgrims and trekkers can spend the night

and get a basic vegetarian meal. A donation is appreciated from non-pilgrims.

From Bhujbasa the trail cuts across boulder scree and moraine to Gaumukh, a trek of about three hours.

Beyond Bhujbasa the trek can be extended to the Gangotri Glacier. One convenient objective is Tapovan, the base camp for expeditions climbing Shivling and the Kedarnath Ranges. To reach Tapovan, which is a grassy plateau above the main glacier at 4463 metres, you must cross the Bhagirathi River well below Gaumukh. Climb to the high ridge to the south of the Gangotri Glacier following a trail marked by a series of cairns through the moraine. Average trek time from Bhujbasa is about five hours. At Tapovan there is a local sadhu who is willing to accommodate trekkers in his cave/shelter. A few rupees a night plus your own supply of food is sufficient.

From Tapovan you can return direct, down-valley to Gangotri, or traverse the Gangotri Glacier to the camp at Nanadavan, the base for climbing the 4500-metre Bhagirathi peak.

The latter involves crossing ice and boulder terrain so take care to avoid the most obvious crevassed sections. This is not for the inexperienced trekker. A guide is essential as is your own tent and supplies, stove and kerosene.

From Nanadavan you can return direct to Bhujbasa along the moraine to the north of the Gangotri Glacier and return to Gangotri the following day.

GANGOTRI TO KEDARTAL

From Gangotri a short trek can be made to Kedartal, a glacial lake set amidst many impressive peaks including Meru (6672 metres), Pithwara (6904 metres) and Bhrigupanth (6772 metres). The trek does not involve any major organisational problems, just a tent, stove and supplies, plus an awareness of acclimatisation, as Kedartal is at 4500 metres.

The initial stages of the trek are up through the Kedar Gorge, a trail followed

by the local shepherds from June onwards. The trail cuts through some particularly beautiful birch forest before reaching the summer grazing pastures and moraine in the vicinity of Kedartal. The choice is yours whether to camp on the ridge above the lake, or by the lake edge after the spring snow melts. Besides the panorama of peaks in the immediate vicinity, the Bandarpunch range beyond Uttarkashi can also be appreciated.

TO DODITAL & YAMUNOTRI

This scenic trek can be undertaken from Uttarkashi. Like the trek to Kedartal, there are no organisation problems and the trek to and from the roadhead can be completed in three stages. Beyond Dodital the trek can be extended to the Sonpara Pass and on to Hanumanchatti and Yamunotri.

From Uttarkashi there is a local bus service to Gangotri, from where you can jeep or trek to the village of Kalyani. From Kalyani the going gets steeper, up through the forest to Agoda village which, at 2280 metres, is the highest village in the vicinity. From Agoda it's a further 16 km to Dodital the following day.

The lake is the source of the Asi Ganga and is quite a considerable size, set amidst oak, pine and deodar. There is a *Forest Rest House*, which can be used as a base for exploring the surrounding terrain. From Dodital you could return to the roadhead in a day, and from there either return to Uttarkashi or on to another trek region of the Garwhal.

If you're continuing beyond Dodital to Hanumanchatti and Yamunotri, two stages are required. The first is over the Sonpara Pass at 3953 metres. This is a highly rewarding stage with superb views of the Bandarpunch range as you drop from the pass along the ridge line to the alpine meadows to camp. The following day's descent to Hanuman Chatti is a steep one with many splits and turns in the rail as it descends through the conifer forest. A local shepherd guide is recommended as far as the village of Nachni. From there it is two km to the *Forest Rest House* at Hanuman Chatti and the main pilgrim trail to Yamunotri.

GANGOTRI TO GHUTTU

The former pilgrim trail from Gangotri cuts across country from the village of Malla, 30 km north of Uttarkashi, to the roadhead at Ghuttu in the Khatling Valley. It is a well marked path and the trek could be completed in four or five stages. From Ghuttu the pilgrims continue via Panwalikantha to Soneprayag and Kedarnath.

KEDARNATH

Kedarnath, at the head of the Mandakini Valley, is one of the most sacred sites dedicated to Shiva, and attracts thousands of Hindu pilgrims each year. Inside the temple Shiva is symbolised by a huge stone representing the hind quarters of a divine buffalo. Its other four parts are worshipped in other places in the Garwhal. Kedarnath is therefore part of the *Panch Kedar*, the five different forms of Lord Shiva.

The shrine at Kedarnath also commemorates the sage Shankaracharya, who died here. He is credited with revitalising Hindu philosophy during the 8th century, and his travels across the Himalaya are well documented.

The Kedarnath shrine is a day's walk from the roadhead at Gaurikund. Pilgrims normally drive from Rishikesh to Soneprayag, five km below Gaurikund, where the Uttar Pradesh authorities have established a tent colony. The following morning the pilgrims continue to Gaurikund and hire porters and bearers for the day ahead. The temple is opened during the last week of April and remains open till the Diwali festival in late October.

There is a *Tourist Bungalow* and a wide variety of *dharmsalas* and shelters near the temple.

The trail from Gaurikund to Kedarnath is well defined through the forested banks of the Mandakini River and up to the village of Rambara, where less physically fit pilgrims spend the night.

From Rambara the trail steepens to the village at Garurchatti, from where the Kedar Valley opens out to reveal some magnificent views of the Himalaya. Several day trips can be made out of Kedarnath. These include a 10 km walk to Chararadi Tal, where Gandhi's ashes were immersed in 1948.

Treks

There are three treks outlined in this section:

1. The Panch Kedar series of pilgrimages.
2. Soneprayag to Ghuttu via Panwalikantha.
3. Ghuttu to the Khatling Glacier.

PANCH KEDAR TREKS

The temples which signify the *Panch Kedar*, the five different forms of Lord Shiva, are at Kedarnath, Madmaheshwar, Tungnath, Rudranath and Kalpeshwar. For the devout Shivite pilgrim a visit to each temple is necessary while in the Kedarnath region. The trek to Kedarnath has been described and the other four temples are a day or so's walk from the nearest roadhead.

Madmaheshwar

To reach Madmaheshwar catch the Rishikesh/Soneprayag bus and get off at Okhimath, the winter residence of the priests of Kedarnath. It is a 30 km trek from Okhimath to Madmaheshwar (3289 metres) along the Madmaheshwar Ganga. En route there are basic shelters for the pilgrims and a *PWD Bungalow* at Okhimath.

Tungnath

At 3680 metres, near the summit of Chandra Shila Peak, Tungnath is the highest temple in the Garwhal Himalaya.

From Okhimath there is a local bus to

Choptra (17 km), from where there's a steep six km climb through forests to the temple. The entrance to the Tungnath temple is guarded by two sculptured lions and behind them rises a short pagoda-like tower capped with a wooden roof and golden spire.

Rudranath

Rudranath is 37 km from Choptra; the first 16 km can be travelled by bus on a fair-weather road. From Mandel the trail to Rudranath branches north and climbs gradually to the temple. The Rudranath temple is dedicated to Rudreshwar (Shiva) who slew the demon Andhakasur here. There is a *PWD Bungalow* at Mandel and basic shelters along the trail.

Kalpeshwar

This shrine at 2786 metres is approachable from the roadhead at Helang on the Rishikesh-Badrinath highway. From Helang the trail turns north-east and climbs 13 km to the temple in the village of Urgam. The architectural construction of the shrine is such that it looks as if it is carved out of a rock. For the more devout pilgrims there is a direct cross-country trail from Rudranath which avoids the road and can be completed in two stages.

SONEPRAYAG TO GHUTTU via Panwalikantha

The trek to Panwalikantha is best made on the return journey from Kedarnath. It starts from Soneprayag and follows the former pilgrim route from Gangotri to Ghuttu and then on to Kedarnath. The development of roads into the Garwhal has restricted the use of the trail, although it is still followed by the more devout pilgrims. For trekkers following the trail from Gangotri the itinerary will be taken in reverse.

Stage 1: Soneprayag-Triyugivarayan

From Soneprayag follow the jeep trail towards Triyugivarayan. There are many shortcuts en route, first through the village of Kemaada and then a steady climb through the forest to an open area below Triyugivarayan, the highest village en route to Ghuttu.

The village is a fair size, with about 100 houses. The ancient temple is dedicated to Lord Vishnu Narayan, and is similar in style and architecture to the Kedarnath temple. *Akhand Dhuni*, the eternal fire which burns in the temple, is said to have been lit on the occasion of Lord Shiva's marriage to Parvati. Pilgrims smear its ash on their foreheads. The duty of tending the flame falls in turn to each family in the village and is supplemented by the logs of wood brought by pilgrims.

For accommodation, there is a *dharmsala* for the pilgrims, and a camping ground about a quarter of a km away, near the village water source. The day's trek is about six km.

Stage 2: Triyugivarayan-Panwalikantha

The route from Triyugivarayan goes south-west along the well-defined pilgrim trail. It initially cuts through forest to the flowered meadows of Maggu Chatti at 300 metres. From the *Bhujkundi Bugyals*, (loosely translated as 'high altitude meadows'), it's about 1½ hours to Bajamdhar where there are good views down to the Bhilanga Valley. Two km beyond Bajamdhar (*dhar* means top) there is a fork in the trail that leads to the Khatling glacier at Gangi village. The trail to Ghuttu bears to the left and goes down through the forest and another series of *bugyals* to Panwalikantha at 3963 metres.

Panwalikantha is a convenient overnight stop with panoramic views of many of the major peaks, from Nanda Devi in the east across to the Kedar peaks and west to the Bandarpunch ridges. There are half a dozen small huts, a *dharmsala* and a *PWD Rest House*.

Stage 3: Panwalikantha-Ghuttu The trail at first climbs a small valley before descending past a series of Gujar shepherd

uts. There is then a steep descent, short-cutting the main trail to the village at Gawana. From there it's another hour to Ghuttu village and the roadhead.

Ghuttu (1526 metres) is a large attractive village, set on both sides of the Bhilanga River and there is a *Forest Rest House* here. From Ghuttu it's a 3½ hour bus journey to Tehri where you can get a connecting bus to Rishikesh.

GHUTTU TO THE KHATLING GLACIER

Khatling is a lateral glacier out of which the Bhilanga River, one of the major Ganges River tributaries, emerges. The glacier is in the heart of the Tehri Garwhal region, with Gangotri to its north and Kedarnath to the north-east. From Rishikesh it is a five-hour bus ride to Tehri and a further three hours to Ghuttu, where basic supplies are available and porters can be hired for about Rs 40 per day.

Stage 1: Ghuttu-Gangi
The trail initially cuts through terraced fields to Deolang village. From there it's an easy 1½ hour climb through the forest to Reeh channi (temporary village) and then a steep climb for an hour to Buranschauri. *Buran* means rhododendron, and the whole countryside is dotted with these trees, providing a particularly magnificent spectacle in March and April when they are in full bloom.

From Buranschauri it's a further two hour climb to Gangi village at 2585 metres. There is no accommodation in Gangi, apart from the small school shelter, and a camping ground further up the track towards Khatling. The only food available are the high altitude potatoes, a village speciality. Gangi's small economy relies on the production of potatoes and wool.

Stage 2: Gangi-Kharsali
The trail drops initially for an hour to Deokhri channi, another winter settlement for the villagers from Gangi. From there it's half an hour through the forest to where the trail forks, just beyond the

Kalyani stream. The left trail leads to Sahastratal Lake (4872 metres), while the trail to Khatling continues straight on, descending gradually before a steep climb through thick vegetation to an open area known locally as Birodh.

Legend has it that this place was either the site of the old Gangi village or a meeting place for all the Bhilang villagers. The site still contains remnants of previous settlements. From there, it is a further two hours to Kharsali, which is a large meadow surrounded by giant conifers and oaks, and an ideal camping site.

Stage 3: Kharsali-Bhedikharg
Cross the bridge over the Kharsali stream and continue further along the forest track to Bhelbagi. The trail follows the river for about two km then rises steeply through thick bush, passing Bhumk Odaar cave to the left of the trail. A further two or three km of climbing brings you to Tamakund cave in an area known for its wildflowers. At Tamakund cave there are bound to be several Gaddi shepherds, on their long migration from Kangra. From there it is just over an hour's walk to another good camping ground at Bhedikharg.

Stage 4: Around Khatling Glacier
Khatling glacier is 11 km beyond Bhedikharg and it takes a full day to get to the glacier and back. There are a number of spectacular hanging glaciers above the main glacial floor and the peaks of Jogin Group (6463 metres), Tholay Sagar (6902 metres), Rudugaira (5364 metres), Kirti Stambh (6402 metres) and Bharte Khunta (6578 metres) make this a spectacular setting.

The return to Ghuttu can be completed in two stages, or you can return to Gangi village and trek direct to Kedarnath (see previous trek section).

BADRINATH
Badrinath has traditionally been the resting place of Vishnu. According to legend it was once the abode of both

Vishnu and Shiva but this arrangement apparently didn't work very well. Shiva offered to move to Kedarnath and Vishnu, as an act of gratitude, stipulated that all pilgrims should visit Shiva first at Kedarnath before making the journey to Badrinath.

The main temple at Badrinath is quite small, and pilgrims often have to wait for a day or more before paying homage to Vishnu. At one stage in the past the temple was used by Buddhist sages but reverted to a Hindu shrine when the teachings of Shankara reconverted the local monks. Since the 8th century the Brahmins who administer the temple have traditionally come from Kerala. Even today the high priest of Badrinath can trace his origins back to southern India.

The temple opens in the first week of May each year and remains open until the last week in October when the priests go down to Joshimath to spend the winter months.

The drive to Badrinath normally ends at Joshimath where porters can be arranged for trekking. It's then a three to four hour drive (44 km) to Badrinath where there are the usual religious shelters, *Tourist Bungalow* and *PWD Rest House*, all of which can be booked in advance from Joshimath.

Interesting day trips can be made out of Badrinath, notably to the Rishis cave at Kesharaprayag above Hara village, and to the famous 'hot water spring' at Tatakund three km beyond the town of Badrinath.

As with the Gangotri series of treks, those out of the Badrinath/Joshimath region can be made in a comparatively lightweight fashion. The immediate trekking attractions, of the Valley of the Flowers and Hempkund, can be undertaken without a tent or supplies, particularly as it is not possible, at present, to trek the entirety of the Bhyuntar Valley (Valley of the Flowers).

With the restrictions on entry to the Nanda Devi Sanctuary, a trek to the Homakund and Rupkund (lakes) is an ideal alternative. The trek again can be undertaken without a huge army of porters. However, a local guide, a tent and supplies must be carried with you as it takes a minimum of a week to explore this spectacular area.

Treks

There are two treks outlined in this section:

1. From Govind Ghat to Hempkund and the Valley of the Flowers, with suggestions for further treks from the valley.
2. From Ghat to Rupkund Lake.

TO HEMPKUND/VALLEY OF THE FLOWERS

Ever since Frank Smythe's discovery of the Valley of the Flowers in the 1930s, the Bhyuntar Valley has been a popular destination. Between mid-June and mid-September the valley is an enchanting vision, filled with a bewildering variety of wildflowers. Snow-clad mountains stand in bold relief against the skyline, forming an impressive backdrop. The valley, which is nearly 10 km long and two km wide, is divided by the Pushpawati stream, into which several tiny streams and waterfalls merge. The huge Ghoradhungi mountain blocks one end.

Hempkund provides a different attraction. In the Sikh holy book, the *Granth Sahib*, the Sikh Guru Govind Singh recounts that in a previous life he had meditated on the shores of a lake surround by seven snow-capped mountains. Hempkund Sahib, Sikh pilgrims have decided, is that holy lake. Each year it attracts many thousands of devotees who immerse themselves in the icy waters at 4370 metres.

Both Hempkund and the Valley of the Flowers can be reached from the roadhead at Govind Ghat, a point 10 km on from Joshimath on the road to Badrinath. Porters and local guides can be arranged at Joshimath, although it's easy to rely, for a few days, on the many tea house/hotels that line the main pilgrim route.

Stage 1: Govind Ghat-Ghangaria

From Govind Ghat it is a 14 km trek to Ghangaria. The trail first skirts a mountainside and then follows the Laxman Ganga (also known as Bhyuntar Ganga) upstream along its right bank through dense forest. The first section of the trail, to Bhyuntar village, is fairly easy but from there it's a stiff four km climb. Hundreds of Sikh pilgrims regularly use this well-marked trail and there are tea shops along the way to relieve the climb.

Ghangaria, also known as Govind Dham, is set between high mountain walls and dense forest at 3084 metres. As a large pilgrim complex, Ghangaria has a *gurdwara* with free board and lodging, small hotels and a *Government Bungalow*. The camping ground is about two km further up the track.

Stage 2: Ghangaria-Hempkund-Ghangaria

Two km above Ghangaria the trail splits; one route goes to Hempkund (Lokpal), the other to the Valley of the Flowers. Take the eastern (right hand) trail. The ascent to Hempkund is quite steep and it takes three to four hours to cover the six km.

Stage 3: Ghangaria-Valley of the Flowers-Ghangaria

This is a short and pleasant trek of 10 km to the valley and back. Take the left trail at the split two km above Ghangaria. About half a km further on it descends steeply down to a narrow gorge and crosses the Bhyuntar Ganga by a bridge. The trail then climbs gradually for two km to *Nandavan*, the Valley of the Flowers. The best time to visit is from mid-August to mid-September, when the whole valley is in bloom.

Options from the Valley of the Flowers
1. Valley of the Flowers-Ghunta Khal

From the Valley of the Flowers, at Bamani Duar, one trail turns west and, after crossing Ghunta Khal (4425 metres), reaches Hanuman Chatti (2548 metres). The latter is a few km before Badrinath on the Govind Ghat side. This is a short trek of two to three days and there are a few stone shepherds' huts along the way which can be used as shelter.

2. Valley of the Flowers-Bhyuntar Pass
A trail leads along the Bhyuntar Ganga to the east, where, after eight km it reaches the Tipra camping ground (3700 metres) near the moraine of Lari Glacier. On the second day, following the left side of this glacier, the trail crosses the Bhyuntar Pass (5090 metres) and reaches Eri Udiar camping ground on the left side of the Bankund Glacier. The trail follows the Amrit Ganga downstream back to Joshimath via Gamsali, Malari, Lata and Tapovan.

3. Valley of the Flowers-Badrinath
Another trail from the Valley of the Flowers heads north-west just above Tipra, at Chakulthela. After crossing

Khulia Ghat (Khulia Pass) at 5000 metres the trail descends to and traverses Khulia Ghat Glacier keeping to its right-hand side until it reaches Chupchapa village near Mana. It is one day's easy trek from there to Badrinath.

Note: The Valley of the Flowers has been declared a National Park and special permission is needed to stay and camp inside. For treks over Khulia Ghat and Bhuinder Pass, permission is also required.

GHAT TO RUPKUND LAKE
At an altitude of 4778 metres, below the 7122-metre high Trisul massif, Rupkund Lake is sometimes referred to as the 'mystery lake', because of skeletons of humans and horses which have been found here. Every 12 years thousands of devout pilgrims make an arduous trek to the lake from Nauti village, near Karan-

prayag. The pilgrims are said to be led by a mysterious four-horned ram which takes them from there through Rupkund to the Shrine of Nanda Devi, where it disappears. A golden idol of the goddess Nanda Devi is carried by the pilgrims on a silver palanquin.

This trek to the outer rim of the Nanda Devi Sanctuary is spectacular. The trails across country can be quite confusing and a guide is well worth hiring from Joshimath. Stone shelter huts and caves seem about it as far as accommodation is concerned, so a tent is necessary, as well as supplies to last you at least a week.

The trek to Rupkund can be undertaken either direct from Joshimath, crossing the Kauri Pass and then on to Homakund and Rupkund, or from the south from the roadhead at Debal, beyond the Pindar Valley.

The simplest itinerary however is to approach Rupkund from the roadhead at Ghat, 20 km from Nandprayag in the Nandakini Valley. From Ghat you can head up-valley to Homakund and from there visit the impressive Shila-Samudru glacier and Rupkund before heading cross-country over the high meadows on the return to Ghat. This trek is easy to organise as porters can be hired at Ghat, although the more experienced men come from Joshimath and Gwaldon. Basic provisions can also be purchased at Ghat, but it is recommended to purchase the bulk of food and kerosene at Joshimath or Nandprayag beforehand.

From Ghat it is a long initial stage to Bandikund. The 20-plus km is usually covered by locals in a day, but you should allow two. Bandikund is a small settlement consisting of log huts and a series of small lakes. There are also two temples dedicated to the goddesses Bhagwati and Kali.

From Bandikund you climb up through the forest to the higher meadows at Sutol, which is essentially a shepherd encampment. Beyond Sutol it is a full day's walk to Homakund (4031 metres) one of the most impressive glacial lakes in the Garwhal. Homakund drains into the Nandakini River and is of particular importance to the local devotees who believe the goddess Nanda Devi worshipped here at a sacred fire.

From a camp in the vicinity of the lake it is a day's hike to the Shila Samudru glacier and back. The glacier marks the head of the Nandakini Valley, and the trail crosses boulder fields and lateral moraines. It is also possible to trek direct from Homakund to the trail just below the Kauri Pass, an interesting diversion but a local shepherd guide is a must.

It is a three hour climb to the ridge between Homakund and Rupkund and from the Junargali Pass (4780 metres) there are clear views of the Trisul peaks and Nandakot.

It is a steep descent over cliff and scree to the water's edge. From Rupkund the trek can be extended to the meadows at Bisla, the first possible camp, and from there to Debal and the Pindar Valley.

Index

LONELY PLANET NEWSLETTER

We collect an enormous amount of information here at Lonely Planet. Apart from our research we also get a steady stream of letters from people out on the road – some are just one line on a postcard, others go on for pages. Plus we always have an ear to the ground for the latest on cheap airfares, new visa regulations, borders opening and closing. A lot of this information goes into our new editions or 'update supplements' in reprints. But to make the most of the info that comes our way we also produce a quarterly newsletter packed full of the latest news from out on the road. It comes out in January, April, July and October every year. Cost of the yearly subscription (including postage) is $7.50; or single copies of the newsletter cost $2. That's US$ in the US or A$ in Australia, write to:

Lonely Planet Publications
PO Box 88, South Yarra, Victoria, 3141, Australia
or
Lonely Planet Publications
PO Box 2001A, Berkeley, CA 94702
USA

We have lots of books on the Indian sub
continent, so if you're travelling furthe
look for:

Trekking in the Nepal Himalaya

If you're planning on trekking in the Nepa
region of the Himalaya as well as th
Indian region this book takes you on all th
major routes including the Everest Bas
Camp trek and the Annapurna circuit.

Kashmir, Ladakh & Zanskar – a trave
survival kit

For more information on the norther
regions of the state of Jammu an
Kashmir this book has all the informatior

India – a travel survival kit

Or if your travels are going to take yo
further afield in India our award-winnin
India guide covers the whole country. I
you're looking for palaces in Rajasthar
beaches in Goa or faded touches of the Ra
almost anywhere, this is the book.

Kathmandu & the Kingdom of Nepal

Few travellers can resist the lure c
magical Kathmandu and the surroundin
mountains. This guidebook takes yo
round the temples and up into th
foothills.

Pakistan – a travel survival kit

We don't forget India's neighbours either
Our guide to the 'unknown land of th
Indus' also has a detailed section o
trekking in the Pakistani Himalaya.

Sri Lanka – a travel survival kit

The island-nation of Sri Lanka offer
everything from the ancient cities to som
of the most beautiful beaches in th
world.

Bangladesh – a travel survival kit

Whether you're riding the famous rive
boats or exploring the Chittagong Hi
Tracts this book has all the informatior

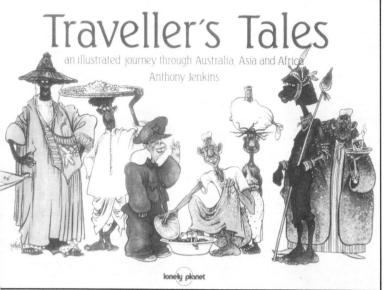

Traveller's Tales

an illustrated journey through Australia, Asia and Africa

Anthony Jenkins

lonely planet

artoonist Anthony Jenkins has spent
veral years on the road, travelling in
countries around the world. Along
e way he has filled numerous sketch-
ooks with his drawings of the people he
et.

This is a book of people, not places. A
ttooed Iban tribesman in Sarawak, a
ango seller in Cameroon, fellow
avellers in Nepal . . . all are drawn with
erception and (in most cases) affection.

Equally perceptive are Jenkins' written
omments and descriptions of incidents
uring his travels. The combined result
like a series of personal illustrated
tters.

This is a traveller's travel book. If you
ave ever endured an Indian train,
atched the world go by in Kathmandu's
urbar Square or tried to post a letter
southern Africa, then opening these
ages will be like meeting old friends
d will probably give you itchy feet to
e on the road once more.

Lonely Planet travel guides
Africa on a Shoestring
Alaska – a travel survival kit
Australia – a travel survival kit
Bali & Lombok – a travel survival kit
Bangladesh – a travel survival kit
Burma – a travel survival kit
Bushwalking in Papua New Guinea
Canada – a travel survival kit
China – a travel survival kit
Ecuador & the Galapagos Islands
Fiji – a travel survival kit
Hong Kong, Macau & Canton – a travel survival kit
India – a travel survival kit
Indonesia – a travel survival kit
Japan – a travel survival kit
Kashmir, Ladakh & Zanskar – a travel survival kit
Kathmandu & the Kingdom of Nepal
Korea & Taiwan – a travel survival kit
Malaysia, Singapore & Brunei – a travel survival kit
Mexico – a travel survival kit
New Zealand – a travel survival kit
North-East Asia on a Shoestring
Pakistan – a travel survival kit kit
Papua New Guinea – a travel survival kit
South America on a Shoestring
South-East Asia on a Shoestring
Sri Lanka – a travel survival kit
Tahiti – a travel survival kit
Thailand – a travel survival kit
The Philippines – a travel survival kit
Tibet – a travel survival kit
Tramping in New Zealand
Travel with Children
Travellers Tales
Trekking in the Indian Himalaya
Trekking in the Nepal Himalaya
Turkey – a travel survival kit
USA West
West Asia on a Shoestring

Lonely Planet phrasebooks
Indonesia Phrasebook
China Phrasebook
Nepal Phrasebook
Thailand Phrasebook

Lonely Planet travel guides are available around world. If you can't find them, ask your bookshop to or them from one of the distributors listed below. countries not listed or if you would like a free copy of latest booklist write to Lonely Planet in Australia.

Australia
Lonely Planet Publications, PO Box 88, South Ya Victoria 3141.
Canada
Milestone Publications, PO Box 2248, Sidney, BC \ 3S8, Canada.
Denmark
Scanvik Books aps, Store Kongensgade 59 A, DK-12 Copenhagen K.
Hong Kong
The Book Society, GPO Box 7804.
India & Nepal
UBS Distributors, 5 Ansari Rd, New Delhi.
Israel
Geographical Tours Ltd, 8 Tverya St, Tel Aviv 631
Japan
Intercontinental Marketing Corp, IPO Box 5056, To 100-31.
Malaysia
MPH Distributors, 13 Jalan 13/6, Petaling Ja Selangor.
Netherlands
Nilsson & Lamm bv, Postbus 195, Pampuslaan 2 1380 AD Weesp.
New Zealand
Roulston Greene Publishing Associates Ltd, E 33850, Takapuna, Auckland 9.
Pakistan
London Book House, 281/C Tariq Rd, PECHS Kara 29, Pakistan
Papua New Guinea see Australia
Singapore
MPH Distributors, 3rd Storey, 601 Sims Drive #03-2 Singapore 1438
Spain
Altair, Riera Alta 8, Barcelona, 08001.
Sweden
Esselte Kartcentrum AB, Vasagatan 16, S-111 Stockholm.
Thailand
Chalermnit, 108 Sukhumvit 53, Bangkok, 10110.
UK
Roger Lascelles, 47 York Rd, Brentford, Middles TW8 0QP.
USA
Lonely Planet Publications, PO Box 2001A, Berkel CA 94702.
West Germany
Buchvertrieb Gerda Schettler, Postfach 64, D34 Hattorf a H.

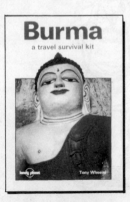

Burma
a travel survival kit

Tony Wheeler